Sentencing the Ethically-Motivated Offender

Sentencing the Ethically-Motivated Offender

Mitigation for 'Ethical' Criminality?

Edited by

JULIAN V. ROBERTS

Emeritus Professor, University of Oxford, UK

LEO ZAIBERT

Andreas von Hirsch Professor of Penal Theory and Ethics, University of Cambridge, UK

JESPER RYBERG

Professor of Ethics and Philosophy of Law, Roskilde University, Denmark

OXFORD
UNIVERSITY PRESS

OXFORD
UNIVERSITY PRESS

Great Clarendon Street, Oxford, OX2 6DP,
United Kingdom

Oxford University Press is a department of the University of Oxford.
It furthers the University's objective of excellence in research, scholarship,
and education by publishing worldwide. Oxford is a registered trade mark of
Oxford University Press in the UK and in certain other countries.

Published in the United States of America by Oxford University Press
546 Fifth Avenue, New York, NY 10036, United States of America.

British Library Cataloguing in Publication Data
Data available

Library of Congress Control Number: 2026946688

ISBN 9780198993018

DOI: 10.1093/9780198993025.001.0001

The manufacturer's authorized representative in the EU for product safety is
Oxford University Press España S.A. of Parque Empresarial San Fernando de Henares,
Avenida de Castilla, 2 – 28830 Madrid (www.oup.es/en or product.safety@oup.com).
OUP España S.A. also acts as importer into Spain of products made by the manufacturer.

Preface

The editors would like to express their gratitude to the following individuals and organizations without whose help this volume would have been impossible. Draft chapters were first discussed at a seminar held in the faculty of Jurisprudence, University of Ferrara in May 2025. We acknowledge the assistance of Gianmarco Bondi, Michele Pifferi and colleagues, as well as the generous support for the event provided by the Faculty of Law, Ferrara. We also thank Principessa Pio and its staff for their hospitality. We would also like to thank Charlotte Kershaw and Fiona Briden from the Oxford University Press for their assistance in bringing this volume of essays into print, and the anonymous reviewers for their comments on an early draft of the book.

Julian V. Roberts, Oxford
Leo Zaibert, Cambridge
Jesper Ryberg, Roskilde
1 May 2026

Contents

PART II. SENTENCING ETHICAL OFFENDING IN PRACTICE: JURISDICTIONAL CASE HISTORIES

Contributors

Hauke Bock is Research Assistant, Faculty of Law, Humboldt-University Berlin, Germany. https://orcid.org/0009-0006-9865-9015

Gianmarco Bondi, PhD is Teaching Assistant and Exam Committee Member in Criminal Law, Department of Law, University of Ferrara, Italy. https://orcid.org/0009-0005-9149-8274

Ivó Coca-Vila, Dr is Associate Professor of Criminal Law, Faculty of Law, Pompeu Fabra University, Barcelona, Spain, Max Planck Institute for the Study of Crime, Security and Law, Freiburg, Germany. https://orcid.org/0000-0002-2507-7974

Netanel Dagan is Senior Lecturer, Hebrew University, Jerusalem, Israel. https://orcid.org/0000-0001-5610-8801

Clémence Demay is Lecturer and Post-Doc researcher, Center for Public Law, Université de Lausanne, Switzerland. https://orcid.org/0000-0001-7394-3083

Benjamin Ewing is Associate Professor, Faculty of Law, Queen's University, Canada. https://orcid.org/0000-0003-0551-5188

Katrin Höffler is Professor of Criminal Law, Law of Criminal Procedure, Criminology and Sociology of Law, Faculty of Law, Humboldt University Berlin, Germany. https://orcid.org/0000-0002-4923-8090

Zachary Hoskins is Associate Professor, Philosophy Department, University of Nottingham, United Kingdom. https://orcid.org/0000-0003-4445-1412

Jonathan A Jacobs, PhD in Philosophy is Emeritus Professor of Philosophy, John Jay College of Criminal Justice of the City University of New York, New York City, United States. https://orcid.org/0000-0003-0676-2519

Florence Lee is Assistant Professor, Faculty of Law, The University of Hong Kong, Hong Kong. https://orcid.org/0009-0006-1091-9514

Julian V. Roberts is Emeritus Professor, University of Oxford, United Kingdom.

Jesper Ryberg is Professor of Ethics and Philosophy of Law, Roskilde University, Denmark.

Carla Sepúlveda, DPhil is Assistant Professor, Faculty of Law, Universidad Adolfo Ibáñez, Santiago, Chile. https://orcid.org/0000-0003-4934-0199

Tim Nicklas Wensien is Research Assistant, Faculty of Law, Humboldt-University Berlin, Germany.

Javier Wilenmann, PhD is Professor of Criminal Law, Universidad Adolfo Ibáñez, Santiago, Chile. https://orcid.org/0000-0003-4237-3537

Bill Wringe is Associate Professor, Department of Philosophy, Bilkent University, Ankara, Turkey, and Honorary Visiting Professor, Department of Philosophy, University of York, York, United Kingdom. https://orcid.org/0000-0001-7979-7689

Leo Zaibert is Andreas von Hirsch Professor of Penal Theory and Ethics, University of Cambridge, United Kingdom.

PART I

SENTENCING ETHICAL OFFENDERS: THEORETICAL ISSUES AND DEBATES

1

Sentencing the Ethical Offender

The Context

Julian V. Roberts, Leo Zaibert, and Jesper Ryberg

1. Introduction

Should people convicted of ethically-motivated crimes benefit from mitigation at sentencing? Legislatures and courts around the world have for years grappled with this question. An earlier collection of essays addressed the case for sentencing mitigation when the state has acted unlawfully towards the offender (Zaibert, Roberts, and Ryberg 2025). For example, when police assaulted an offender during or after arrest. In such cases, both the punishing authority and the individual being sentenced are at fault. In a merging of roles, the punishing or censuring party has itself acted wrongfully.[1]

This volume explores another context in which the parties' standings differ from conventional proceedings: the sentencing of offenders acting from benign rather than malign motives. Here the sentencer must determine whether the offender is entitled to mitigation in recognition of an 'honourable' or otherwise laudable motive. Sentencing frameworks generally assume that perpetrators seek to benefit themselves at the expense of others. The offender is seen as malignantly motivated and is punished accordingly. Yet is this approach appropriate when the offender seeks no obvious gain, and aims to benefit society or the world? Rational agents generally act from motives, and few offenders conform to Coleridge's description of Iago as hunting for motives, as he acts out of what appears to be motiveless malignity.

Laws are sometimes broken in order to improve society. Legislatures, courts, and sentencing councils and commissions now confront a wide range of such offending. But honourable motives need not be directly linked to efforts to

[1] For other discussions of whether and how state wrongdoing should be taken into account at sentencing, see e.g., 2001); Tadros (2009); Beade (2019).

Julian V. Roberts, Leo Zaibert, and Jesper Ryberg, *Sentencing the Ethical Offender* In: *Sentencing the Ethically-Motivated Offender*. Edited by: Julian V. Roberts, Leo Zaibert, and Jesper Ryberg, Oxford University Press.
 DOI: 10.1093/9780198993025.003.0002

benefit society: Antigone (in Sophocles' play), for example, does not benefit society, and yet her motives are nevertheless honourable. In that play, the eponymous heroine defies the ruler's express prohibition of any burial rites for her brother. Antigone argues that the legal prohibition is immoral, hence her defiance of lawful authority.

As this literary example shows, breaking the law for an 'honourable cause' is neither a new nor a rare phenomenon. Over the centuries, many people have committed offences while claiming to improve society or to otherwise be acting laudably. The suffragettes broke the law to achieve gender equality in Edwardian society, as did Rosa Parks when she refused to obey racist laws during the 1960s in the United States. Such forms of offending are often situated within the framework of civil disobedience. All western nations have experienced a rise in criminal behaviour motivated by a 'just cause'. Perhaps the most prevalent (and publicized) recent example concerns climate change protesters. Environmental activists have disrupted daily life in a wide range of ways in order to draw public and political attention to the global climate crisis (Eckes 2025). It is unsurprising, therefore, that many contributors to this volume explore the sentencing of climate change protesters. Yet the spectrum of cases involving claims of 'honourable' motive mitigation is wider and includes:

- Offenders who impede construction projects or highway expansion in an attempt to protect the natural habitat.
- People who break the law to draw attention to threats to violations of fundamental values such as democracy or even basic human decency.
- Defendants who offend to protest against one country's attack on, or occupation of, another country.
- Defendants who offend to prevent a worse crime by other offenders (but short of a legal excuse).
- Offenders who act against known perpetrators when it is clear that the criminal justice system cannot or will not act—such vigilantes may argue they are in some unofficial capacity 'upholding the (moral) law'.
- 'Robin Hood' offenders who steal from wealthy individuals or companies and distribute the proceeds to suffering third parties and who do not themselves benefit from their crime.
- Defendants who end the life of a terminally ill relative or spouse, to spare the patient further suffering.
- Defendants who offend in conformity with strictures or requirements of a recognized or official religion. They regard their offending as being justified by reference to the ethics of their belief.

- Defendants who victimize executives or employees of organizations which they deem to have acted illegally.
- 'Whistle blowers' who unlawfully disclose confidential documents in order to expose wrongdoing by powerful organizations.

This introductory chapter sets the stage for the remainder of the volume. We begin by highlighting some key issues and questions which are subsequently addressed by the contributing authors. Some of these are conceptual in nature and apply across a range of ethical criminality. We then focus on the sentencing of ethically-motivated offenders, noting the challenges confronting courts. The chapter concludes by noting the specific contributions made in both parts of the volume.

Motives matter, in the criminal law as in daily life—despite the famous 'irrelevance of motives' maxim in criminal law theory discussed by several contributors to this volume. Whether an individual is furious or forgiving with respect to a friend who borrows his car without asking depends on the explanation offered.[2] If the friend had had to drive someone to hospital, there would be little (or nothing) to forgive. If he had borrowed the car merely for his own convenience (and the owner had to walk home), anger may be a more appropriate response. The words 'intent' and 'motive' are often used interchangeably, although they are distinct concepts (see e.g. Husak 1989, and several contributions to this volume).

By definition, aside from offences of strict liability and some crimes of omission, a criminal conviction implies a culpable mental state: it is usually the case that the offender has violated a legal provision for some personal benefit or for some other immoral purpose. Proving malign intent, or at least a culpable state of mind, is necessary for a conviction. Intent often determines the nature of the crime committed. In most jurisdictions throughout history, an intent to kill generally distinguishes murder from lesser offences such as manslaughter. Intent is therefore important to the charging decision and is often contested by the parties at trial. ('My client only intended to harm the victim who unfortunately died'). Motive, as in the underlying purpose which drove the criminal intent, is harder to define and to manage. The offender's motivation is often bundled into a category of 'personal mitigation' along with diverse other factors.

[2] For an overview of moral psychological reseach on how motives affect assessments of the ways in which people act, see e.g. Carlson et al. (2022).

Motives affect decisions taken throughout the criminal process. The nature of a suspect's motives for their actions may influence the police decision to resolve an allegation by means of an out of court disposal. In England and Wales, assisting suicide is a criminal offence. When deciding whether a prosecution is in the public interest, the Crown Prosecution Service will consider the motive of a person suspected of assisting another's suicide. The prosecution service may charge a suspect acting from a selfish motive while declining to prosecute someone acting purely to alleviate a relative's incurable suffering. At trial, the defendant's motive may result in the jury returning an acquittal even in the face of an overwhelming prosecution case. Several juries in England have acquitted environmental protesters, even though the defendants had accepted responsibility for the criminal acts.

The offender's motivation has risen to prominence as an issue for courts at sentencing. This is as true for aggravation as it is for mitigation. Most jurisdictions have legislated sentencing enhancements for crimes motivated by bias, hatred, or prejudice with respect to specific profiles of victim (Hessick 2006; Roberts 1999). Offenders assaulting a member of a racial minority are deemed more blameworthy for generalizing their animus to whole communities. The harm is also enhanced in recognition of the additional fear experienced by other members of the community (see Hurd and Moore 2003; Mellgren et al. 2021). Some ideologically motivated offenders are also deemed more culpable for threatening the state (along with the specific individuals harmed by their terrorist crimes). It is not only the retributivist concern with blameworthiness that matters: motivation also counts from a preventive perspective. Sentencers are likely—understandably—to regard hate-motivated and terrorism offenders as higher risks for reoffending. When this is the case, courts are authorized to impose harsh sentences for the purposes of deterrence or incapacitation. If motive is relevant to aggravation, it is even more significant as a factor relevant to mitigation.

Our volume focuses on prosocial or ethical motives as a potential source of mitigation at sentencing. Contributors address a series of questions now confronting courts around the western world:

- How should the law deal with the possibility of 'honourable' criminality?
- To what extent should an 'honourable' motive affect sentencing, if at all?
- Should a court decide whether the offender's cause is legitimate enough to justify at least some mitigation?
- If honourable motives are relevant to the sentencing decision, how much mitigation is appropriate?

- Is there a degree of proportionality between the gravity of the problem to which criminal protesters draw attention—preventing global warming, say—and the seriousness of the crime committed? Should the harmfulness of the crime or the culpability of the offender be considered in light of the gravity of the problem giving rise to the offence?
- Do preventive theories adopt a different approach vis-à-vis retributive theories?

We have noted the range of criminal conduct arising from a positive motive. Some people break the law to benefit society by highlighting a pressing social problem. Others become defendants through criminal actions seeking to redress an injustice or spare another person from suffering. The forms of positively motivated offending vary greatly. In terms of the caseload of the courts, however, one particular category accounts for a particularly high volume of cases: social, political, or environmental protests. It is unsurprising therefore, that most contributors, whether discussing the issue at the theoretical or practical level, discuss this category of offending.

2. Challenges for Courts at Sentencing

A number of jurisdictions have codified a mitigating factor in acceptance that an honourable intention should mitigate sentence, at least under certain circumstances (see, e.g., Chapter 13). However, these provisions do not enumerate the motives or causes which might justify mitigation. That challenge is left to courts to resolve. Sentencing guidelines contain a wide range of mitigating factors for courts to apply at sentencing, although so far, no sentencing commission or council has included 'honourable motive' or a similarly worded circumstance in its guidelines. Yet trial and appellate courts routinely hear claims for mitigation on this ground, and often reduce sentence as a result.

Determining whether (and how much) to mitigate sentence in recognition of an ethical motives raises challenges for a sentencing court, the most obvious of which concerns the legitimacy of the motive. How is a court to determine whether the offender's motive is honourable or dishonourable, and when it is sufficiently honourable to justify recognition and trigger mitigation? People breaking the law to protest against the current war in Ukraine may act on behalf of either of the combatants. Should a court mitigate sentence for both categories of protester to the same degree? In some jurisdictions, constitutionally recognized values may offer some guidance, legitimizing some motives and excluding others. Yet the decision to award mitigation will remain a matter for judicial discretion.

These sorts of challenges may be addressed in several ways. One populist solution would draw upon community views. Lawyers sometimes point to a strong level of public support for their client's cause, or the right to protest even when this involves breaking the law. If a clear majority of the population acknowledged the ethicality of a given cause, this might authorize or legitimize a court's decision to award mitigation. Yet public opinion evolves constantly and may well be an unreliable guide to the ethicality of the cause motivating the offender. While 'majoritarianism' plays a prominent role in politics, it is simply not a reliable normative guide—and for this reason it is commonly rejected by moral theorists. Community views were unsympathetic towards advocates of gender enfranchisement in Edwardian England or slavery abolitionists in earlier centuries. It is possible, moreover, that the majority of the US population nowadays supports its government bombing boats in the Caribbean, or targeting particular minorities for potential deportation. Moreover, it is unclear why the relevance of motive should be determined be reference to public opinion if this is not the case for other sentencing factors.[3]

Another approach to determining whether mitigation is appropriate would examine the proportionality between the harm which the offender seeks to prevent or mitigate, and the harm caused by the offence.[4] Blocking an airport runway to draw attention to the high cost of air travel seems disproportionate to the disruption caused. Yet the same act committed to highlight the potential global climate catastrophe may seem more acceptable, and more worthy of mitigation at sentencing. The gravity of the offence may also limit the application of mitigation more generally. An offender who harms property owned by a corporation that is guilty of corporate wrongdoing may attract some mitigation. Yet if the same individual assaults company employees, mitigation may be deemed inappropriate.

The role of the state is also contested. If an individual breaks the law to protest unlawful state actions or inactions, the state's wrongful act or omission may link to the offence and justify some mitigation. But if the same person breaks the law to bring to light wrongdoing by a private actor, does this relieve the prosecuting state of any obligation to award mitigation?

[3] For a general discussion of the moral relevance of public opinion to sentencing, see Ryberg and Roberts (2014a), (2014b).

[4] The magnitude of the problem has long been set against the minimal nature of the unlawful protest as ground for sentence mitigation. For example, in 1977 anti-nuclear protesters who committed criminal trespass by blocking access to a nuclear power plant argued that this minor transgression was justified by the much more serious and existential threat to the planet (see Richardson 2020).

Awarding mitigation in recognition of the cause animating the ethical offending inevitably draws the court—and the state on whose behalf punishment is imposed—into the political arena. When a court mitigates sentence to recognize that the defendant has a legitimate motive for the crime, this mitigation confers a degree of legitimacy on the cause espoused. Similarly, when a court rejects pleas in mitigation, there may be an implicit message that the cause advocated lacks legitimacy.

A key question is the extent to which conventional sentencing regimes should modify their sentencing principles and practices to accommodate the ethical offender. People being sentenced for ethically-motivated crimes claim a status different from that of other defendants. They claim mitigation on several grounds. Their crimes are necessary to address a greater wrong than their offence, they attract no personal benefit, or they have a sound ethical basis. The 'greater evil' argument is raised as a defence as well as a source of mitigation. Environmental protest groups such as Extinction Rebellion or Just Stop Oil assert the legitimacy of their otherwise illegal acts on the basis that they are justified in order to prevent a climate catastrophe (see Cunningham 2019).

If courts are directed by statute to mitigate sentence, or if they award mitigation *sua sponte*, some guidance is surely useful, or even necessary (Hessick 2006). A statutory mitigating factor which authorizes mitigation for the ethical offender offers no assistance in determining the degree of sentence reduction. As several contributors to this volume note, left to their own discretion, judges will vary in the extent to which they reduce sentence to reflect an ethically-motivated crime. Even in jurisdictions where the law permits sentence reductions, disparity exists between courts, and the appellate courts have offered little in the way of practical guidance.

Transparency and predictability are hallmarks of a legitimate sentencing regime. Citizens need to know, or be able to ascertain, whether specific acts carry criminal liability. More than this, they also need to know the grounds on which sentences are based, and this includes key aggravating and mitigating circumstances. The diversity of ethical motives and offender profiles makes the task of devising guidance difficult. Yet it must be attempted (but see Chapter 2, where considerations related to equity and mercy suggest complications attendant to this attempt). A sentencing commission or court of appeal can suggest limits on the mitigation, as well as circumstances which justify higher or lower levels of reduction. Environmental protesters, for example, who take steps to ensure that their unlawful protests are both targeted and designed to minimize harm deserve more mitigation than those who simply disrupt public business without regard to who is harmed, or to what degree.

Courts may need to consider the extent to which lawful means exist for advancing the cause that animates the offending. A defendant who ends the life of a terminally ill and suffering relative is likely to have exhausted all alternative means of alleviating the patient's suffering. The claim for mitigation is less compelling if, for example, the defendant has ample opportunities to protest. Courts in jurisdictions which have removed citizens' right to protest have greater reason for mitigating sentence.

3. Contents of the Volume

The book comprises two parts. The remaining chapters in Part I address a range of cross-cutting questions which apply across many forms of such offending. In order for the courts to develop theoretically sound approaches to sentencing these forms of offending, a clear understanding of the conceptual challenges is necessary. These first nine chapters provide a critical examination of a range of competing perspectives. Part II of the volume examines the different ways in which these efforts play out in several representative jurisdictions.

Chapter 2, by Leo Zaibert, seeks to understand ethically-defensible criminality in broad terms. Self-evidently, ethically-*motivated* criminality constitutes a significant part of the former, but other elements can render certain prima facie wrong actions less wrong than they initially appear. Thus, Zaibert analyses influential calls for broadening the scope of what the criminal law may deem relevant. He argues against comprehensive legislative reform or radical expansions of our understanding of culpability as strategies to try to cope with ethically-defensible criminality. Finding inspiration in the classical distinctions between justice, equity, and mercy, Zaibert suggests that the proper occasion for addressing ethically-defensible criminality is at sentencing—and that ethically-defensible wrongdoing is a prime candidate for either equitable or merciful judgment.

Even when restricting the discussion of the manifold circumstances that may affect the normative evaluation of human action to sentencing, difficulties remain. Many of these are captured by the famous 'irrelevance of motive' maxim, with which several authors in the first part of the book engage. This engagement is largely critical, or sceptical: the general view is that motives are relevant at sentencing. While Zaibert, for example, offers a generous reading according to which what is meant by the maxim is that in order to impute liability we do not *need* to investigate motives, others, like Ryberg, explore the complexities of motives. As Ryberg observes, motives can be obscure, contradictory, over-determined, and at times unclear even to the actors themselves. Identifying *the* central motive can be a very difficult challenge. And these difficulties are not merely epistemological: what exactly is a motive (or what exactly is necessary for a motive to be the central motive explaining our actions) are difficult metaphysical questions. And yet, most contributors agree that these complexities do not warrant the conclusion that motives have no normative importance.

One contribution—by Benjamin Ewing—engages with the extent to which the notion of motive can be extended to include circumstances related to socio-economic disadvantage. As the title of his contribution—'Are disadvantaged offenders ethically motivated?'—implies, it is an open question whether socio-economic disadvantages can be seen as motivational, or as giving rise to motives that should be admitted as ethically defensible. In the end, Ewing is sceptical about an affirmative answer to this question—but not about the idea that some mitigation for socio-economic disadvantage may be adequate.

Several authors explore a possible justification of mitigation for ethically-motivated criminality related to communicative rationales. Ivó Coca-Vila and Bill Wringe, for example, highlight the ways in which these types of wrongdoers engage in wrongdoing in order to send messages—messages that sometimes can be not only defensible, but downright admirable. These 'wrongdoers' do not typically seek personal gain, at least not the sort of personal gain that 'ordinary' wrongdoers seek. Far from being selfish, for instance, climate protesters seek to send messages that, if heeded, shall (in their view) benefit society at large—and they do this putting themselves at risk, sometimes considerable risk. (The analogies between this view of ethically-motivated criminality and civil disobedience are obvious and are discussed by several contributors.) When criminality can be seen as a form of protest—as some of the cases discussed in this volume can—then the 'social meaning' of those acts changes, and to the extent that one sees punishment by the state as also at least partially communicative, then the whole 'crime and punishment' enterprise can be seen as a dialogue. Within this framework, certain mitigations can be usefully seen as (appropriate) interventions in this dialogue. Moreover, as Ivó Coca-Vila highlights, it is sometimes the case that at least part of the complaint of protesters who have engaged in (municipal) criminality concerns failures by the state to live up to its own international obligations. In such cases, the state's legitimacy, and its standing to punish, is itself questionable and thus offering an avenue toward mitigation.

Other contributors—Zachary Hoskins, Julian Roberts, and Netanel Dagan—examine the reasons for mitigation based on ethically-defensible motivation that arise in each of the common justifications of punishment. Hoskins concludes that the communicative (the communicative-retributive version, to be more exact) justification of punishment is the best equipped to do that. At sentencing, a court communicates a message of censure which should reflect the offender's level of blameworthiness. On his view, then, the state should recognize that ethically-motivated offenders are reasonably deemed less blameworthy than people who break the law for profit or other selfish motivation. Roberts and Dagan, for their part, also see the retributive concern with culpability and proportionality as offering the best way of punishing ethically-motivated criminality. While they recognize the relevance of motive in some exceptional cases (such as merciful intention killing) they see limited grounds for mitigation in more common crimes. One of their claims in justification for this position is that mitigating sentences for activist offending inevitably politicizes the judicial role.

Several authors, then, endorse the view that we should indeed provide mitigation for ethically-motivated criminality, and they base this view on both communicative and retributive elements. Not all authors, however, are equally inclined to mitigate ethically-motivated criminality, or to deviate from the reasons to mitigate that attach to ordinary criminality. Roberts and Dagan, for example, cite 'principled and practical objections' to granting mitigation to ethical criminality. While their practical objections are variegated, these objections are all related to retributivism's concern for proportionality. Not surprisingly, among the reasons for mitigation, they focus on first-time offending, and they emphasize that ethically-motivated offenders should be as susceptible to mitigation as they are to aggravation—in ways not too dissimilar from those applicable to garden-variety (ie non-ethically-motivated) offenders.

This last point is also stressed by Jonathan Jacobs, who points out that 'the fact that conduct makes a moral point . . . can cut both ways', noting that sometimes protesters (even if protesting the right things) are in fact engaged in moral theatrics or other morally dubious motivations, particularly when there is little risk to themselves. (Here again the problems with overdetermination and obscurity of motivation explored by Ryberg and others become relevant.) In recommending caution when thinking about mitigation for ethically-motivated offenders, these contributors counterbalance the positions of several others in the volume, perhaps most exemplified by Zaibert's mobilization of the age-old literature on both equity and (above all) mercy. This literature embraces an asymmetry between aggravation and mitigation that assigns priority to the latter. In suggesting that ethically-motivated offenders are not that different from ordinary offenders Jacobs goes even further than

Roberts and Dagan, for he additionally suggests that sometimes grounds for mitigation can 'be more uncertain than grounds for aggravation'—and for this reason (amongst others) special care should be exercised when contemplating mitigation. In so doing, Jacobs interestingly turns the classical asymmetry between aggravation and mitigation on its head. These chapters offer a variety of perspectives on a set of questions which are at once difficult, timely, and important for many societies.

4. Part II: Sentencing Ethical Offending in Practice: Jurisdictional Case Histories

Part II of the volume turns from the conceptual to practical. It contains a series of jurisdiction-specific analyses which reveal the diversity of approaches to sentencing offenders who act from an honourable motive. Sentencing theory and practice often evolve independent of each other. Even a cursory review of sentencing judgments and statutes will show that in many instances these appear inconsistent with foundational theoretical perspectives. For their part, scholars often discuss penal theory without regard to current practice. In compiling this collection of essays, we hope to strengthen the link between theory and practice. In pursuing this objective, we solicited contributions from legal scholars from a range of jurisdictions.

The five selected countries address the same challenge discussed in the first part of the book: how to sentence well-intentioned offenders. We include countries which represent very different experiences. The authors in this part shed light on these different responses of courts to some of the problems identified in Part I. For example, courts in Switzerland and legislators in Italy appear more open to considering an ethical motivation as grounds for mitigation.[5] A limited international review suggests that most jurisdictions have declined to recognize in statute the relevance of a pro-social motive for offending. In this respect, Italy and Switzerland present an interesting model for these other jurisdictions to consider. These jurisdictional case histories also highlight the political context in which pro-social offending occurs. Thus, in considering

[5] In contrast, courts in England and Wales have adopted a more restrictive view, and this is manifested in more punitive sentencing of the 'ethical offender'. For example, in 2024, the Court of Appeal upheld a sentence of 24 months' immediate imprisonment on Phoebe Plummer, a young adult (21 years old). Although the offender had a history of unlawful protests on behalf of 'Stop Oil' the Court noted that a pre-sentence report had documented that she was a 'vulnerable young person who was easily influenced by others and who displayed deficits in understanding the impact of her decisions on others' (*R. v Hallam and Ors* [2025] EWCA Crim 199 [188]).

sentencing of protesters in Chile and Hong Kong it is important to understand the recent and past history of political protest.

Hong Kong is the first jurisdiction examined. Florence Lee examines how the courts there approach sentencing pro-democracy protesters within Hong Kong's evolving national security framework. Following a period of social unrest, sentencing decisions have assumed increased importance, reflecting a delicate balance between recognizing offenders' motives (their pursuit of democratic ideals) and upholding the government's priority of maintaining stability. The sentencing of pro-democracy protesters in Hong Kong remains a source of tension in the struggle to uphold traditional common law values amidst a changing political landscape. Lee notes that on one hand judges strive to uphold principles like proportionality which require a careful balance of assessing culpability and harm. However, the Security Law prioritizes deterrent sentencing, reflecting the prevailing political environment. The result is a complex sentencing landscape in which an offender's commitment to pro-democratic ideals is acknowledged but often seen as a reason to impose tougher sentences to deter others.

Clémence Demay discusses judicial responses to crimes of civil disobedience in Switzerland. She argues that the distinction between political and ethical motives for offending is logically untenable as a justification for sentence mitigation. She advocates employing the European Court of Human Rights (ECHR) framework as this offers a stronger, rights-based method for assessing and sentencing civil disobedience cases. Although courts rarely apply the ECHR to such cases, the framework provides a principled, consistent, and rights-based method for determining when offenders convicted of crimes of civil disobedience warrant mitigation. Moreover, this approach it circumvents the conceptual and practical pitfalls of the 'honourable motive' doctrine, avoids engaging individual judges' political preferences, and is more likely to promote consistency and clarity in outcomes.

Katrin Höffler, Hauke Bock, and Tim Nicklas Wensien examine the judicial response to sentencing climate activists in Germany. In order to shed light on the sentencing in cases of climate protesters, they analyse a number of judgments in which custodial sentences were imposed on the offenders. The sentencing in the cases reviewed reveals the inadequacy of the criminal law in addressing the underlying issue. Prison sentences are unlikely to resolve the anomic condition that motivates the offenders, and this leaves the repressive response of the courts open to serious normative challenge. The sentencing statute directs judges to assess motivations when evaluating culpability and this permits findings of low or very low culpability, resulting in mitigated sentences.

Gianmarco Bondi explores the issues in Italy, one of the few jurisdictions which legislated a specific mitigating factor which recognizes an offender's positive motivation. The mitigating factor applies to any criminal offence and permits up to a one-third reduction of the sentence. However, the provision is vague, and has been interpreted in an overly restrictive way, to the detriment of meritorious defendants. Bondi makes several suggestions for reform which would introduce greater coherence in the application of ethical offending mitigating. First, courts ought to adopt a more generous test, awarding mitigation even when the ethical motive does not enjoy universal approval or when it co-occurs with less commendable motives. Greater flexibility avoids the injustice of applying a simple dichotomy. Second, he suggests founding pro-social mitigation in states' constitutions and international human rights charters. This would strengthen the legitimacy of this form of mitigation and promote greater consistency of application. He concludes that the judicial response in Italy demonstrates that engaging with the moral dimension of offending at sentencing is both possible and appropriate.

Chile is the final jurisdiction included in the volume and the state response to protest-related offending provides a clear contrast with the others. Javier Wilenmann and Carla Sepúlveda note that Chile has experienced both peaceful and violent demonstrations connected to widespread socio-economic inequality. In response, Chilean legislation has treated protest-related conduct as aggravating the seriousness of the base offence, particularly with respect to property crimes. Security concerns predominate in this area of law. Accordingly, a mandatory aggravating factor was introduced for offences committed at the time of public disorder. General deterrence emerged as a recurring preoccupation: sentences seeking not merely to sanction the individual but to deter other, potential protesters. Courts have drawn a sharp distinction between the commendable aim of climate protection and unlawful disruptions. Particularly in cases of persistent offending, courts have felt compelled to mark the boundaries of lawful protest through the imposition of custodial sanctions. Paradoxically, a distinctly different approach was adopted with regard to sentencing white-collar crimes. The authors argue that there is no principled impediment to extending the white-collar reasoning to all forms of offending, including crimes committed as part of political or other forms of protest.

Can we draw any general conclusions from the varied experiences in these five jurisdictions? One obvious lesson would be that there is no single approach to sentencing social activists or other honourably-motivated defendants. The nature of the state response will reflect the country's social and judicial culture, as well as its recent political history. In this respect, there may be no near-universal approach to sentencing positively-motivated offenders. Some sentencing principles guiding courts may be common to many societies and exist independent of local culture; proportionality may be one such principle. A diversity of jurisdictions require courts to sentence offenders in a way that respects retributive proportionality. The approach to sentencing the forms of offending discussed in this volume may be more jurisdiction-specific.

A second conclusion is that for such contested issues, the democratic legislature should debate and legislate some direction to courts. Some societies will support the approach taken in Italy of recognizing a positive motivation. In other countries the populace may be less sympathetic towards such offending, and oppose any statutory recognition of this mitigating factor. Without some guidance from the legislature, courts will likely assume different positions, awarding mitigation in some cases but not others. The legitimacy of the judicial reaction may be called into question: individual judges apply the law and do not necessarily reflect the views of the community.

None of the jurisdictions examined appears to have developed a satisfactory response to punishing ethical offenders. The judicial response has evolved without sufficient consideration of fundamental sentencing principles. The jurisprudence on this issue has emerged sporadically and piecemeal, in response to the forms of offending prosecuted. Elsewhere, courts have attempted to accommodate ethical offending within existing sentencing regimes which developed to respond to more conventional offences and offenders. What is needed is a more comprehensive examination of the issue. The legislature should initiate such a review, in order to resolve the question of whether this form of offending could or should be treated more leniently. Many legislatures around the world conducted such an exercise prior to placing sentencing enhancements for hate-motivated crimes. A similar legislative initiative should examine the potential for mitigation when the offender's motivation is benign rather than malign. This accomplished, appellate courts could interpret any statutory factor and issue further guidance to ensure greater consistency across trial courts.

5. Conclusion

The chapters of this volume represent different, sometimes conflicting perspectives on the question of ethical-offending mitigation. No clear consensus emerges on the key question of whether mitigation is appropriate, although there appears to be general recognition that an offender's motive for offending is potentially relevant to sentencing. Disregarding an individual's motives entirely would be unjust; it would fail to distinguish between offenders whose crimes reflect very different ethical situations. Some authors are sympathetic to the claims for mitigation, particularly with respect to issues of global importance such as the environmental crisis. As a result, they see sentence mitigation as an appropriate state response.

Others are more sceptical and warn that the ever-changing and contested nature of society and public opinion suggests that courts should be wary of recognizing honourable causes which may not attract sufficient consensus. Several of the more theoretical chapters highlight the complexity of ascertaining what the motives of our actions really are: these are sometimes opaque, self-contradictory, or in fact not known even to the actors themselves. This theoretical complexity may shed light on some of the peculiarities of the ways in which this concern with the broader context behind certain criminal actions plays out even in those specific jurisdictions that are open to this sort of examination. We believe that this interplay between the theoretical and the more practice-oriented chapters will advance our understanding of the issues and lead to more theoretically coherent approaches to sentencing ethical offending.

Sentencing ethically-motivated offending presents a long-standing and complex challenge for courts and indeed for our legal systems as a whole. One reason is that the cause giving rise to the offending behaviour changes over time, evolving in response to emerging problems such as international conflicts and climate change. Despite these (and other) challenges explored herein, it should be possible to derive some core principles to guide courts at sentencing. This volume represents the first scholarly effort towards mapping the conceptual terrain and clarifying the principles relevant to sentencing the 'honourable' defendant.

References

Beade, Gustavo. 'Who Can Blame Whom? Moral Standing to Blame and Punish Deprived Citizens' *Criminal Law and Philosophy* 13 (2019): 271–281.

Carlson, Ryan W. et al. 'How Inferred Motives Shape Moral Judgements' *Nature: Psychology* 1 (2022): 468–478.

Cunningham, Neil. 'Averting Catastrophe: Environmental Activism, Extinction Rebellion and Coalitions of Influence' *King's Law Journal* 30 (2019): 194–202.

Duff, Antony. *Punishment, Communication, and Community*. Oxford: Oxford University Press, 2001.

Eckes, Christina. 'Dissensus in Europe: Climate Protesters Before Court' *European Political Science* 24, no. 3 (2025): 532–552.

Hessick, Carissa B. 'Motive's Role in Criminal Punishment' *Southern California Law Review* 80, no. 1 (2006): 89–150.

Hurd, Heidi and Michael Moore. 'Punishing Hatred and Prejudice' *Stanford Law Review* 56 (2003): 1082–1147.

Husak, Douglas. 'Motive and Criminal Liability' *Criminal Justice Ethics* 8, no. 1 (1989): 3–13.

Mellgren, Caroline et al. 'For Who does Hate Crime Hurt More? A Comparison of the Consequences of Victimization Across Motives and Crime Types' *Journal of Interpersonal Violence* 36 (2021): 1512–1536.

Richardson, Benjamin. 'Protesting Against Climate Breakdown: Novel Legal Options'. *Australian Environmental Review* 35 (2020): 21–25.

Roberts, Julian V. *Legislative Responses to Hate-motivated Crime: An International Survey.* Ottawa: Department of Canadian Heritage, 1999.

Ryberg, Jesper and Julian Roberts. 'Exploring the Moral Significance of Public Opinion for State Punishment'. In *Popular Punishment: On the Normative Significance of Public Opinion,* edited by Jesper Ryberg and Julian Roberts, pp. 1–13. New York: Oxford University Press, 2014a.

Ryberg, Jesper and Julian Roberts. *Popular Punishment: On the Normative Significance of Public Opinion.* New York: Oxford University Press, 2014b.

Tadros, Victor. 'Poverty and Criminal Responsibility' *Journal of Value Inquiry* 43 (2009): 391–413.

Zaibert, Leo, Roberts, Julian V. and Ryberg, Jesper. *Responding to the Culpable State: Is Sentence Mitigation Appropriate?* Oxford: Hart Bloomsbury, 2025.

2

How to Deal with Ethically-Defensible Criminality; or On Deep Sentencing

Leo Zaibert

1. Introduction

The question as to whether or not legal systems ought to consider the sometimes ethically defensible motivations of some wrongdoers is more complicated than it may first appear.[1] While I am rather sympathetic to the idea of treating ethically-motivated offenders with leniency (more so than are other contributors to this volume),[2] advocating for that is not the main goal of this chapter. The goal here is more modest, or more preliminary: to explore the (perhaps surprisingly) difficult question as to *where* within the legal system this proposed leniency for ethically-motivated crime is to be located. To a considerable extent, then, this chapter is an exercise in conceptual cartography. As will be apparent shortly, my answer will differ from very influential (and supposedly very intuitive) answers.

My starting point is the criminal law's understanding of wrongdoing. The criminal law declares actions it deems wrongful criminal (it *criminalizes* them), and then it punishes them. Important differences between instances of wrongdoing tend to be overlooked. A questionable—or an ethically-motivated—crime is still a crime, in a sense similar to that in which a meagre estate is still an estate, a husk of a marriage is still a marriage, and so on. The criminal law thus treats disparate wrongs as all wrong in essentially the same homogeneous and simplified way—or so I will suggest.

This suggestion, however, should immediately invite scepticism, for at least two reasons. First, because the criminal law evidently recognizes that some of

[1] With thanks to the participants in the workshop at the University of Ferrara in May 2025, and, for incisive written comments, to Julian Roberts and Jesper Ryberg.
[2] See Jacobs, this volume, and, in a way, Ryberg, this volume.

Leo Zaibert, *How to Deal with Ethically-Defensible Criminality; or On Deep Sentencing* In: *Sentencing the Ethically-Motivated Offender*. Edited by: Julian V. Roberts, Leo Zaibert, and Jesper Ryberg, Oxford University Press.
 DOI: 10.1093/9780198993025.003.0003

these actions are *more* wrong than others—murder, for example, is (understandably) seen as much more wrong than, say, offences against the public order—and that is why they attract more severe punishments. Second, because the criminal law already considers a variety of factors as it distinguishes particular instances of wrongdoing. Even if we restrict ourselves to a hypothetical in which identical proscribed outcomes are brought about by two different agents (acting independently of each other, etc.), it is typically *not* the case that the criminal law would visit identical punishments upon these two agents. In other words, when confronted with particular occurrences of wrongdoing, the criminal law regularly considers what we can call certain 'stories' that add depth to its response, allowing for excuses, justifications, and mitigating (and aggravating) circumstances. (I use the term 'story' deliberately, trying to highlight a connection with literature to which I will return below.)

My response to these two interrelated sceptical responses is to underscore this (undeniable) fact: the criminal law does consider *some* stories that complexify wrongdoing—but not all the stories that matter, or all the stories the criminal law *should* consider. In the face of wrongdoing, the criminal law operates with a rather fixed cast of characters and entities. There is of course the state itself, which is taken to be in an unproblematic position to inflict just punishment, at least in the sense of not being in the wrong (see Zaibert et al. 2025). Then there is the defendant who is unproblematically taken to have done wrong, and thus to have set the wheels of the criminal justice system in motion. (There is also the victim, who is unproblematically taken to be a passive sufferer of harms—see (Bergelson 2009).) For cases in which the criminal law's formulaic approach breaks down, consider Lee's chapter in this volume. And, finally, there is the wrongdoing itself, which, *qua* wrong, is always equally wrong in the sense just sketched.

The homogenization of wrongdoing I have in mind is reflected, for example, in the doctrines of complicity, attempts, general mitigations, and aggravations. In principle, these apply equally to murder and to assault, to arson and to embezzlement, and so on. The very existence of these 'general part' doctrines assumes that it is possible to distil a certain essence common to all (or at least to the majority) of the specific crimes. Such distilled essence contains the over-simplified sense in which these crimes, stripped of many differences, are all instances of wrongdoing.

Some over-simplifications of this sort are not only unavoidable, but often useful. Still, we should not lose sight of the fact that that is what they are: over-simplifications. Trying to not lose sight of that fact, I propose scrutinizing the way in which the criminal law cares about certain complexities regarding wrongdoing. I propose to do this by examining the range of *stories* that a criminal law could potentially consider. Below I will discuss the connection between these stories and literature, but I can at once note their wide variety.

At one extreme we find the narrow attitude at play in the context of, say, strict liability offences, in which virtually no story matters: someone performs the proscribed action (say, she drives over the speed limit), then she receives the prescribed punishment. That some of her motives may be ethically defensible is irrelevant. At the other extreme we find the extraordinarily capacious attitude captured in the famous saying *tout comprendre c'est tout pardoner*, according to which virtually any story can be relevant to our response to perceived offences. Here not only ethically defensible motives may exculpate, but almost any factor will. Both extremes militate against the very central goal of punishing wrongdoers justly. One extreme is blinkered by its blanket dismissal of crucial moral aspects of what is essentially a moral matter; the other extreme is blinkered by its allowing so many considerations to affect our moral judgment so as to contextualize it out of existence. A just, defensible criminal law would evidently fall somewhere between these two extremes. But where (and how) to determine the exact point within this continuum where the boundary between relevant and irrelevant stories ought to be fixed is more complicated than is typically assumed.

2. Overview

In the next two sections of the chapter, I argue against efforts to account for moral complexity—of the sort exhibited by ethically-motivated wrongdoers—via changes in the areas of legislation or criminal procedure, and of culpability. This leads me to suggests, in section 5 (and in the brief conclusive paragraph), that the appropriate location for considering moral complexity (including that of the ethically-motivated offender) is sentencing. This suggestion, in turn, assumes (or necessitates) considerable discretion for courts.

3. National Pride at the *Palais de Justice*

I will start with one specific real-life, concrete case of ethically-motivated offending—surely a contender for the most noteworthy such case in modern times, the famous Schwartzbard Trial (see (Arendt 1994)), where she suggests that emulating Schwartzbard may have been a preferrable course of action for the Israeli commandos who abducted Eichmann from Argentina. See also (Schur 2007) and (Johnson 2012)).[3]

These (for current purposes) are the essential elements of the case: Sholom Schwartzbard shot Simon Petliura dead in broad daylight, on the busy and hip Parisian Boulevard Saint-Michel, and then patiently waited for the police to arrest him. As Anna Schur has put it: 'when a gendarme arrived, Schwartzbard was still standing over his victim, making no effort to flee the scene or to resist arrest. He handed in the empty revolver and declared that he had killed a great murderer' (Schur 2007: 16). Schwartzbard's stated rationale for killing Petliura was to avenge the latter's alleged role in carrying out pogroms against the Jewish population in Ukraine, which had in fact killed members of Schwartzbard's own family, alongside scores of other innocent Jews.

It is irrelevant for current purposes to determine whether Schwartzbard was correct in his assessment of Petliura's role in the pogroms. I care more about two other facts. First, that Schwartzbard himself *thought* that he was avenging innocent victims, that he was really seeking the most elevated form of justice—that he was embarked on a mission of profound moral significance. Second, that the French court—and seemingly the French *populace*—agreed with him. Schur's summary of the trial captures the mood well: 'On October 18, 1927, the Schwartzbard trial opened at the Paris Palace of Justice in a courtroom packed with 400 spectators. Eight days later the trial was over; it took just thirty-two minutes for the jury to reach a verdict' acquitting Schwartzbard. 'Upon hearing the verdict, the courtroom exploded with triumphant cries of 'Vive la France!' As Schur points out, Schwartzbard's lawyer did not even need to bring to the stand some of the luminaries that were included in his list of potential witnesses: 'Albert Einstein, Henry Bergson, Maxim Gorky, and Paul Langevin' (Schur 2007: 16). Schwartzbard's *story* was sufficient for the jury to acquit him.

What I wish to highlight is that the jury took itself to be doing *justice*—and the nationalistic outburst that followed the acquittal can best be seen as a self-congratulatory celebration of the French's court ability to achieve such lofty virtue. The jury did *not* see itself as granting mercy or forgiveness. In the eyes of the jury, the details of Schwartzbard's story—his ethically defensible motives—*dictated* his acquittal. Justice, as the French jury understood it, was thus inexorably linked with *equity*—with the perfectioning of our response to wrongdoing in light of details that are typically (and best) absent from the text of the law.

[3] Schwartzbard's very name is dropped out of the title of the trial report by Schwartzbard's defence attorney—the famous Henri Torrès—*Le Procès des Progromes* (Torrès 1928).

One explanation for the exclusion of such details from statutes is practical: no law could possibly enumerate all potential circumstances such as those found in Schwartzbard's case. But I would suggest that even if we could imagine a superhuman legislature with the foresight to specify and include all relevant foreseeable details, these details should not be included in the text of the law. Important as these details may really be, *legislators* should not take them into account.

This begins to highlight the radically different roles of the legislative and the judicial branches of government. Imagine that you agree with the French court that Schwartzbard's story made his acquittal appropriate. That would not, I think, mean that you would want to modify the legal prohibition against homicide so as to include an exception for those who kill political figures suspected of heinous crimes. Drafting laws in such a way would be a very bad idea. In order to see why, I propose turning now to another real-life episode—this time not an actual criminal trial, but an actual proposal by a noted contemporary legal scholar for dealing with (a different form of) ethically-motivated offending.

Alan Dershowitz has infamously proposed the use of 'torture warrants' (Dershowitz 2002, 2004). His reasoning is roughly this: notwithstanding its own laws, the state—*any* state—is going to engage in torture (if it thinks that there are overwhelming moral reasons for doing so). There is just no avoiding this example of *Realpolitik*. Now, any decent person should oppose (and any decent legal system should prohibit) torture; so, we had better *regulate* this deplorable practice rather than allow it to fly under the radar, so to speak. That is, we should require state officials who are convinced that a compelling moral reason for torture exists—that is, ethically-motivated torturers—to formally present their evidence to a judge and allow the latter to issue (or not) a torture warrant. Dershowitz thinks that this is a more civilized and honest way of dealing with what he sees as the problem posed by the unavoidable use of torture as an investigatory tool.

Not surprisingly, Dershowitz's position has attracted widespread condemnation. There are many reasons why, despite the possibly superficial appeal of his alleged desire to regulate a practice he claims to detest, his position truly is to be rejected. One of these reasons is relevant for current purposes. Some actions are so morally wrong, so offensive to some of our most fundamental values that their 'unwavering prohibition' is apt, even if one could imagine hypotheticals in which violating such prohibition may be morally permissible. Elaine Scarry has exposed the uninspiring poverty of Dershowitz's argument (Scarry 2004). Imagine someone convinced that she needs to torture someone in order to save an entire city. Scarry reminds us that 'it is unlikely that any saviour of the city would actually be inhibited by the lack of preexisting moral and legal assurances of immunity' (Scarry 2004: 281). As Scarry even more penetratingly puts it, Dershowitz's 'entire argument is premised on the idea that the population lacks the simple attribute of courage' (Scarry 2004: 282). In other words, if someone has enough moral courage to go ahead and torture a person in order to save the city, she would be precisely the sort of person who would neither need nor want immunity beforehand.

Imagine how differently Schwartzbard would have looked—to us and to his court—had he not embraced the consequences of his action (facing trial, risking his liberty, etc.) *without* any assurances. He neither wanted nor needed to strike an immunity deal with the French authorities before killing Petliura: the very point of his moral heroism was predicated on taking the risk he took, on *not* having any immunity. Again, this is not to say that Schwartzbard was correct—either about the facts or about morality—but it is to insist that the sort of ethical motivation that animated him is at odds with Dershowitz's recommendation.

The case can of course be generalized to other forms of ethically-motivated behaviour. Activists of all stripes violate legal prohibitions because they believe that their moral cause is very important—in ways structurally similar to Schwartzbard's. Evidently, their behaviour evinces a certain arrogance (if also a certain courage)—but they could be correct: just as courage does not guarantee correctness, arrogance does not guarantee incorrectness. And in cases of ethically-motivated offenders, moral correctness and moral arrogance are in tension.[4] Crucially, part of what their arrogant courage seeks to do is to call attention to the loftier goal they pursue, an attention that is, again, at odds with the idea of securing immunity beforehand. They seek to highlight certain moral principles precisely by means of putting themselves (or their interests, etc.) on the line.

The myopia of Dershowitz's proposal is further exposed by noting how he fails to realize that the idea of 'torture warrants' erodes the fundamental principle that torture should be *prohibited*. If Dershowitz really wants to curb torture, the way to do that is to *strengthen* the prohibition, not to weaken it by introducing these warrants. The crucial point, however, is that a steadfast

[4] Insofar as ethically-motivated offenders *can* sometimes be correct, their recidivism is different from that of ordinary offenders. Think of someone who repeatedly refuses to help Nazis round up Jews (thus violating Nazi law): I would not want to punish this person with escalating severity. The escalating severity that rightly applies to recidivist ordinary wrongdoers seems misplaced in the context of recidivist ethically-motivated wrongdoers.

defence of some important prohibitions of the criminal law—such as the prohibition of torture, or the protection of human lives and basic human interests—militates against building complex stories within the very text of the law.

The law on the books—both substantive and procedural—in which foundational moral principles are enshrined, should not be tailored (even if that could be successfully accomplished) to include every conceivable exception, including those possibly arising from ethically-motivated behaviour. It is precisely the great importance of some moral principles that recommends limiting the specificity of the stories with which the law, as such, should concern itself.[5] But this creates a paradox. Imagine we think that the French jury reached the right decision in the Schwartzbard case—how can we think this without thereby also thinking that our commitment to prohibitions against killing or against vigilantism should be more nuanced?

The answer is that deeply flawed approaches such as Dershowitz's are not our only option. There are ways to consider complex stories without affecting the way in which laws are drafted. As announced earlier, one promising way of doing this is to highlight the differences between legislating and sentencing. As I will suggest below, the sentencer has more room to manoeuvre here: it is incumbent upon her to look at more stories than it is permissible for the legislator, without thereby eroding commitments to some fundamental prohibitions. Before turning to that discussion in earnest, I wish to discuss a related misplacement of the discussion of complex stories such as those of ethically-motivated offenders.

4. The Irrelevance of Motive

Another strategy for trying to expand the stories which concern the criminal law shifts our focus away from legislation itself and towards matters of culpability. The move seems reasonable: after all, what, if not a special culpability, distinguishes Schwartzbard (and other ethically-motivated offenders) from common offenders? But this move too faces obstacles which are in fact structurally similar to the ones we have already encountered. The most immediate obstacle is that in killing Petliura, Schwartzbard accomplished essentially what he *intended* to accomplish, and the same can of course be said of both many ethically-motivated offenders and many non-ethically-motivated offenders.

[5] My sympathies toward moral particularism (Zaibert 2018) do not fully apply within *legislative* theory.

So, to the extent that all of these offenders share exactly the same degree of culpability (as we are stipulating), then this strategy also appears unconvincing.

There is, however, something so intuitively appealing about the difference between Schwartzbard and any ordinary (not ethically-motivated) killer (even if one believes that he was mistaken or employing the wrong means, etc.), that to summarily dismiss this strategy seems inappropriate. So, an idea suggests itself: calling into question the way we think about culpability as such, and in particular about its apparently narrow focus on intentions to the detriment of motives. Perhaps Schwartzbard's *intentions* are indeed not significantly different from those of ordinary killers, but this is because what really distinguishes him from ordinary killers are his *motives*. If our received theory of culpability cannot account for this obvious difference between intentions and motives, well, so much the worse for it. As Douglas Husak, among many others, has put it: 'a good motive might mitigate punishment . . . and a bad motive might aggravate punishment' (Husak 1987: 144). It really is hard to disagree with him (and others) about this (even if one can disagree with his more radical claim that 'a laudable motive should *preclude* liability' (Husak 1987: 148, emphasis added)).

And yet, noted criminal law theorists have defended 'narrow' versions of culpability. Taking 'motive' to mean 'ultimate reason for action', George Fletcher, for example, has stated that 'an actor's ultimate reason for acting may not bear on his liability. It does not matter whether he steals in order to buy Christmas presents for his children or to support his heroin habit. In some legal systems, it does not matter whether he kills out of jealousy or in order to prevent the decedent from testifying in a criminal trial' (Fletcher 2000: 452). If Fletcher were right, of course, then we could not easily distinguish between ethically-motivated offenders such as Schwartzbard and ordinary offenders in the way we are now contemplating.

Evidently, Fletcher is presupposing a sharp distinction between motives and intentions. The problem for Fletcher is that attempting to 'distinguish intentions from motives' is to enter a 'murky field', as he has recognized himself (Fletcher 2000: 452). The field is murky even outside of penal theory—as seminal works on action theory attest: motives are sometimes seen as forms of intentions ('ulterior intentions'), other times intentions are supposed to be answers to the same type of questions whose other answers include motives. In her celebrated *Intention*, for example, G.E.M. Anscombe asserted: 'motive-in-general is a very difficult topic which I do not want to discuss at any length' (Anscombe 1963: 20). Despite this warning, she evinces sympathy for the 'popular' (i.e., the ordinary language) view that motives are not terribly different from intentions (Anscombe 1963: 18 ff. and *passim*), and she herself equates 'forward looking motives' with 'intentions' (Anscombe 1963: 21). On the other hand, she unequivocally tells us that 'revenge and gratitude are motives' (Anscombe 1963: 20), apparently unaware of how hard it would be to think of these as intentions. A 'very difficult topic' indeed.

For current purposes, however, Anscombe's most remarkable admission is that: 'as for the importance of considering the motives of an action, as opposed to considering the intention, I am very glad not to be writing either ethics or literary criticism, to which this question belongs' (Anscombe 1963: 19). I shall return to the proximity between ethics and the literary (already noticeable in my emphasis on *stories*) in the next section; but for now: to the (obvious) extent that our discussion includes irreducible normative dimensions, we cannot cordon them off as easily as Anscombe does. Only a terribly impoverished—in fact a wholly sterile—criminal law theory can avoid a discussion of motives, or without the concomitant space for treating offenders whose motives may be ethically defensible differently from those whose motives are ethically reprehensible. Alan Norrie has posed the question pithily 'Why has legal justice [in ignoring motives] never got beyond the standpoint of the small child?' (Norrie 2014: 42), and he directly tells us that 'it is indeed "childish" to imagine that culpability can be properly evaluated with reference to intention alone' (Norrie 2014: 53).

A few years ago, as it turns out, the influential *Buffalo Criminal Law Review* published an entire special issue on 'The New Culpability: Motive, Character, and Emotion in Criminal Law'. Guyora Binder opened the lead article of the volume distancing himself from the American jurist Jerome Hall's famous dictum 'hardly any part of the penal law is more definitely settled than that motive is irrelevant' (Binder 2002: 1; Hall 2010: 88). On the other side of the Atlantic, Norrie cites a similarly celebrated British criminal law theorist to the same effect: as Glanville Williams put it 'a crime may be committed from the best of motives and yet remain a crime' Norrie 2014: 42; Williams 1961: 31). Binder and Norrie—among many others—oppose the 'irrelevance of motive' maxim of the common law. Husak, to mention but one of those many others, compellingly concludes that while this maxim 'fails to withstand critical scrutiny' it has nonetheless 'had a pernicious impact on the disposition of a number of cases' (Husak 1987: 148).[6]

[6] Husak's main example: cases of euthanasia, where a refusal to engage with the motives of the 'mercy killer' renders her indistinguishable from any other killer.

I dislike the irrelevance of motive line and yet I do not wish to join the ranks of the 'new culpability' champions. I wish to create space both for the relevance of motives *and* for a recognition of the value of a traditional culpability largely focused on intentions. My reasons will soon emerge, but they can be seen as analogues within the area of culpability proper of the sort of situation we encountered before concerning the problems of adding too many details to the text of the law itself. So, while I am not unsympathetic to the sort of 'ideology critique' of traditional culpability that Norrie, for example, advances (according to which the criminal law hides behind a flatfooted individualism in order to avoid complicated moral issues), I will try to suggest a way in which a traditional—and yes, individualistic—culpability focused on intentions is worth our continued endorsement.

Interestingly, Williams's remark as to the persistence of crime as crime despite good motives is meant to be an explanation why the classical theory of '*mens rea* of English law' may not be sufficiently responsive to retributivism's concern with justice (Williams 1961: 30).[7] In fact, the remark prompts Williams to admit that 'the phrase *mens rea* is somewhat misleading' and to rhetorically ask 'What, then, does legal *mens rea* mean?' (Williams 1961: 31). Williams is in a way agreeing with the spirit of Norrie's critique: *mens rea* seems to be a bit *superficial*—or, to put it in terms I will use below, a bit *thin*.

There *is* a point in linking *mens rea* centrally to intentions (as opposed to motives)—a stance that goes back, with understandable modifications, for millennia (Zaibert 2005).[8] It is a stance connected to the fact that of all the ways in which human beings can relate to their actions, to intend them is the most intimate. It is not necessary here to delve deeply into the technicalities of action theory in order to appreciate this. Contrast, for example, intentions, on the one hand, to desires, wants, wishes, hopes, on the other. The contents of the latter group of mental states can be almost anything whatsoever: I may desire to be taller, hope that I win the lottery, want to defeat Rafa Nadal in tennis, wish that I composed more beautiful songs than Leonard Cohen did, and so on. But I cannot *intend* any of those things: I can only intend my own actions—I can only intend those things that I believe are up to me. I can of course want or wish that I were able to defeat Rafa Nadal in tennis—but I cannot possibly intend to do so (unless we engage in contrived scenarios in which my intention is to drug him before our match and things

[7] The problems Williams sees in the *mens rea* of English law transcend retributivism (see Williams 1961: 30).

[8] For more on the opacity of motives, see Ryberg, this volume.

like that): on pain of irrationality, I cannot intend to beat him at an actual tennis match.

Moreover, intentions are 'self-referential' in a way that the other mental states need not be. If I desire to lose weight, and while I sleep you kidnap me and perform a liposuction on me, so that I wake up 10 kilos lighter, my *desire* has been satisfied. But if I *intend* to lose weight, I have envisioned a way of doing so (say, dieting)—if I lose weight because of the unforeseen liposuction, then my intention has not been satisfied. Intending to do something entails not merely desiring it and not merely believing (even wrongly) that it is up to me but also desiring that it comes about as a result of my own agency, as a result of a specific plan that I have formed. Unsurprisingly, the connection between intentions and actions is so intimate that some have defined an action as the 'condition of satisfaction of an intention' (Searle 1983), or as an 'event which can be described as intentional under at least one description' (Davidson 1980).

There is, then, an intuitive distinction between intentions and motives. We have motives for all sorts of things. Some of those motives can be very significant. But nothing prevents these motives from remaining in the background, even dormant. I have, for example, a motive to lose weight, but this motive does not lead me to actually undertake a diet as forming such an intention would: only the latter directly gets, in the standard case, my agency in motion.[9] In many relevant contexts, saying that we have a motive to do something is like saying that we have a *reason* to do something. And, again, there are countless reasons for me to do countless things that I am unlikely to ever even attempt to do. Our intentions say much more about who we are than do our motives, our reasons, and our desires. Intending to do something entails a certain intimate identification with that something. *This* distinction between motives and intentions does not strike me as particularly murky.

Of course, it is possible to also form intentions without acting on them. But this is not typical. A person who regularly formed intentions on which she did not act would be irrational to a considerable degree—we may even say that she does not know what an intention *is*. A person who had all sorts of desires on which she did not act would not be irrational to the same degree (if to any degree): there is nothing particularly irrational about daydreaming. So, when an act is criminal, the intention to do it reveals—by itself—a commitment to offending that is already highly culpable.

To say that someone is culpable because she intended to do something bad is not 'childish', even if it is problematic to end the evaluation of human action

[9] I ignore here akratic behaviour.

there. It is, and mobilizing now the thin–thick distinction I flagged earlier, a very *thin* way of telling the story. Following Williams (2006), Walzer (1994), and Geertz (1973), we can think of thin terms as very general—or, in a sense, *superficial*—descriptors. Right, good, wrong, bad—and, importantly, also culpable—are thin; courageous, elegant, cruel, deceitful are thick. Although a case can possibly be made as to a certain overreliance on thin terms in post-Enlightenment normative theorizing, the appropriateness of thick or thin concepts varies by context. It would seem misguided to describe criminal law's prohibitions too thickly. We can, in matters of legislation or culpability in general, live with broad distinctions—say, between crimes and misdemeanours, or between the intended and the unintended. Contrariwise, within the context of determining the recipients of a certain medal (say, recognizing courage), we need to examine thick concepts.

Traditional culpability is indeed thin/superficial, and this is, in general, good. Just as within the context of criminalization the message 'torture is wrong' drowns out thicker messages (such as 'torture is despicable, or cowardly', etc.), within the context of culpability the message 'you are to blame for this' drowns out thicker messages (such as 'what you did is despicable, or cowardly', etc.). Again, this is not to say that thicker considerations have no place whatsoever in the criminal justice system—although it *is* to push back at once against abominations such as Dershowitz's torture warrants and against misconceived ideas such as the need for a new culpability. And it *is,* moreover, a reminder of the importance of the respectability of thinness within legislation proper and culpability proper.

Wanting traditional culpability to be much thicker than it is risks *misplacing* the importance of thick stories and considerations. Recall Robert Nozick's useful distinction between moral constraints and moral goals, and in particular his objection to the view that 'a moral concern can only function as a moral goal' (Nozick 1974: 28). To briefly summarize his point: imagine that you are alive to the problematic fact that utilitarianism does not much care for *rights*, since what it cares about is the maximization of utility (even at the expense of rights). Thus, you endeavour to devise a theory which would in effect minimize the violation of rights—what Nozick calls a 'utilitarianism of rights'. But a utilitarianism of rights still allows for their violation—even if it seeks to minimize it. Nozick's insightful rejection of the utilitarianism of rights invites us to think of rights (or their non-violation) as 'side-constraints': not as goals per se, but as so important that they should be seen as restricting our choices *ab initio.*

This is a useful (if imperfect) *model* for understanding the theoretical place for these stories that enrich our understanding of offenders' actions and culpability.

They had better not belong fully in the text of the law itself (again, even if that were possible). And they had better not belong, either, in our analysis of culpability, understood as the fundamental way of connecting offenders to their offences, lest we risk diluting such connection. These two things—that a crime was committed and with enough of a 'guilty mind'—are crucially connected to a form of superficiality, to a certain thinness, which is not problematic in every context.

The Nozickian model is imperfect for my purposes in that I am not quite invoking his distinction between goals and side-constraints. Rather, I am focusing on what I take to be a more basic insight that some things we care about—some of our moral concerns—can be *misplaced* in our normative theorizing: that not every moral concern should be a moral goal is but an instantiation of this more general insight about misplacement. There is again an undeniable air of paradox here: if we care so much about the non-violation of rights, what can be wrong with striving to have as few such violations as possible? As Nozick shows, the answer is that to treat the non-violation of rights as a goal of our ethical theory is in fact sub-optimal, because this approach will permit *some* violations. Instead, treating the prohibition against rights violations as a side-constraint will not permit *any* rights-violation. The most generous way of interpreting Dershowitz's plea for torture warrants is to see it as exhibiting the logic of Nozick's 'utilitarianism of rights': by misplacing his facially morally respectable motive (of reducing instances of torture), however, Dershowitz evinces remarkable moral myopia.

Under this light, the 'irrelevance of motive maxim' is itself to be interpreted humbly—that is, thinly or superficially: as a mere reminder of the fact that (bad) motives are, logically speaking, not *necessary* for establishing legal liability. Proving that someone intended to commit a crime is (*ceteris paribus*) generally logically *sufficient* for liability, independently of motives. Put differently: the fact that someone lacks a motive in no way suggests that she may not be guilty of having committed a crime: having a *motive* is not *necessary* for liability. We rest content with a culpability that does not plumb the depths of human motivation in anything approximating its immense complexity, and with laws that do not seek to foresee and react to every possible relevant complicating story. We can understand that this superficiality is better suited for the proper functioning of a criminal justice system—and this is so *not* because we do not care at all about complications but *rather* because we see that those are not the places in which to care for them.[10]

[10] There are interesting affinities between my plea for 'superficiality' in legislation and culpability here and Matthieu Queloz's defence of superficiality regarding 'voluntariness' in Queloz (2022), where

5. Deep Sentencing, Equity, and Mercy

In using the term 'stories', I have meant to emphasize both the type of entity that actual stories—of the sort we typically find in literature—are, and the sensibility and judgment that is often nurtured by engaging with them. I am taking a cue here from Martha Nussbaum's inspiring work on this subject, particularly her erudite and influential 'Equity and Mercy' (Nussbaum 1993; see also Nussbaum 2016). I wish to echo her view that 'legal, and especially judicial, reasoning can be modeled on the reasoning of the concerned reader of a novel' (Nussbaum 1993: 110). Nussbaum's 'literary judge sees defendants as inhabitants of a complex web of circumstances, circumstances which often, in their totality, justify mitigation of blame and punishment' (1993: 110–111).

Two important points Nussbaum makes deserve underscoring. First, it is not just motives (as contrasted to intentions) that sentencers should investigate, but all manner of *circumstances* in a very general sense. We may calibrate sentences for reasons other than respectable motives alone, including *being right* about those motives (as discussed above). Think about how you may judge a tax-evader in Nazi Germany, even independently of her mental states. Or, think about your assessment of Billy Budd (in Melville's eponymous novella) based on circumstances not directly related to his mental states (Zaibert 2018: 209–242). This capacious sense of 'circumstances' further strengthens the view I defended above that classical culpability may not be the best (and surely not the only) place to deepen our analyses of complicated offenders. Second, and even more importantly, that the distinction to which Nussbaum alludes, almost *en passant*, between legal and judicial reasoning is absolutely crucial. It is precisely *judicial* reasoning—unlike legislative reasoning—that should become thicker and more literary; it is here where giving free rein to our moral and literary imagination is particularly appropriate. (It seems to me that this is what Nussbaum believes as well, but it is not important for my purposes whether that is so.)

In emphasizing this distinction between specifically judicial reasoning and generic legal reasoning, I do not mean to *rank* these different contexts. Just as there is a certain 'dignity of legislation' as Jeremy Waldron pithily put it, there is also a 'dignity of sentencing' (Waldron 1999). What I wish to highlight in

he discusses 'situations in which deeper scrutiny of the conditions that led up to a superficially voluntary action has people revise their perception of the action as voluntary and withhold blame as a result. *Tout comprendre, c'est tout pardonner*, as the old adage has it—to understand all is to excuse all'—and that such depth is not always a good thing (2022: 1614). Ryberg's insistence (in his chapter in this volume) on the potential obscurities regarding motives also can recommend superficiality.

this final section is that the peculiar appeal of some forms of superficiality that I have sketched and defended above is greatly diminished within the context of sentencing. Here, more than anywhere else, is where depth has a place—hence my dubbing the sort of sentencing I envision vis-à-vis ethically-motivated offenders *deep sentencing*.

Naturally, some rules apply here too—particularly those connected to individual protections afforded to defendants, say, by the principle of legality—but, still, sentencers ought to be much freer in their deliberations than legislators. (For a partly different route to largely a very similar conclusion, see Du Bois-Pedain (2017).) French society's celebration of Schwartzbard's acquittal was not, to the best of my knowledge, accompanied by proposals to change their laws so as to decriminalize killing in some circumstances, or to create a new and thicker culpability. The French celebration appeared predicated on the conviction that it was right for the jury to decide roughly as it did, even if there was nothing wrong with the law being roughly what it was.

Unsurprisingly, Nussbaum's pleas for sentencers to embrace the nuanced sensibility of the concerned reader of novels are related to her overarching concern with mercy—a concern that I share (Zaibert 2009, 2024). There is an affinity between an interest in mercy and the nuanced sensibility typical of literary authors, critics, or readers—a sensibility attuned to thick stories. It is very hard to imagine granting mercy—understood as a gracious or supererogatory act—without relying on some stories of this nuanced and complicated sort.

I cannot here engage with the historical analysis as to why normative theorizing, particularly after the Enlightenment, has (consciously or otherwise) looked askance towards mercy. That dismissal relates to ideals of predictability, uniformity, and systematicity that the concept of *justice* appears better suited to enshrine. Insofar as mercy, by definition, is gracious or supererogatory—never a duty—it is very hard to systematize. Were 'mercy' to be legislatively mandated, for example, it would—already as a definitional matter—cease to be mercy. While there is nothing inherently wrong (and much that is very good) about those Enlightenment ideals, it is easy to overstate their importance, or to miss their potential drawbacks.

Malcolm Bull has explored the intellectual demise of mercy in normative (mostly political) theorizing and has insightfully suggested that 'mercy is thicker than justice'; in fact, that 'it is difficult to imagine what would serve as a thin account of mercy' (Bull 2019: 117). It is in virtue of thick stories that mercy could ever be appropriate. If mercy is to have a place within the law, as Nussbaum and Bull and I believe, it is crucially within sentencing, where deontic strictures are considerably looser than in other areas. Deep sentencers *can* grant mercy in ways that legislators cannot—and often it is good that they do. The overall functioning of the legal system is not jeopardized if we afford sentencers the latitude to judge deeply and imaginatively—quite the opposite.

I wish to end by delineating two aspects of my views on mercy's relationship to punishment, and on mercy's relationship to one other important source of thick stories. These emerge clearly by contrasting my position with Nussbaum's.

Nussbaum sees mercy above all as an *alternative* to 'a retributivism that is brutal in its neglect of human complexity'—better than a 'deterrence-only view' (which she also deems 'brutal') (Nussbaum 1993: 115).[11] The upshot of Nussbaum's *tour de force* on ancient Greek history is that the justice paradigm (primitive, brutal, superficial, and *thin*) should *give way* to the mercy paradigm (mature, subtle, profound, and *thick*). Nussbaum thus slides too far toward one of the two extremes described at the outset. For she may (unwittingly?) endorse a position in which just punishment simply vanishes into thin air—since in every case mercy would be a better (thicker, etc.) response to wrongdoing than it.

Despite Nussbaum's demonization of retributivism, mercy and retributivism are much more intimately connected than typically acknowledged.[12] Furthermore, it is simply not true that modern justifications of punishment—whether retributive or consequentialist—are as 'brutal' as Nussbaum contends. Contemporary retributivism has very little in common with the 'archaic' approach to cosmic processes, such as that contained in Anaximander's talk of an 'encroachment' of winter's sphere into the sphere of summer (and vice versa), and for which, he thought, 'retribution must take place' (Nussbaum 1993: 88).[13] Contemporary consequentialist approaches are, similarly, much more sophisticated than this, alive to all manner of qualifications and safeguards. If the avoidance of an imaginary brutality in retributivism were indeed the reason to turn toward mercy, we would be better off looking for another one.

Pace Nussbaum, to care about justice (in the way that, say, retributivists do) is not to be 'brutal', not to thereby engage in 'magical thinking' (Nussbaum 2016: 24 ff. and *passim*), and, most importantly, *not optional*: (retributive)

[11] For criticisms of Nussbaum's views on retributivism see Zaibert (2018).

[12] Surprisingly, only retributivists can (as a matter of sheer logic) *be* merciful. See Zaibert (2025a).

[13] At least once Nussbaum distances herself from the tendentious (but nonetheless prominent in her article) linking of contemporary retributivism with archaic Greek views such as Anaximander's, when she chides Andrea Dworkin (also prominent in Nussbaum's article) for embracing a view of 'justice' 'so resolute in its denial of particularity that it resembles Anaximander's *dike* more than it resembles most modern retributive schemes' (Nussbaum 1993: 124).

justice matters. The fact that contemporary criminal justice systems often display horrific excesses is no reason to dismiss the problem of justice—in fact, many of those awful excesses are most compellingly denounced by pointing to their injustice. Part of the difficulty in fixing the exact point along the continuum that goes from strict liability to *tout pardonner* derives from the tension between the value of justice and the value of mercy.[14]

In demonizing 'brutal' justifications of punishment Nussbaum evades the general and complicated interplay between depth and superficiality which I have explored above. Her version of the criminal justice system seems to lack precisely the sort of depth and complexity that literary stories often display: her story is too lineal and naïve to tackle this complexity.[15] While I explicitly agree with Nussbaum in wanting (above all) sentencers to exhibit depth and to be detail-oriented (etc.), these characteristics are not unalloyed goods. They do not belong everywhere within the legal system, and they do not exhaust all that matters. Things are much more complicated than Nussbaum recognizes. We want *both* mercy's thickness and justice's thinness.

And this brings us to that other aspect of my views on mercy crucial for my purposes here. Mercy itself is but *one* important tool for dealing with ethically-motivated and other complicated offenders—one among many. Sometimes the proper way of treating ethically-motivated offenders may involve no mercy at all. As suggested above, I do not think that the jury (or the public) in Schwartzbard's trial saw the case as one in which Schwartzbard had been treated *mercifully*—on the contrary, their view seems to have been that Schwartzbard was treated *justly* ('brutally' so, to use Nussbaum's inapt term), even if in a way that the law in the books could not, on its own, have prescribed. While I am not interested here in actual statistics, my suspicion is that, more often than mercy, sentencers can invoke other notions as they deal with ethically-motivated offenders—of particular importance, equity. And it seems to me that it was above all equity—and, again, not mercy—that the court in the Schwartzbard case had in mind when it acquitted him.

Despite appearing in its very title, equity sits uncomfortably within Nussbaum's famous article. At times she appears to flatly *reduce* mercy to equity—in what is, in fact, a very common reductive approach to mercy.[16] For example, Nussbaum tells us that 'tragedy is thus a school of equity, and

[14] The criminal justice system serves many purposes, not all directly connected to justice. Those other purposes further complicate matters. See Roberts (2015); Zaibert (2025b).
[15] In contrast, several chapters in this volume seek to explore, in different ways, this complexity.
[16] Masterfully discussed in Tasioulas (2003).

therefore of mercy' (1993: 95), that a good reader of novels 'is already prepared for equity, and in turn, for mercy', and remarks of a similar tenor (1993: 105). Admittedly, equity shares with mercy a heightened concern with the details and the complexity of life. But there is a crucial difference between the two notions: equity has traditionally (and rightly) been seen as an important dimension of the administering of 'brutal' justice, whereas mercy is best seen as operating on a different plane altogether.

Juan Iglesias has usefully summarized the classical understanding of equity, current at least since the heyday of Roman law: 'there are matters that the law leaves unanswered, in light of its own inarticulacy, or in light of the intrinsic limitations to which texts are subject, or because the spirit of new times has aged the law and rendered it obsolete' (Iglesias 2010: 69—my translation). Versions of this intimate connection between equity and justice can be traced from ancient times to our own day (Beneduzi 2021). The essence of equity is that it *perfects* justice in the concrete case. Equity accomplishes this perfecting by means of rightly thickening *at sentencing* what was—sometimes rightly, sometimes deliberately—left *thin* in the law itself. Equity thus shares another characteristic with mercy: it is out of place in *legislation*. Just as legislators can hardly be merciful, they can hardly be equitable. These tools are emphatically *not* out of place in the legal system as a whole, for they do belong in sentencing, where they often play protagonist roles.

Both mercy and equity are valuable tools in the arsenal of the deep sentencer, as she deals with ethically-motivated offenders and other complicated cases. And both involve engaging with thick stories of the sort that are common in literature. Stressing equity is *helpful* for my purposes because, insofar as equity has been historically connected to the law, the interpretative freedom it recommends is perhaps less objectionable (because more limited) than the one that flows from appeals to mercy. 'Mercy scepticism', after all, is much more common than 'equity scepticism'.[17] Independently of mercy, an *equitable* concern with details may lead to a juster (and in principle more lenient) treatment of ethically-motivated offenders. And stressing mercy, in turn, is *helpful* for my purposes because it shows how truly broad the space of deep sentencing I envision is: it is not just the classical 'perfecting' of justice that belongs there, but the very *overcoming* of justice by way of its merciful remission.

[17] Mercy scepticism comes in many versions: note the differences between, say, Harrison (1992), Kekes (2009), and Duff (2007).

6. Conclusion

I trust that by now a series of closely interrelated conclusions should have emerged from this exercise in conceptual cartography. First, there is ample room within the law for dealing with ethically-motivated offenders. Secondly, responding to them involves a certain 'deepening' of the way in which we evaluate what they do. Thirdly, this deepening cannot happen just anywhere in the legal system—and it would be a mistake to attempt to always introduce such depth within legislation, or as a reason for championing a 'new culpability'.[18] Structurally, the law and traditional culpability may be fine as they are:[19] depth is not always, and at any rate not everywhere, good. Fourthly, that the proper place for this deepening is sentencing, understood as a rather autonomous legal space. And, fifthly, that insofar as *both* equity and mercy are pertinent when judging ethically-motivated offenders, the relatively autonomous legal space of sentencing ought to be recognized as very ample indeed.

References

Anscombe, G.E.M. *Intention.* Cambridge MA: Harvard University Press, 1963.

Arendt, Hannah. *Eichmann in Jerusalem: A Report on the Banality of Evil.* New York: Penguin, 1994.

Beneduzi Renato. *Equity in the Civil Law Tradition.* Cham: Springer, 2021.

Bergelson, Vera. *Victims' Rights and Victims' Wrongs: Comparative Liability in Criminal Law.* Palo Alto CA: Stanford University Press, 2009.

Binder, Guyora. 'The Rhetoric of Motive and Intent', *Buffalo Criminal Law Review* 6 (2002): 1–96.

Bondi, Gianmarco. 'Sentencing Ethically-Motivated Offenders in Italy', Chapter 13 of this volume.

Bull, Malcolm. *On Mercy.* Princeton NJ: Princeton University Press, 2019.

Davidson, Donald. 'Agency' in his *Essays on Actions and* Events, pp. 43–62. Oxford: Oxford University Press (1980).

Demay, Clémence. 'Sentencing Crimes of Civil Disobedience in Switzerland', Chapter 11 of this volume.

Dershowitz, Alan. *Why Terrorism Works: Understanding the Threat, Responding to the Challenge.* New Haven CT: Yale University Press, 2002.

[18] I do not here discuss cases in which motives are already built into legislation (or culpability). Neither do I wish to claim that motives *never* belong in the law itself (or culpability), only that they *often* do not belong there, because their natural home is sentencing proper. See Bondi (this volume) and Demay (this volume), for examples of jurisdictions that include mitigation for the ethically-motivated wrongdoer within the law itself.

[19] No closet conservatism is to be inferred here: existing law and culpability may be 'fine as they are' *in the sense that we are discussing here*—that is, in connection to the complexity that we may wish them to exhibit.

Dershowitz, Alan. 'Tortured Reasoning', in *Torture: A Collection*, edited by Sanford Levinson, pp. 257–280. Oxford: Oxford University Press, 2004.

Du Bois-Pedain, Antje. 'In Defence of Substantial Sentencing Discretion' *Criminal Law Forum* 28 (2017): 391–435.

Duff, R.A. 'The Intrusion of Mercy' *Ohio State of Journal of Criminal Law* 4 (2007): 361–387.

Fletcher, George P. *Rethinking Punishment*, Oxford: Oxford University Press, 2000.

Geertz, Clifford. *The Interpretation of Cultures*, New York: Basic Books, 1973.

Hall, Jerome. *General Principles of Criminal Law* (3rd edn). Clark NJ: Lawbook Exchange, 2010.

Harrison, R. 'The Equality of Mercy' in *Jurisprudence: Cambridge Essays*, edited by H. Gross and R Harrison, pp. 107–126. Oxford: Clarendon Press (1992).

Husak, Douglas N. *The Philosophy of Criminal Law*. Ottowa: Rowman & Littlefield, 1987.

Iglesias, Juan. *Derecho Romano: Historia e Instituciones* (18th edn). Barcelona: Sello Editorial, 2010.

Jacobs, Jonathan. 'Is Sentence Mitigation More Problematic than Aggravation in the Context of Ethical Offending?', this volume.

Johnson, Kelly Scott. 'Sholem Schwartzbard: Biography of a Jewish Assassin', doctoral dissertation at Harvard University (2012), available online: https://dash.harvard.edu/server/api/core/bitstreams/5f7bd6ec-f5ea-425e-b2fe-3b6b8f494d02/content, last visited 8 August 2025.

Kekes, John. 'Blame Versus Forgiveness', *The Monist* 92.4 (2009): 488–506.

Lee, Florence. 'Sentencing Pro-democracy Protesters in Hong Kong', Chapter 10 of this volume.

Norrie, Alan. *Crime, Reason, and History: A Critical Introduction to Criminal Law*, Cambridge: Cambridge University Press (3rd ed.), 2014.

Nozick, Robert. *Anarchy, State, and Utopia*, Oxford: Blackwell, 1974.

Nussbaum, Martha. 'Equity and Mercy', *Philosophy and Public Affairs* 22.2 (1993): 83–125.

Martha, Nussbaum. *Anger and Forgiveness: Resentment, Generosity, Justice*, Oxford: Oxford University Press, 2016.

Queloz, Matthieu. 'The Essential Superficiality of the Voluntary', *Philosophical Studies* 179 (2022): 1591–1620.

Roberts, Julian V. *Criminal Justice: A Very Short Introduction*, Oxford: Oxford University Press, 2015.

Ryberg, Jesper. 'Sentencing Honourable Offenders: On the complexities of assessing human motives', Chapter 3 of this volume.

Scarry, Elaine. 'Five Errors in the Reasoning of Alan Dershowitz' in *Torture: A Collection* (Sanford Levinson, ed.) Oxford: Oxford University Press (2004): 281–290.

Schur, Anna. 'Shades of Justice: The Trial of Sholom Schwartzbard and Dovid Bergelson's *Among Refugees*', *Law & Literature* 19.1 (2007): 15–43.

Searle, John R. *Intentionality: An Essay in the Philosophy of Mind*, Cambridge: Cambridge University Press, 1983.

Tasioulas, John. 'Mercy', *Proceeding of the Aristotelian Society* 103 (2003): 101–132.

Torrès, Henry. *Le Procès des Progromes*, Paris: Editions de France, 1928.

Waldron, Jeremy. *The Dignity of Legislation*, Cambridge: Cambridge University Press, 1999.

Walzer, Michael. *Thick and Thin: Moral Argument at Home and Abroad*, Notre Dame: Notre Dame University Press, 1994.

Williams, Bernard. *Ethics and the Limits of Philosophy*, London: Routledge, 2006.

Williams, Glanville. *Criminal Law: The General Part*, (2nd ed.), London: Stevens & Sons, 1961.

Zaibert, Leo. *Rethinking Punishment*, Cambridge: Cambridge University Press, 2018.
Zaibert, Leo. *Five Ways Patricia can Kill her Husband*, Chicago: Open Court, 2005.
Zaibert, Leo. 'Mercy' in *The Oxford Handbook of the Philosophy of Punishment*, (Jesper Ryberg, ed.) Oxford: Oxford University Press (2024): 423–440.
Zaibert, Leo. 'The Paradox of Forgiveness' *Journal of Moral Philosophy* 6 (2009): 365–393.
Zaibert, Leo. 'Le pardon et la rétribution', in *La justice pénale aux frontières du pardon*, (Nayfield, et al., eds.) Paris: Classiques Garnier (2025a): 109–129.
Zaibert, Leo. 'Pluralism in the Justification of Punishment', in *Sentencing, Public Opinion, and Criminal Justice*, (Marie Manikis and Gabrielle Watson, eds.), Oxford: Oxford University Press (2025b): 83–97.
Zaibert, Leo, Julian Roberts, and Jesper Ryberg (eds.), *Responding to the Culpable State: Is Sentence Mitigation Appropriate?*, Oxford: Hart, 2025.

3

Sentencing Honourable Offenders

On the Complexities of Assessing Human Motives

Jesper Ryberg

1. Introduction

The image of an offender as someone who has decided to break the law and who has a malicious motive corresponds to popular conceptions of offenders and is prevalent in all genres of crime fiction. However, it does not always represent the reality in criminal courts. There are cases where an offender's behaviour, although clearly illegal, becomes more understandable as the context of the offence emerges. There may be cases where the offender's motive attracts sympathy or even admiration. In short, some crimes are committed out of good motives.

There are several ways in which such motives may be taken into account in criminal justice systems. Even though it has sometimes been stated almost as criminal law wisdom that motives are irrelevant when it comes to the determination of liability, in reality this is often not the case.[1] For instance, motives play an important role in justification defences which may exculpate a defendant. They may also have a direct impact on the type of crime of which a defendant is convicted. More importantly, they may play a role at sentencing. Not only is this descriptively true; there are also many criminal law theorists who hold that this is normatively plausible. It has been underlined that in contrast to binary considerations of liability, the sentencing phase is well-suited to dealing with issues concerning motives of various kinds. Models have even been proposed for how this might be done in a more systematic manner. For instance, Carissa Byrne Hessick has proposed a classification system consisting of five motive categories: highly mitigating, partially mitigating, neutral,

[1] An oft-quoted example of this view is Jerome Hall's contention that 'Hardly any part of penal law is more definitely settled than that motive is irrelevant' (1960: 88). For an informative and critical discussion of the view that motive is immaterial to liability, see e.g. Husak (1989).

Jesper Ryberg, *Sentencing Honourable Offenders* In: *Sentencing the Ethically-Motivated Offender*. Edited by: Julian V. Roberts, Leo Zaibert, and Jesper Ryberg, Oxford University Press.
DOI: 10.1093/9780198993025.003.0004

aggravating, and highly aggravating. Different motives are then *ex ante* placed within this continuum (Hessick 2006: 236). The idea is that there should be an initial presumption that an offender has acted out of an 'ordinary motive', but that evidence of deviations from this default position can be accounted for by moving up or down along these categories (i.e. by ascribing larger or smaller mitigations/aggravations).[2]

The focus of this chapter is on the role of honourable and dishonourable motives as a sentencing factor. On the one hand, I believe that such motives should sometimes be taken into account at sentencing. For instance, there are reasons to treat the mercy killer differently from the contract killer. On the other hand, it also seems to me that the idea that motives should count in the determination of sentences opens a Pandora's box of theoretical issues that have as yet only been tentatively addressed. This means, for instance, that a procedure for the invocation of motives, such as the model sketched by Hessick (discussed later in this essay), may be plausible in principle, but very hard to apply in practice. The purpose here therefore is not to argue definitively for or against the moral significance of motives at sentencing. More modestly, I will highlight some of the theoretical challenges that arise if motives are accepted as a mitigating or aggravating factor at sentencing.

2. Overview

In order to address these challenges, the chapter proceeds along the following lines. Section 3 presents an hypothetical scenario of offenders who all commit the same type of crime while acting out of very different motives. The scenario serves as an example that will illustrate the ensuing considerations. Section 4 considers distinguishing between good and bad motives. The purpose is not to focus on the practical issue of what can serve as sufficient evidence to establish a good or bad motive, but simply to consider what we are even talking about when this distinction is made. The same is the case in section 5 which concerns the question of how one should distinguish between different degrees of a good motive. What does it mean to hold that one motive is better than

[2] It is not clear to me what precisely Hessick has in mind when she talks about the 'neutral' category of motives. Apparently, this category comprises 'ordinary motives' for a particular crime. However, it is not obvious why an ordinary motive should be regarded as a morally neutral motive. Could there not be cases where particular crimes are ordinarily committed out of malicious motives? Presumably, the most plausible interpretation is that this category consists of motives that do not seem either good or bad independently of whether these motives are ordinary.

another? Section 6 concerns cases where an offender may have conflicting motives and considers what this means for the assessment of the motive behind a crime. Section 7 focuses on the significance of the fact that a crime may often not be performed out of a single motive. If an offender acts out of mixed motives, such as both a good and a bad motive, then this presents an obvious challenge to the idea that motives should be taken into account at sentencing. Some of the ways in which courts have dealt with mixed motives are considered. Section 8 addresses what I believe constitutes the most important challenge to the inclusion of motives as a mitigating or aggravating factor; namely, that an offender's action may be motivationally over-determined. When this is the case, it no longer seems to make sense to try to identify the real or true motive behind a crime. It is suggested that motivational over-determination may well not be a rare phenomenon and that this means that there are cases where motives will be difficult to account for at sentencing. Finally, section 9 summarizes and concludes.

Before proceeding further, a few comments should be added on the scope of the discussion. First, I will not provide a definition of the concept of a motive. For example, I shall not attempt to draw a clear line between motives and intentions. It is indisputable that these concepts are imprecise, and several attempts at developing definitions have been presented.[3] Nonetheless, the following considerations will not be contingent on one particular definition. Secondly, although some of the considerations may also be relevant in relation to specification of types of crime and to the question of criminal liability, I will, as noted, focus exclusively on motives as a sentencing factor. Thirdly, I shall not discuss what it will take to prove that an offender acted out of a particular motive or, more generally, how we tend to infer motives from the way people behave.[4] These are of course important questions and there are studies that indicate that our attribution of people's motives is far from always accurate.[5] However, such evidentiary questions will be left untouched. Fourthly, I will not engage in a discussion of how different good or bad motives should be translated into mitigations or aggravations of varying degree. In order to substantiate the idea that motives should be taken into account at sentencing, it is necessary to say something about how large a mitigation should be if an

[3] A definition provided in a recent psychological review on research on motives is that 'motives refer to psychological states that direct an individual towards an end that they actively want to obtain' (Carlson et al. 2022: 470). For a discussion of different attempts at defining motives, see e.g. Husak (1989).

[4] For an overview of research on the latter question, see Carlson et al. (2022).

[5] For instance, some studies suggest that we tend to over-attribute self-interest as a motive for others' actions (see Carlson et al. 2022: 474).

offender has acted from a particularly good motive, and vice versa with regard to a bad motive. How this should be done is a complicated question that depends on the theory of punishment to which one subscribes. However, I shall not consider this question except by underlining here that an answer is crucial for a theory of motives as related to sentence mitigations or aggravations to be workable.[6] Finally, I will not address the question of how the criminal justice system should respond to civil disobedience. It is obvious that motives play a key role in discussions of civil disobedience, and some of the hypothetical scenarios that I will present and draw on in the following seem to fall in this category. However, there is wide disagreement about how precisely civil disobedience should be understood, and entering into this conceptual discussion will not serve the purposes of this chapter. More importantly, as the example of the mercy killer versus the contract killer illustrates, the question of the significance of motives reaches far beyond the discussion of civil disobedience.

3. An Hypothetical Scenario: A Day in Activist City

To provide a context for the ensuing discussion of the role of motives at sentencing, let us start with the following hypothetical (but not unrealistic) scenario. In Activist City, the streets are crowded with people. Climate activists have initiated a campaign to protest against the current use of fossil fuels in a world that is burning. In order to direct public attention to the urgency of the problem, a crime is committed as part of the campaign. However, not all citizens of Activist City share the views of the climate activists. In a nearby street, a group of climate sceptics have initiated a 'Drill, baby, drill' demonstration to protest against possible restrictions on the use of fossil fuels. They also commit a crime to underline the importance of their cause. However, other issues are being contested in Activist City. In another neighbourhood, a group of pro-abortion activists have taken to the streets to fight for women's right to abortion. As part of their protest, a crime is committed. The same is the case on the other side of the street where abortion opponents commit a crime to underline the significance of their pro-life message. Although the general level of activist engagement is thus high in Activist City, there are still some citizens who have

[6] The question of how a particular factor should be translated into a particular degree of mitigation (or aggravation) obviously also arises in relation to considerations of other mitigating factors. For more thorough discussions of this challenge in relation to different types of sentencing factors, see e.g. Ryberg (2014, 2023, 2025a, 2025b).

other business to do, and for one person, a member of a non-activist group, this involves being paid to commit a crime, which he consequently carries out.

Now, suppose that the persons who committed the crimes in each of the four protest groups and the one non-activist group have been identified and that there is no doubt about the guilt of each of these five persons. Suppose, further, that the crime that has been committed—let us call it C—is in all cases identical (e.g. vandalism). The only difference across the cases is that the crimes have been committed for very different causes. How should the criminal court of Activist City respond to these crimes? Should any of the offenders receive a sentence that differs from the one that is usually imposed when C is committed out of 'ordinary motives'? If so, which offender(s) and for what reasons?

4. Benign and Malign Motives

Many theorists have defended the view that motives should play a role at sentencing. In fact, some have advocated a view that relates closely to some of the above scenarios; namely, that climate activists, due to their honourable motives, should be treated more leniently. In order to give content to these views, it is of course necessary to distinguish between good and bad motives. Without this distinction, there will be no ground for mitigation or aggravation. But how should this distinction be made? A liberal reader may perhaps find it easy to sympathize with the climate activist or the pro-abortion advocate. However, this sympathy cannot constitute sufficient grounds for a judge to award mitigation to offenders belonging to these two groups, or for sentencing more harshly the climate sceptic or the pro-life activist. After all, a more conservative judge's sympathies might well run in the opposite direction. Therefore, what is needed is a more principled way of drawing a distinction that reaches beyond mere personal preferences. But what would this look like? An obvious answer might be to consult some of the reasons that have been advanced in favour of regarding motives as a relevant factor at sentencing. Let us see if a criterion can be derived on any of these grounds.

One way of sustaining the view that motives should play a role at sentencing is to consider what theories of punishment would imply.[7] Several theorists have underlined that retributivism provides support for the penal ethical significance of motives. For instance, Hessick contends that 'motive's role in punishment is strongly supported by both retributive and expressivist theories

[7] For a comprehensive presentation of modern theories of punishment, see Ryberg (2025c).

of punishment' (2006: 112). Might it therefore be the case that a retributivist approach to punishment helps us distinguish between the moral quality of offender motives?

It is difficult to see how this is the case. The basic view shared across different versions of retributivism is that an offender should receive his or her just deserts and that the severity of the punishment should reflect the seriousness of the crime. Therefore, if a crime is less serious when it is committed out of a good motive, then the offender should be punished more leniently. However, this does not tell us anything about how motives should be assessed. On the contrary, a retributivist approach to punishment needs to be supplied with a theory of what should be regarded as good or bad motives in order to be able to take such aspects of a crime into account. Thus, Hessick might be right in the simple sense that a retributivist theory of punishment may be *compatible* with the idea that some motives may warrant different punitive responses insofar as these mental attitudes contribute to the seriousness of a crime, but this does not in itself provide us with a criterion for how good and bad motives should be distinguished. Rather, it seems to presuppose such a distinction.

Another possibility might be to draw on considerations of the consequences associated with different motives. This can be done in different ways. A first argument that has been given in favour of seeing motives as a factor at sentencing, is that this may have desirable consequences in terms of crime prevention. For instance, Hessick contends that 'while the conventional view of deterrence theory may not provide much support for an expanded role for motive in punishment, a broader view of deterrence, which recognizes that the perceived legitimacy of criminal law and informal controls play determinative roles in the promotion of lawful behaviour, strongly supports a larger role for motive' (2006: 118). Following this view, a good motive would be one that, when it is accounted for in the criminal justice system's response to crime, contributes to crime prevention by reflecting a general perception of the criminal justice system as a fair system.

Another broader consequence-based view might be that a good motive is one that generally promotes desirable outcomes (in the same way as David Hume suggested that the distinction between virtues and vices should be based on how such character traits systematically contribute to good consequences).[8] I shall not here engage in further considerations on the plausibility of these criteria. But it should be noted that if, as is the case on both accounts, motives are not per se good or bad, but rather *become* good or bad depending on the

[8] For considerations of this view, see e.g. Driver (1995).

consequences they generally have or the consequences that follow from the way the court reacts to them, then the possibility of accounting for such motives at sentencing will be contingent on empirical information that it may not always be easy to obtain. For instance, it will not be easy to establish that sentence mitigation in a criminal case contributes to the more general perception of the criminal justice system in a way that affects the level of crime. And when it comes to the general consequences of various types of motive, there will also be many cases where these will be quite difficult to assess (e.g. what are the more general consequences of acting out of pecuniary motives?). Finally, these criteria presuppose that we are able to identify the motives for a crime. As we shall see shortly, this in itself turns out not to be an easy task.

It may perhaps be felt that the previous considerations amount to some sort of philosophical nit-picking. After all, is it not usually the case (as a US Supreme Court judge once stated in relation to pornography) that we know it when we see it?[9] As indicated, I am not suggesting that there may not be some motives that strike us as obviously good or bad. Psychological studies on motives have shown that we generally regard altruistic motives as better than self-interested motives (see e.g. Carlson et al. 2022). However, I also believe that the examples of the activists and the non-activist in Activist City indicate that the distinction may not always be obvious, and that reasons that may help us to reach beyond mere intuition will therefore often be desirable.

5. Comparing the goodness of motives

Suppose that we are generally able to distinguish between good and bad motives. The next question is how to distinguish between motives that qualitatively fall in the same category. Benign motives are not all equally good. Presumably a plausible theory of the role of motives at sentencing will imply that some good motives are better than others, and that the size of the mitigation should depend upon how good a motive is. As we have seen above, this is

[9] It might perhaps be suggested that the moral quality of motives should be determined on the grounds of what are regarded as good or bad motives within the society; that is, that it should be determined by public views on the matter. Whether such a criterion would be plausible will depend upon penal theoretical considerations. For instance, if such a view is defended within a retributivist theoretical framework, then one will have to consider whether this way of attributing significance to public opinion when it comes to mitigations/aggravations is consistent with the more general way in which the severity of punishments is determined (e.g. it may generate a tension to hold that public views should count when it comes to motives, but not with regard to other dimension of punishment severity). I do not pursue these questions here, however; for a discussion of the role of public opinion in penal theory, see e.g. Ryberg and Roberts (2014a, 2014b).

precisely what Hessick suggested in her model for the ranking of motives. But what reasons can be given in favour of the view that one motive is better than the other? It should be noted that while we may feel we have an idea of which motives are good and which are bad, the task of comparing motives within each of these two categories is much less straightforward. Thus, some sort of theoretical guidance on the relative comparison of good motives would be desirable in order to substantiate the view that motives should play a role in sentencing.[10]

If one consults arguments that have been presented in favour of regarding motives as a sentencing factor, then it might be hoped that they will also provide some grounds for a relative comparison of motives. One such argument has been presented by Ivó Coca-Vila, who holds that climate activists should receive a sentence mitigation when they commit a crime in relation to their protests. What he contends is that 'although the wrongdoing [of climate protesters] is not objectively less serious, the message conveyed regarding the validity of the law violated and the legal systems as a whole is substantially different' (2024: 583). Thus, the view is based on the idea (also defended by other penal theorists)[11] that crimes that are equally harmful may nevertheless send different messages, and that the quality of these messages should be taken into consideration in the overall assessment of the crime and the appropriate sentence. Could this idea help us when it comes to the relative comparison of the valence of good motives? That is, might it be held that the quality of such crime messages provides a way of justifying differences in the size of motive-based sentence mitigations?

The idea that crimes may send different messages is of course a claim that needs empirical support. In my view, such claims are sometimes used a little carelessly by theorists without providing any evidence to answer what in the end is an empirical question. However, even if we set this point aside, the idea

[10] Another more detailed question that arises with regard to the comparison of good motives is whether these should be compared only in purely ordinal terms; that is, whether all we need to say is that one motive is better than another, or whether some sort of *interval* comparison will be required which accounts for the possibility that one motive may be much better than another. When the severity of punishment has been discussed within a retributivist context it has often been underlined that mere ordinal comparison is insufficient. However, it is obvious that an interval comparison will be much more demanding. For a general discussion of the complexities of different scales for the ranking of crime gravity, see e.g. Ryberg (2004).

[11] See e.g. Kahan (1996). He illustrates this point by asking his reader to compare the 'the actions of a white supremacist who kills an African-American out of racial hatred and a mother who in anger kills a man who has sexually abused her child. Both acts are wrong, and their consequences are in some sense equivalent—there is one dead person in each case. Nevertheless, the racist's killing is more worthy of condemnation precisely because his hatred expresses a more reprehensible valuation than does the mother's anger' (ibid: 598).

of focusing on the messages of crimes is of little help if we do not have a way of comparing the quality of the messages that are conveyed. Coca-Vila suggests that climate activists violate legal norms 'as a means of effecting a change in public policy that can be considered reasonable' (2024: 583). But what does that mean? Consider again the perpetrators in Activist City. Should we say that the message conveyed by the crimes of the climate activists concerns a more reasonable policy change than the message conveyed by the climate sceptics? What if the climate sceptics' protests are based on empirically mistaken assumptions (e.g. that there is no climate problem or that it will be resolved through technological development)—is it then reasonable to assess the quality of their motives on the grounds that the message is unreasonable? And even if this is the case, what should we say when it comes to the comparison of the crimes committed by the climate activists and the abortion proponents? Recall that they committed the same crime, but is there a difference in the reasonableness of the conveyed messages that would support the conclusion that the motive is better in one group than in the other? Should this ultimately depend on an ethical analysis of whether it is more important to change climate policy than to ensure women's right to abortion? What these questions indicate, in my view, is that the idea of assessing motives on the grounds of the messages conveyed does not seem to have much to offer. It is of little help to move the delicate question of the relative valence of good motives to a question of the relative reasonableness of crime messages if we do not possess a clear way of assessing the latter. Once again, my point is not that there are no policy changes that are more reasonable than others. It is rather that there is no simple relation between a motive and the message that is conveyed and, further, that an assessment of the wish for policy changes in many cases will presuppose thorough ethical analysis (which it will definitely be difficult for a sentencing judge to carry out as part of their work at the court).

Furthermore, there is another aspect of motivation that complicates an assessment of the relative ranking of good motives; namely, that such an assessment is not mono-dimensional. Suppose that it is found that motive A is better than motive B. This still will hardly exhaust the assessment of the motive behind the way a person behaves. Another aspect that seems relevant is the *strength* of the motive. As Carlson et al. note in their recent review of motive studies, we tend to evaluate others 'along the dimension of valence (whether the agent's motives are generally good or bad) and strength (the power of the agent's movies to translate into motive congruent acts)' (Carlson et al. 2022: 473). The strength dimension of a motive may be indicated by the degree to which someone is exerting more (rather than less) effort to realize what one is striving for, or the degree to which one is willing to incur greater costs in bringing about a certain result. But if a motive assessment is two-dimensional, then we cannot conclude that a crime committed out of motive A relative to one committed out of motive B should result in greater mitigation. Not only the valence, but also the strength will have to be taken into account. And if A scores better in terms of valence than B, but is less strong, then it may become even more complicated to make an overall relative moral assessment of crimes committed out of motive A and B. Thus, even if it is possible to make the kind of classification system suggested by Hessick where motives are *ex ante* placed on a continuum, this would still (given the presumption that such a continuum is only valence-based) be an incomplete guide to how motives should be handled in individual criminal cases.

6. Conflicting motives

The previous considerations all focused on cases where an action is driven by a single motive and where the task therefore is to assess the valence and strength of this motive. However, as documented in psychological studies,[12] human motivations can be more complex. What we are going to consider now and in the following sections are cases that involve more than a single motive. As will be clear, such cases can take many different forms.

For instance, a person may have conflicting motives, that is, one can be placed in a situation in which motives pull in opposite directions. To return to the offenders in Activist City, we can imagine that the climate activist is driven on the one hand by an altruistic motive to prevent the various calamities that follow from the use of fossil fuels and global warming, but also feels a reluctance to commit a crime in light of the collateral consequences that a conviction and punishment may have for their future. It is also possible to imagine cases where the motives that pull the person in opposite directions are respectively a good motive and a bad motive. How should such cases be handled if motives are considered as a factor at sentencing? There seem to be two possibilities.

The first possibility is to hold that only the motive that triggered the act should count in a sentencing context, and to consider the other motives to be irrelevant. If this is the case, then conflicting motives will not constitute a challenge. Even though a person's decision-making may (given the conflicting

[12] For a fine overview and further references, see Carlson et al. (2022).

motives) have been more complicated for the person herself, this is not relevant at sentencing. However, the question is whether this possibility is consistent with the reasons that might be given in favour of taking motives into account. Suppose that it is the case that a person having conflicting motives implies that the overall force behind the action that is ultimately decided on is less strong than if the person had not also had a countervailing motive. This does not seem psychologically implausible. In that case, there seems to be a conflict between holding, on the one hand, that the strength of a single motive matters (as considered in the previous section), while also holding, on the other, that it should not be taken into account if a person's impetus for acting in a certain way is reduced because of a pull in the opposite direction generated by a conflicting motive. This, at least, indicates that it is not obvious that a motive that conflicts with the one that led to an action can plausibly be ignored at sentencing.

The second possibility is to assert that conflicting motives should be taken into account insofar as they affect a person's overall inclination to engage in criminal conduct. However, it is obvious that it will turn into a rather complicated task to compare a single motive of a certain valence and strength with a set of conflicting motives of varying strength and valence that ultimately drew a person into crime. But as we have seen, such a comparison is what is needed if the motivational background for crimes should be translated into mitigations of varying magnitude.

7. Mixed motives

Another way in which a person's motivational structure can be affected by several co-existing motives is when there are several motives driving a person in the same direction. While conflicting motives require that a person engages in the process of balancing conflicting reasons, the co-existence of motives pulling in the same direction makes personal decision-making much simpler. But it may nevertheless complicate the assessment of the person's motives for committing a crime. Suppose, more precisely, that a person had two motives for acting in a certain way and that the motives are both necessary in the sense that if the person had only had one of the motives, he or she would not have carried out the action. It is easy to see that such a situation complicates the assessment. If the two involved motives are both good motives, but nevertheless vary in valence and strength, then one will have to find a way of comparing this to a case where a single good motive has driven an action. The same is the case if the two motives are respectively a good motive and a bad motive. For instance, a climate activist may commit vandalism in order to attract attention to widespread political inaction on climate change, but may also decide to carry out the vandalism against a property owned by someone he or she dislikes. The former would seem like an altruistic good motive while the latter would be a personal and malicious motive. How should a judge deal with such situations of mixed motives?

There is no easy answer to this question. Obviously, one might try to engage in some sort of balancing of the valences and strengths of the involved motives, but the problem is that it is unclear how this should be done. It is of course not surprising that courts are confronted on a regular basis with cases that involve mixed motives, and different procedures have been developed in different jurisdictions with the purpose of identifying a single relevant motive in cases where the motives are from the outset mixed.[13] For instance, one approach is the 'substantial motivating factor test' (see e.g. Hessick 2006). According to this test, a motive counts insofar as it has contributed *substantially* to the action under scrutiny. However, this test has little to offer in a case involving mixed motives. Even if it is the case that two motives are not equally strong for an agent, it will not help to single out one motive if, as assumed, it is the case that both were necessary for the action to be performed. Both will have contributed substantially, in the sense that the action would not have been carried out had it not been for the coexistence of both motives. Thus, this test is of no help. The same is the case with regard to what is known as the 'primary motive test' which focuses on the reason that first and foremost motivated an action (see e.g. Verstein 2019). Once again, if two motives were both necessary for the performance of the action it seems arbitrary to only focus on the strongest motive and ignore the fact that the action would not have been performed had it not been for both motives. At the least, this way of narrowing the attention to one motive rather than another would require some sort of justification. Another test that has been used is the 'but for' test, according to which a (typically bad) motive should only count if an action would not have been performed had it not been for this motive. However, the point here is that when there are several motives that together drive a certain action, this criterion will not leave us with a single motive but will rather imply that both (necessary) motives should be considered. Thus, none of these standards (typically used as liability tests) seem to have anything

[13] For a comprehensive discussion of several of the tests that have been used by US courts, see Verstein (2019).

to offer in cases where several motives together lead an offender to commit a crime.

8. Motivational Over-determination

Cases where several motives propel a person to perform a certain act constitute only one way in which our behaviour can be affected by a multiplicity of motives. There is another and, in my view, overlooked way in which we can be motivated to act, which in a more direct way seems to undermine the possibility of identifying a particular motive behind the action. Consider the following example, from outside the criminal justice context, presented by Robert Goodin:

> Bishop Tutu goes to Oslo to collect the Nobel Peace Prize. Why? Well, there are various reasons we might mention. It is a high honour and a lucrative purse. Those seem to be egoistic considerations, at least at first brush. But it is also a rare chance to speak out against the evils of apartheid from an enormously influential platform, perhaps thus hastening an end to the suffering of oppressed peoples across South Africa: that looks like a principled, altruistic concern on almost any reading. Which, you ask, was the Bishop's real motive? (Goodin 1989: 406).

Goodin's point, and I believe that in this he is right, is that there may well not be an answer to this question. A more formal way to put it is that a decision to act in a certain way may be *motivationally over-determined*. Each of the motives which Bishop Tutu might have had for going to Oslo would per se have constituted a sufficient internal reason. And, importantly, when there are many converging reasons for an agent to perform a certain action, there is no reason for the agent to engage in speculations of the relative magnitude of each reason or to consider how he or she would have acted under counterfactual circumstances where some of these reasons were removed. There may perhaps sometimes be an *external* interest in the identification of a true motive. For instance, as Goodin also underlines, we often have an interest in predicting other people's future behaviour. Understanding why someone acted as he or she did can help us to predict how they will act in the future. However, from an internal point of view, there is not the same interest. It is usually not relevant for an agent to make estimates of how he or she will act in the future by enquiring into present motives. All that matters is to reach a decision. As Goodin appositely puts it: 'From our own point of view, other's actions are to be predicted; our own are to be chosen' (1989: 411). In fact, not only do we not have a reason to engage in considerations of our true motive when we have more than enough reasons to act in a certain way; we may perhaps sometimes even have reason *not* to engage in such an enquiry. For instance, Goodin suggests that the identification of a true motive may generate a feeling that we are committed to act in a certain way in future situations. Conversely, a lack of identification of such a motive leaves us uncommitted, which may be more pleasant. Whether this is psychologically true is not something that we need to consider any further. The crux of the matter is that if there is a superfluity of converging motives, then it no longer makes sense to talk of the real or true motive behind an action.

If indeed we act from a multiplicity of motives, what does this imply for the possibility of invoking motives as a mitigating or aggravating factor at sentencing? The first problem once again is that if a person has several motives, then there is no reason to believe that these will all have the same valence or strength. As we have just seen, a set of motives may include motives that are both bad and good, or motives that are all good or all bad but to varying degrees.[14] The second and principal problem is that while it might be the case that some procedure could be developed to handle cases involving mixed motives as considered in the previous section—that is, a procedure for how motives should be balanced when they all play a role as drivers of an action—such a procedure would no longer be applicable in cases of motivational over-determination. The challenge, as we have just seen, is that there are no specific sets of motives that are all true in the sense that they have all contributed to the action. On the contrary, it no longer makes sense to talk of the true motives when an action is motivationally over-determined. More generally, motivational over-determination constitutes a serious challenge if motives should be included in considerations of sentence mitigation and aggravation. In particular, this is so, as Goodin suggests, if such an over-determination is not a rare exception, but rather a typical phenomenon in the structure of human motivation.

[14] What this means is that if a person has many motives, then it will be highly unlikely that these motives are all of the same valence and strength. Therefore, to suggest that it does not constitute a challenge if there is a superfluity of motives as long as these motives are of the same quality—that is, that an assessment need not then presuppose the identification of the real motive—may be correct, but this is also a highly unlikely situation. This cannot provide a general answer to the challenge of motivational over-determination.

9. Conclusion

Despite the variation across different jurisdictions, a defendant's motive is often considered in legal proceedings. Motives may well be incorporated into the sentencing phase of a criminal case. Furthermore, as we have seen, there are several theorists who have argued that this is as it should be; an offender's motive is a morally relevant factor in the evaluation of a crime. In this chapter, I have not attempted to resolve this discussion of the significance of criminal motives. Before turning to the summary of my main argument, it is important to first make clear what I have not argued.

I have not suggested that an assessment of offenders' motives should play no role in the criminal justice system. As noted, I believe that there may well be good reasons to treat a mercy killer differently from a contract killer. One possibility might be to account for this distinction at the guilt phase of the criminal process by regarding the two types of misconduct as separate categories of crime. Whether this is the best solution, however, is not something that will here be considered any further. Also, I have not excluded the possibility that there could be some cases where taking a motive into account may be relatively straightforward. However, what I have argued is that this is definitely not always the case. On the contrary, the invocation of motives as a sentencing factor opens up a range of complexity.

First, if we do not wish assessment of an offender's motives to end up as a question of mere personal preferences (such as whether a judge sympathizes more with an abortion proponent than with a pro-life activist) then some criterion for distinguishing between good and bad motives is necessary. Second, insofar as different motives are held to warrant mitigations/aggravations of varying size, an assessment criterion for distinguishing between motives within the same category is also required. This task was complicated by the fact that the quality of a motive may both be the result of its valence and strength. Third, we have seen that it is far from obvious that motives that pull an offender in the opposite direction of what they ultimately decide to do should be ignored in the overall assessment of their motivational background for committing a crime; and that this adds to the complexity of the assessment. Fourth, we have seen that an agent may act out of mixed motives that all together play a contributing role in driving an action, and that this makes it even more complicated to assess the background of a crime and to determine an appropriate mitigation/aggravation. Different legal standards for the identification of a single crucial motive in cases of mixed motivation turned out to be clearly insufficient. Last but not least, it was underlined that there may well be cases where an agent has more than enough reason to perform a certain action; that is, where the action is motivationally over-determined. When this is so, it no longer makes sense to talk of a real or true motive behind a crime. In sum, there are many theoretical obstacles on the road if one wishes to treat offenders' motives as a mitigating or aggravating factor at sentencing.

References

Carlson, Ryan W. et al. (2022). 'How Inferred Motives Shape Moral Judgements'. *Nature: Psychology* 1 (2022): 468–478.

Coca-Vila, Ivó. 'Punishing the Law Citizens? On the Climate Necessity Defence'. *Res Publica* 30 (2024): 567–387.

Driver, Julia. 'Monkeying with Motives: Agent-Basing Virtue Ethics'. *Utilitas* 7, no. 2 (1995): 281–288.

Goodin, Robert E. 'Do Motives Matter?' *Canadian Journal of Philosophy* 19, no. 3 (1989): 405–419.

Hall, Jerome. *General Principles of Criminal Law*. Indianapolis: Bobbs-Merrill, 1960.

Hessick, Carissa B. 'Motive's Role in Criminal Punishment'. *Southern California Law Review* 80, no. 1 (2006): 89–150.

Husak. Douglas. 'Motive and Criminal Liability'. *Criminal Justice Ethics* 8, no. 1 (1989): 3–13.

Kahan, Dan M. 'What Do Alternative Sanctions Mean?'. *University of Chicago Law Review* 63, no. 2 (1996): 591–654.

Ryberg, Jesper. *The Ethics of Proportionate Punishment. A Critical Investigation*. Dordrecht: Kluwer Academic Publishers, 2004.

Ryberg, Jesper. 'Punishing Adolescents: On Immaturity and Diminished Responsibility'. *Neureoethics* 7 (2014): 327–336.

Ryberg, Jesper. 'Guilty Plea Sentencing Discount and Retributivism'. In *Sentencing the Self-Convicted*, edited by Julian Roberts and Jesper Ryberg, pp. 35–50. Oxford: Hart Publishing, 2023.

Ryberg, Jesper. 'Responsibility, Mental Capacities, and Socially Deprived Offenders'. *Neuroethics* 18 (2025a): 18–32.

Ryberg, Jesper. 'Standing to Punish, Sentence Mitigation and the Applicability Challenge'. In *Responding to the Culpable State: Is Sentence Mitigation Appropriate?* edited by Julian Roberts, Leo Zaibert, and Jesper Ryberg, pp. 61–78. Oxford: Hart Publishing, 2025b.

Ryberg, Jesper. *The Oxford Handbook of the Philosophy of Punishment*. New York: Oxford University Press, 2025c.

Ryberg, Jesper and Julian Roberts. 'Exploring the Moral Significance of Public Opinion for State Punishment'. In *Popular Punishment: On the Normative Significance of Public Opinion*, edited by Jesper Ryberg and Julian Roberts, pp. 1–13. New York: Oxford University Press, 2014a.

Ryberg, Jesper and Julian Roberts. *Popular Punishment: On the Normative Significance of Public Opinion*. New York: Oxford University Press, 2014b.

Verstein, Andrew. 'The Failure of Mixed-motives Jurisprudence'. *University of Chicago Law Review* 86, no. 3 (2019): 725–796.

4

Sentencing Climate Protesters

Honourable Motivation and State Misconduct as Sentence Mitigation

Ivó Coca-Vila

1. Introduction

Offenders often commit crimes not for personal gain but rather to promote some ethical cause. The current climate crisis has inspired many people to break the law in order to draw public attention to global warming and to urge their governments to take action on this and other environmental issues. In recent years, disruptive climate protest has become increasingly common in western democracies. Some of these protests involve the commission of (minor) criminal offences—usually offences of coercion, trespass, public nuisance, or damage to public or private property. The disruptive climate protests usually respond to the model of indirect civil disobedience: activists fight against a climate policy they deem unjust or unwise by breaking legal norms that are not per se objectionable. The criminal offences of climate activists, thus, are basically a mechanism for (political) expression (Chrisman and Hubbs 2021a, 2021b; Wringe 2026).

Although nowadays climate activists—unlike the ideal civil disobedient in the classic liberal account of civil disobedience presented by John Rawls[1]—generally do not passively accept prosecution and punishment, but instead mount defences, they are often convicted. The two central arguments in favour of justifying criminal climate protests are largely rejected by the criminal courts.[2] First, the courts, adopting what Richard Martin (2024) calls the 'offence-centric paradigm', generally deny that disruptive climate protests can

[1] Rawls's definition remains the most influential within the legal and philosophical debate (1971: 320): civil disobedience is a public, non-violent, non-evasive, conscientious, yet political act contrary to law done with the aim of bringing about a change in the law or policies of the state.

[2] For discussion, see Coca-Vila (2024), Coca-Vila, Feldman, and Lefkowitz (2026).

Ivó Coca-Vila, *Sentencing Climate Protesters* In: *Sentencing the Ethically-Motivated Offender*. Edited by: Julian V. Roberts, Leo Zaibert, and Jesper Ryberg, Oxford University Press. © Ivó Coca-Vila 2026.
DOI: 10.1093/9780198993025.003.0005

be justified on the basis of constitutional rights. Even if it is acknowledged that protests can be considered 'political speech', it would be an abusive exercise of a fundamental right. In a democratic system, so the argument goes, climate activists can express themselves through legal means. Second, the courts, with few exceptions, also deny the possibility of justifying the offences of climate protesters by appealing to the necessity defence. Activists cannot, with their protests, avoid a greater evil (climate change) than the one they are inflicting, nor do they respect the 'no legal alternatives' requirement. Where citizens can vote, organize, demonstrate, run for office, appeal to the courts, and so on, civil disobedience cannot be legally justified because it is an objectionable attempt to circumvent the democratic process.

Although there are a few dissenting voices,[3] both courts and legal scholars generally assume that climate activists' offences are, in general, wrongful—culpably committed—acts that must be prosecuted and that deserve to be punished. This is also the premise of this chapter.[4] However, refusal to justify or exculpate climate activists' offences does not mean that the fact that they are committed as a form of political expression is completely irrelevant to criminal law. Leaving aside how political motivation should influence policing and prosecution (Monaghan 2023; Smith 2013), the question remains as to how and whether the political motivation of the activist is relevant in sentencing. As far I can see, there are three main possible answers to this primary question.

First, civil disobedients could be punished more harshly than regular offenders (for discussion, see Greenawalt 1987: 273). One could argue that politically motivated acts—not only harming the specific interest protected by the violated law—also threaten the stability of the legal system as a whole. Since they encourage repetition, the principle of deterrence supports harsher punishments to prevent social unrest arising from escalating and multiplying illegal activities. This may also explain why some prosecutors seek to punish members of climate movements for an additional offence, namely participation in a criminal organization.

Second, it could be argued that there is no reason to treat civil disobedients differently from regular offenders. Both types of offenders would be guilty of the same legal wrong. Proportionality and uniformity in the application of the

[3] In the literature, see e.g. Magnus (2024); Zimmermann (2025), both arguing in favour of acquitting climate protesters. In the case law, see e.g. Tribunal d'Arrondissement de Lausanne, PE 19.000742, 13 January 2020 (Switzerland); Tribunal de Grande Instance de Lyon, 19,168,000,015, 16 September 2019 (France); or AG Flensburg, 07.11.2022–440 Cs 107 Js 7252/22 (Germany).

[4] My argument is not that civil disobedience can never be morally or politically justified, even under a just legal system. It is possible to believe that certain forms of civil disobedience are morally justified while also defending that they should be punished.

law would argue against treating civil disobedients differently. This is the conclusion reached by those authors who seek a criminal law that is independent of motives, binding on all equally (Hörnle 2024), and applied by judges who interpret the law free from ideological influences (Kubiciel 2024).[5] According to this line of thought, permitting sentencers to bring their own conceptions of a just social order to bear on what an offender deserves risks introducing far too much 'political theatre' into the criminal justice system or, as Jonathan Jacobs writes (this volume, p. 155), 'a troubling kind of subjectivity and undisciplined discretion' into sentencing.

Third, some criminal law scholars, along the lines advocated by some courts, argue for leniency for climate protest offences.[6] Three reasons are classically given for mitigating the punishment of climate activists. First, it is argued that activists act under a partial defence related to classical justificatory defences. For example, it is said that even if their acts cannot be justified by appealing to the necessity defence—insofar as they are acting to avoid an evil (consequences of climate change)—their punishment should be mitigated as a proxy form of necessity. Secondly, there are those who, by appealing to the political rights of activists, argue that even if one accepts that their exercise through criminal offences is abusive or illegal, punishment should be mitigated insofar as the criminal acts continue to move within the broad space of basic rights. This would also avoid the potential chilling effect of severely punishing acts that are still linked to the exercise of those basic rights. Thirdly, some authors (and courts) accept that the political motivation of climate activists, understood as an honourable or ethical motive, could also count as a mitigating factor, at least in cases where the offence committed and the damaged caused is trivial. To the extent that activists are acting to draw attention to an issue of common concern—seeking to put an end to a climate policy that is perceived to be unjust or unwise—their acts could merit a mitigated sentence.

The aim of my chapter is twofold: first, I will try to show why, in the context of a liberal democracy, contrary to what some criminal law scholars suggest, it is possible to invoke (political) motives to defend mitigation based on a lesser wrong. Motives matter in sentencing, not as a subjective factor that mitigates

[5] This conclusion is also supported by Ryberg (2026), but on a different basis: since considering motive as a mitigating factor raises a number of unresolved challenges (e.g. distinguishing between good and bad motives, or the fact that human behaviour may be the result of conflicting, mixed motives), the criminal justice system should rather not consider this factor in sentencing. However, this approach leaves open the question of why, in the case of unresolved challenges, the system should opt for the higher punishment rather than the more lenient one, for example by invoking the principle of parsimony.

[6] For a general framework of the debate, see Coca-Vila (2024: 582–584).

culpability, but because they affect the seriousness of the wrong, and in the case of climate protesters, they must generally be seen as honourable motives that lead to mitigation. Secondly, I will show that the recent debate on sentencing climate activists, which has focused on motives and deterrence, has overlooked an equally, if not more, important factor in determining deserved punishment. Namely, the fact that the states that are about to prosecute and sentence climate activists are failing to meet their international commitments to mitigate climate change and reduce its emissions under the Earth Summit and the Paris Agreement. Moreover, in the last few years, some constitutional courts have explicitly recognized the state's failure to respect fundamental rights (constitutional or conventional) as a result of its inadequate climate change policies. Although state failure has been widely explored as a mitigating factor in cases of social exclusion, it has not been considered in the sentencing of climate activists. This contribution aims to fill this gap in order to provide a cross-jurisdictional answer to the question of how to sentence criminal climate protesters.

2. Overview

This chapter is structured as follows: section 3 clarifies the motives of standard criminal climate protests and shows why (political) motives matter for sentencing. It also explains why the punishment of climate activists should be mitigated when the communicative dimension predominates. Section 4 considers whether the failure of western states to reduce carbon dioxide emissions should influence the sentencing of climate protesters who commit minor offences to denounce this systematic failure to address climate change. I argue that this state failure is a ground for a 'just desert' mitigation based on a relational account of responsibility and sentencing. Section 5 answers the question of how much mitigation is appropriate for climate activists and why classic aggravating factors such as lack of remorse or recidivism should not lead to more severe sentences when dealing with politically motivated offenders. Finally, section 6 provides the principal conclusions of this chapter.

3. Climate Concern as Mitigating Factor

Some climate protests, while fulfilling the elements of a criminal offence, are essentially expressive in nature, seeking to draw the attention of the general public to the real dimension of the climate challenge and contributing to collective reasoning; for example, think of activists throwing biodegradable paint on the methacrylate protecting a work of art in a museum. Others, however, have a more coercive dimension, seeking to create such a degree of disruption and damage to general and individual interests that public authorities are prompted to change their climate policies. While the first form of protest still implicitly assumes the possibility of engaging in dialogue with the community and public authorities by generating interest through high-profile events, the second assumes the need to coerce public authorities that have been co-opted by a fossil industry that has distorted the democratic balance of power. The main goal is not to persuade, but rather to express anger and frustration, assuming that there is no hope of finding common ground with the defenders of the status quo. Consider long-term road blockades or the sabotage of airports and other critical infrastructure, causing major disruption.

Regardless of the more or less disruptive or coercive nature of the protest, climate activists are generally motivated by a relatively concrete and shared motive, namely to get states to substantially change climate policies that are considered wrong and will have catastrophic consequences for all citizens of this planet. They speak out in a sincere and good-faith manner against a climate policy that is seen as unwise or unjust (evaluative element), and they demand change in order to avoid catastrophic consequences (prescriptive element). It is thus a common interest, the matter of how we live together in civic society (common good), that serves as the main reason for climate activists to appeal to (criminal) protests. Although activists are generally aware that their actions cannot directly mitigate the effects of climate change, they aim to bring about fundamental changes in climate policy over the medium to long term.[7]

Although the climate crisis may not mechanistically cause the crime in a way that exculpates the offender,[8] it is impossible to fully understand activists' actions without considering their underlying motivations. State inaction on global warming has a major impact on the practical reasoning of activists who undertake civil disobedience. This may be true from a psychological or sociological perspective. But should the motivation behind an offence play a role in the criminal justice system?

[7] While it cannot be ruled out that some activists may in some cases act for other reasons—some not necessarily honourable, such as an interest in fame—or for mixed reasons (Ryberg, this volume), the cases of interest here are those where it is possible to identify a common good motive as the dominant one.

[8] Protesters' decisions are not classically conscientious acts. Both politically motivated acts and acts of conscience are decisions taken by subjects oriented towards the categories of right and wrong, with the difference being that conscientious actors assume that acting contrary to the order is unconditionally obligatory, since a (religiously based) normative system takes precedence. On this distinction, see e.g. Montenegro (2021).

One of the maxims of criminal law orthodoxy is that motive plays no role in a liberal criminal law (Eldar and Laist 2017; Timm 2012: 161–197; Peralta 2012; Husak 2010; Hessick 2006). In a nutshell, the liberal (or neutralist) thesis assumes the possibility of distinguishing between intentions and motives and claims that a criminal law that aims to punish facts and not personal characteristics or ways of life can only take into account the harm (culpably) caused by the offender, but not her emotions or motives (Hörnle 2024; Hurd and Moore 2004). According to this train of thought, recourse to motives means, first, blaming offenders for something beyond their control, since no one is responsible for their emotions or motivations. Secondly, it is argued that appealing to motives is a departure from the ideological-political neutrality that should govern the application of criminal law (Kubiciel 2024). Punishment should depend on what offenders (whether intentionally or not) do, not on the legislator's or judge's personal assessment of the political or ideological reasons that led offenders to act. This would be particularly important in a fragmented multicultural society where it is almost impossible to assess the positive or negative character of a particular motivation.

As those authors who are opposed to taking motives into account themselves recognize, both contemporary criminal codes and the courts of most western states tend to give relevance to motives when determining punishment, both as an aggravating factor and as a mitigating factor. Here, I cannot undertake to argue why I believe that motives are relevant in criminal law, in particular, at the sentencing stage.[9] Rather, I am content to argue specifically for their mitigating relevance in climate activist cases.

My starting premise is that the primary purpose of punishment is to express the censure that offenders deserve for their crimes and that the quantum of punishment should respond to two main foundations: the seriousness of the culpable wrong committed by the offender, and the political legitimacy of the state to inflict punishment (Silva Sánchez 2025: 1930–1932; Manikis 2022: 303). Contrary to what Heidi Hurd and Michael Moore (2004: 1085–1093) claim, I argue that motives are relevant to determine the seriousness of the legal wrong committed. Let us see why.

It is true that motive does not determine greater (or lesser) material or psychological damage, and it may also be true that motive per se does not produce

[9] Criticizing the 'irrelevance of motives' thesis, see e.g. Binder (2002: 45–65). For an opposite view in the continental debate, see Peralta (2012: 151–174). In the Anglo-American debate, see Hurd and Moore (2004), which is still essential reading for the case against taking motive into account in criminal law. There is a more nuanced view in Duff (1998: 173–175): courts must not attend to motivation factors that are not declared relevant by the law.

greater (or lesser) victimization. But criminal wrongdoing, unlike civil wrong, is not limited to the harm that the offender inflicts on someone's tangible interests. Rather, it constitutes an expressive violation of the law—an act that demonstrates a lack of respect for the victim's autonomy or for the institution safeguarded by the violated norm.[10] The amount of this wrongfulness is therefore not something empirically measurable, but instead something that responds to a conventional attributional judgment of 'social meaning'. Although no actual harm is caused in an attempted crime, few seriously doubt that some attempts still constitute criminal wrongdoing. That this attribution of meaning depends on a set of pre-established social conventions is obvious.[11] Nor is there any doubt that motives, good or bad, necessarily condition this judgment of social attribution of meaning. Motives, whether perpetrators like it or not, give meaning to what they do. Just as the interpretation of human conduct becomes unduly reductionist when motives are disregarded, so too would a conception of criminal wrongdoing that fails to account for the communicative dimension of the offender's conduct.

That said, the complexity of assessing offenders' motives and taking them into account as sentencing factors (Ryberg, this volume), does not preclude one from arguing that the social meaning of climate activists' offences is generally different from that of offences committed by criminals acting out of a conventional motive such as greed. Those who act in order to denounce policies that they consider unwise and that will have negative consequences, that is, motivated by a common interest, express something substantially different from the 'ordinary' offender (Payer 2024: 290–291). And this is valid regardless of whether one wants to understand the action of an activist as an individual or to interpret that action as part of a collective action of a group that jointly expresses a common message. Climate protesters, in short, should be punished less severely because their motives lessen the severity of their wrongdoing: the offence (also) reflects that they value the right things, albeit slightly too much relative to other things they ought to care about.[12] As Roger Douglas (1994: 104–105) points out, the more the communicative dimension dominates, the more lenient the punishment should be.

[10] For a defence of the expressive account of criminal wrongdoing, see Hampton (1992: 1666–1685). In a similar vein, Kahan and Nussbaum (1996: 351–352). In the continental debate, see e.g. Günther (2014); Frisch (2001: 252–254).

[11] Therefore, offenders cannot choose what they express by their criminal acts: actions speak. On the general idea that actions carry meanings, see Lessig (1995) and Sunstein (1995).

[12] In this vein, Kahan (2001: 178).

But does every politically motivated act deserve a mitigated punishment? In my view, the answer must be no. What is decisive for the assessment of wrongfulness is not so much the motivation of the offender per se, nor the seriousness of the offence committed, but the inter-subjective understanding of the politically motivated act. Where the communicative-political dimension is pre-eminent, the political motive being honourable, the wrongfulness will be lessened, and the offence should attract a mitigated punishment. However, when the activist's act—regardless of its motivation—is particularly serious or involves the direct instrumentalization of individuals, interpreting it primarily as a form of climate-related expression would be far-fetched. As a result, the harm will remain preeminent and the punishment will not be reduced. An example illustrates the point: someone who kills a businessman to highlight the dangers of climate change does not convey a message substantially different from that of someone who kills without any particular reason—even if the victim is an executive directly responsible for a company contributing to climate change. The act of killing overshadows any political message.

From my point of view, mitigation must be the case, regardless of whether offenders passively accept the legal consequences of their acts or plead a justifiable defence.[13] Attempting to defend oneself in the process may somewhat diminish the political force of the act of civil disobedience, but it does not prevent one from accepting the mitigation. In short, mitigation does not apply exclusively to the 'ideal' civil disobedient who submits to arrest and prosecution, pleads guilty in court, and does not complain about the punishment received.

There are at least three objections to my approach. First, some will say that paying attention to motives, even if only to mitigate, means treating climate activists in an unfairly privileged way, since no one is responsible for their motives, either good or bad (volitional objection). This mechanistic approach to motives, however, forgets that motives are not relevant as causal determinants of criminal acts. Climate activists—even if we assume that their altruistic motives depend on a long series of second-degree determinants such as their education, their tastes or preferences, their commitment to social practices,

[13] For an opposite view, see McEwen (2012: 991–993). In the philosophical literature, acceptance of the legal consequences by disobedients is seen as a condition both by defenders of the 'standard' liberal conception of civil disobedience, as the proof of disobedients' fidelity to law (Rawls 1971: 320). See also Fortas (1968), who claims that the agent's acceptance of punishment makes her respect the rule of law and serves to reconciling the moral obligation to disobey unjust laws and our primary legal obligation; and Nussbaum (2018: 173–174), who claims willingness to play the legal penalty has a double function: it expresses the depth of one's conscientious commitment, and it expresses respect for law. On the case against the non-evasion requirement, see, e.g. Moraro (2018).

etc.—freely choose to act on their motives, generally bearing the costs associated with arrest and prosecution. But even if individuals are not responsible for the motives underlying their actions, such motives nonetheless shape the meaning of those actions and may mitigate their criminal wrongdoing.

Second, some will object that mitigating the punishment of climate activists on the basis of their motivations is an unacceptable affront to the principle of neutrality of criminal law (the liberal objection). Especially in pluralistic and fragmented societies, it is essential for judges to refrain from introducing political evaluations when setting the quantum of punishment (Hörnle 2024: 38). There are also those who believe that sentencing judgments should move to a high degree of abstraction, one that abstracts from the particularities of individual cases and individual motivations and omits many of the subtler features that would be relevant to a thorough moral judgment on offenders. Such abstraction would be necessary to protect individuals from overly intrusive judicial inquires (Norrie 1993: 31–32, 223–225).

In response to the 'liberal' objection, some argue that the application of the law is never neutral, whether politically or ideologically. My main argument for refuting this objection in the case of climate activists is, however, a different one: motive can be a mitigating factor only in an indirect way, insofar the (unlawful) protest is a way of contributing to a debate of public interest in a democratic society. For example: *ceteris paribus*, the anti-nuclear activist and the pro-nuclear activist deserve the same punishment when they illegally occupy a similar space with similar consequences to give greater force to their political acts in relation to nuclear energy. Just as a theory of civil disobedience cannot be based on whether those who participate in the disobedience are right (Dworkin 1985: 105–106), the mitigation of politically motivated crimes cannot depend on the political or ideological assessment of the message expressed.

In short, mitigation does not depend on the inter-subjective ethical or moral assessment of the content of the expressed message, but rather on the social value of the political contribution to an ongoing public debate. Such a distinction is certainly normatively laden. It does not provide a normatively neutral basis on which to distinguish 'valuable' from 'non-valuable' contributions to a public debate. However, it does provide a way to decide how criminal law should address political protests when sentencing. As Clémence Demay makes clear in her contribution to this volume (pp. 207–210), the 'public interest debate' argument invoked by the ECHR provides a good criterion for deciding which cases deserve mitigation, regardless of the specific content of the political expression. Certainly, there will be cases where the social value of a contribution in the form of disruptive protest might be doubtful, for example, because of the unreasonableness of the empirical grounding of a political claim. But this is no reason not to mitigate the punishment of those offenders who are in fact participating in a socially valuable debate. For example, accusing the world's leading scientists of hiding the existence of current technology that would allow the earth to survive with our CO2 reductions is not a contribution to a socially valuable debate. However, farmers who block roads to protest against high taxes on diesel fuel as an unfair way of solving the climate conflict deserve the same respect as climate activists who block the same roads to demand a ban on diesel fuel.

Third and finally, some argue that the mitigation thesis cannot be accepted due to practical consequences. Insofar as the crime committed by the civil disobedient presents a risk of generalization, severe punishment is essential to achieve an adequate level of deterrence (Rönnau 2023: 114–115). How can a state mitigate the sentence of a recidivist offender who has blocked a railway five times, causing major disruption? In the face of this argument, leaving aside the general argument that a just or deserved punishment is not necessarily the ideal one for deterring a specific offender, the following can be simply objected here: it is questionable whether the severity of the punishment plays a significant deterrent role in the case of a truly politically motivated offender. It should be noted that the reduction of the punishment in no way affects the wrongfulness of the act, which remains wrongful. Activists expose themselves to arrest, persecution, and criminal conviction. The idea that a state should not mitigate the punishment of recidivist offenders in order to incapacitate them through imprisonment is also highly questionable. For a democratic criminal legal system, excluding dissenters is not the appropriate approach to sentencing politically motivated offences.[14]

4. State Misconduct as a Mitigating Factor

The contemporary debate about sentencing climate activists has so far focused on deciding whether their motivation should operate as a mitigating factor. This debate has overlooked a second reason for mitigation: the eroded legitimacy of the state that seeks to punish the offence committed by climate activists.

Even at the risk of over-generalizing, it is fair to say that climate activists resort to criminal protests in order to demand, in essence, that western states

[14] Resorting to disproportionate custodial sentences may sometimes be necessary for a society to protect itself from politically motivated offenders, but such sentences cannot be justified as a legitimate form of punishment.

begin to fulfil their commitments to reduce emissions, as enshrined in the Kyoto Protocol (1997) and reinforced through the Paris Agreement (2015). Among scientists, the dominant thesis is that western democracies are not adopting the policies that would allow the ideal objective of limiting global warming to 1.5°C above pre-industrial levels. In fact, scientists assume that if things continue as they are, the most likely scenario is that global warming will reach 3°C above pre-industrial levels.[15] The climate policies pursued so far would, in short, condemn states to breaching their international commitments. Moreover, in some western states, climate activists are protesting against policies or laws that have already been declared unconstitutional or contrary to the European Convention on Human Rights (ECHR). This is the case in Germany, for example, where the Constitutional court has ruled that the Federal Climate Protection Act insufficiently protects the constitutional right to the natural foundations of life and animals;[16] or the case of Switzerland, which according to the European Court of Human Rights (the Court) was in breach of its positive obligations to protect the health, well-being, and quality of life of Swiss citizens from the impacts of climate change. This violation was attributed to the Swiss government's failure to implement the robust regulatory framework necessary for fulfilling its commitment to reduce emissions as set out in the Paris Agreement.[17] In Europe, already in 2019, the Parliament approved a resolution declaring a climate and environmental emergency, asking to the Commission to ensure that all relevant legislative and budgetary proposals are fully aligned with the objective of limiting global warming to under 1.5 °C.[18]

According to Thomas Groß (2024), it is fair to say that western states, which are primarily responsible for climate change, are failing dramatically, as they seem unable to take the necessary measures to achieve the political goals that these same states have accepted since 1992.[19] However, international law does not provide sufficient mechanisms to enforce treaty objectives or obligations against individual states, due to the traditional structure of the order of states. In fact, the Paris Agreement is only seen as setting forth objectives and primarily procedural obligations and obligations of conduct, but not of result (Rajamani 2024). Something similar happens when a state violates the ECHR.

[15] A summary of the current findings can be found in the Intergovernmental Panel of Climate Change (IPCC)'s 6th Assessment Report, available at https://www.ipcc.ch/assessment-report/ar6/.

[16] Order of 24 March 2021—1 BvR 2656/18, 1 BvR 288/20, 1 BvR 96/20, 1 BvR 78/20.

[17] *Verein KlimaSeniorinnen Schweiz and Others v Switzerland* [GC]—53600/20.

[18] European Parliament resolution of 28 November 2019 on the climate and environment emergency (2019/2930(RSP)).

[19] For an overview of states' (non-)compliance, see the Climate Change Performance Index 2025, at https://ccpi.org/.

Although Article 46 of the ECHR states that the Committee of Ministers shall supervise the execution of the judgments of the Court, which are binding on the Contracting Parties, there is no mechanism to effectively enforce the decisions of the Court.

It is also undisputed among legal scholars that neither violations of international law nor violations of fundamental rights per se can justify or exculpate a criminal offence. In short, the violation by the state does not provide a right to act against the law, so criminal climate protest cannot be seen as a defensive harm justified by appealing to principles of self-defence, nor does it modify the guilt of the perpetrator of the offence.[20] But can this state failure undermine its political legitimacy in a way that is relevant to sentencing?

As is well known, legal scholarship has long considered this possibility in relation to the problem of social exclusion.[21] Many voices are in favour of denying the state the possibility of holding socially excluded individuals responsible for offences, at least when it comes to *mala quia prohibita* offences. However, other voices have argued for (only) reducing the punishment of the socially excluded. In both cases, the idea is the same: although the wrongs remain unaltered, the state responsible for the social exclusion loses the political legitimacy to blame such offenders. There is no agreement on the specific reasons that would explain this loss of political legitimacy: while some resort to the argument of hypocrisy to deny the state the possibility of reproaching others for what it itself does (Ryberg 2025), others argue that punishment should be reduced in proportion to the erosion of citizenship status experienced by the socially excluded (Coca-Vila and Irarrázaval 2022). Finally, there are those who resort to the argument of complicity: the state, which is complicit in the crimes of the socially excluded insofar as it contributes to their emergence by creating criminogenic conditions, cannot legitimately punish their offences (Tadros 2009).

Here, I cannot provide an in-depth analysis of how the loss of political or moral legitimacy should affect sentencing. My goal is simply to defend the thesis that climate activists who commit crimes to protest state misconduct in addressing the climate challenge deserve less punishment because of the eroded legitimacy of the punisher (the state).

The starting premise is that a state's inability to fulfil its international obligations, and in particular its inability to change climate policies that are

[20] For discussion on the political legitimacy of coercive rioting as a form of self-defence exercised by an oppressed community, see Pasternak (2018).

[21] For discussion, see e.g. Manikis (2022).

conflicting with fundamental rights, undermines its political legitimacy.[22] From this, my second premise, in line with what I have argued elsewhere,[23] is that eroded political legitimacy also affects the response to criminal offences. Since the loss of political legitimacy in a democratic state is unlikely to be such as to deny a duty of obedience and submission to the law, it is still possible for a non-ideal state to attribute criminal responsibility to offenders. However, if political legitimacy is taken as a scale that can be used to assess the varying degrees of legitimacy that states have in the real world, it seems reasonable to recognize that eroded political legitimacy will at least be reflected in the determination of the quantum of punishment. The loss of political legitimacy demands less censure, which can be achieved through less hard treatment. Again, this is not because the citizen's guilt or the harm caused is less, but because the state lacks the ideal standing to have the right to rule over its citizens.[24]

Does this erosion of legitimacy lead to mitigation in all cases? It is reasonable to make mitigation dependent on a particular connection between the cause of the erosion of legitimacy and the offence to be punished. Although states that are unable to adopt effective climate policies to address climate change do not create a criminogenic context conducive to crime, their failure to comply with legally binding international obligations, as well as the violation of fundamental rights, contributes to the politically motivated crimes committed by activists. In a sense, activists engage in a kind of (illegal) self-protection to force the state to do what it should do. It is the failure of the state that ultimately triggers climate activists' resort to illegal forms of protest. And unlike in the case of social exclusion, the identification of state failure is somewhat easier from a legal point of view, since it can be specified in terms of the specific violation of constitutional rights and freely assumed international obligations. In short, the objection that constitutional rights are too vague to allow certain conclusions to be drawn in the application of criminal law does not apply with equal force to the climate case: foreseeable violations of climate commitments are verifiable, and in the Swiss case, for example, it was the Court itself that declared Swiss climate policy to be incompatible with the European Convention.

[22] I understand the notion of political legitimacy here not as a binary condition, but as a scalar one. That is, political legitimacy is not defined by a set of necessary and jointly sufficient conditions, but by a regulative ideal. For discussion, see Brinkmann (2024). This ideal includes a state that fulfils international obligations and scrupulously respects constitutional texts.

[23] See Coca-Vila and Irarrázaval (2022: 65–67). In a similar vein, see Martí (2017); Ryberg (2025); Silva Sánchez (2025: 1970–1972).

[24] Contra Bergelson (2025: 51), I argue that the state also loses part of its legitimacy to punish wrongs against third parties who have not wronged the defendant. In a different vein, see Duus-Otterstrom (2025), who assumes that politically non-obligated offenders—due to lack of legitimate authority—are less culpable, other things being equal, than politically obligated ones.

Should the above apply to any crime committed by climate activists? The answer must be no: the crime committed must be interpreted as a proportionate response to a specific failure of the state. In general, the crimes classically committed by climate activists—such as coercion, occupation of public spaces, or damage to property—can indeed be read in this light, as long as the communicative, denunciatory dimension predominates over the purely harmful one. But the link between state misconduct and offence must be assessed case by case.

5. Sentencing Climate Protesters

In the previous two sections I have argued that there are two different reasons in favour of mitigating the punishment of activists who protest by committing criminal offences: while their motivation—interest in the common good—diminishes the wrongfulness of the crime, the failure of the state erodes its legitimacy to censure them for their offences, which should be channelled into a mitigation. Having reached this point, however, there are two important questions that remain to be answered. First, how should the two factors described affect the appropriate punishment for activists? Secondly, are there typical circumstances in civil disobedience cases that might qualify as aggravating factors, thereby offsetting the aforementioned mitigating considerations? In particular, in the case of politically motivated offenders, the question of whether their moral or political conviction and willingness to repeat their crimes favours a harsher punishment is strongly raised. Let's look at both issues in detail.

What kind of mitigation is appropriate for a climate activist who acts for a laudable reason and protests against a state whose political legitimacy appears to be eroded? This question cannot be answered with a mathematical formula, much less with any claim to universal application. I will content myself with pointing out two things. First, I believe that the two factors mentioned, although separately they could determine a minimal mitigation, when added together, speak in favour of a significant attenuation. Secondly, I believe that both factors allow for a sentence reduction that is not only quantitative, but also qualitative. This applies to both acts of direct and indirect civil disobedience. David Lefkowitz, in distinguishing between the dimensions of censure and harsh treatment in punishment, affirms that the moral right to civil disobedience only prevents the state from punishing, but not penalizing, those who engage in such behaviour (Lefkowitz 2007: 218–222; 2018:. 279–280). In other words, it would not be legitimate to censure these offenders, but it would be legitimate to inflict some kind of harsh treatment on them (fines, temporary imprisonment, etc.) to address the risk of excessive civil disobedience. Similarly, the legal philosopher Gustav Radbruch (1924) argued that ideological offenders motivated by conviction cannot be censured, since the state does not appear to be ethically superior. Only preventive measures (*custodia honesta*), that is, non-condemnatory hard treatment, can be taken against them.

I argue that the state should take the opposite approach: it is essential that the state declare the criminal responsibility of political protesters and censure their unlawful actions. However, since the message expressed by such offences is for the common good, and the legitimacy of the punisher is undermined, judges should mitigate the severity of punishment. Given that offences committed by climate civil disobedients are in general minor crimes, the mitigation advocated here should generally lead to non-custodial sanctions (for example, fines, community service orders, and reparation orders).[25] If the legal system requires that judges impose custodial sentences, the same mitigating factor speaks in favour of suspending custodial sentences. Likewise, given the political nature of the offences, the deprivation of the right to political participation (active or passive suffrage) is an unacceptable response within the framework of a pluralist democracy. This kind of punishment, of very dubious legitimacy in general,[26] is especially illegitimate when it comes to censuring the actions of civil disobedients: the response of a democratic state to dissidents cannot be their exclusion from the political forum.

Therefore, the approach advocated here differs only slightly from that of the advocates who excuse civil disobedients. Nor does it differ too much from those who understand that the deservingness of punishment is reduced to such an extent that the act should not be punished at all, resorting to a non-exculpatory defence (Günther 1992: 216–218; Fernández-Perales 2022: 783–792; Zimmermann 2025; Silva Sánchez 2025: 1599–1600). The main difference, however, lies in the fact that the mitigation solution makes it possible to affirm the criminal responsibility of offenders by publicly censuring their acts through criminal sentences. This solution, similar in its consequences to the 'Guilty but Civilly Disobedient' verdict proposed by Matthew Hall (2007), does justice to criminal civil disobedience: it takes offenders seriously as civil disobedients, recognizes their particular motivations and the political significance of their acts, without infantilizing them by declaring

[25] In a similar vein, see Busche (2023: 107).

[26] For discussion on exclusionary forms of punishment, see Coca-Vila (2020).

them to be not criminally responsible. This also reinforces individuals' rights and the validity of the laws broken.

As noted earlier, sentencing civil disobedients depends on an overall judgment in which some factors suggest more severe punishment. As a rule, politically motivated offenders do not repent their acts, do not admit guilt, and, at least in cases of direct civil disobedience, do not recognize the legitimacy of the rules they have violated. As disobedients become organized, there is even the possibility of accusing them of participation in a criminal organization, which is, in most jurisdictions, a separate criminal offence. Thus, it is not surprising that at trial, civil disobedients express their intent to commit the same or similar offences again and again. This lack of remorse is often considered to be an aggravating factor when sentencing, as is recidivism. Does this mean that political motivation is a sentencing factor that ultimately should not affect the quantum of punishment by offsetting the positive effect with the negative one? I argue that the answer must be in the negative.

Although criminal law statutes tend to set the aggravating factor of recidivism as an automatic factor, such that someone who has already committed a crime of the same nature should be punished more severely the second time, I believe that there are good reasons to understand that those factors should not aggravate punishment in 'standard' civil disobedience cases.[27] In fact, offenders' insistence on the moral or political legitimacy of the acts of civil disobedience often amounts to little more than compelling proof of the sincerity and personal conviction with which they act. Lack of repentance does not suggest disloyalty or indifference to the legal system, but rather a firm commitment to the cause for which disobedients are willing to violate the law. What does not make sense is that the political motivation only mitigates punishment for civil disobedients who change their minds during the process and show their determination not to resort to communicative law infringement again. In most cases, this would suggest a contradiction with the earlier act, possibly intended as an instrumental defence strategy.

6. Conclusion

To summarize, the sentencing of climate protesters must reflect both the particular nature of their offences and the broader context in which these offences

[27] For a similar result reached via a different rationale (integrity principle), see Cammiss, Hayes, and Doherty (2025).

occur. Disruptive climate protests, when politically motivated and primarily communicative in nature, convey a public-spirited commitment to democratic deliberation and the common good. Such motivation lessens the gravity of the wrongs committed, not by exonerating offenders, but by altering the social meaning of the offences—thus warranting mitigation.

At the same time, the state's failure to meet its constitutional and international obligations regarding climate change erodes its political legitimacy, diminishing the authority with which it can condemn such acts. When these two factors converge—honourable political motivation and compromised legitimacy of the punishing authority—a compelling case emerges for mitigated sentences. This mitigation should manifest in proportionately reducing the severity of punishment. Finally, aggravating considerations such as recidivism or lack of remorse must be carefully re-evaluated in this context. They should not outweigh the mitigating force of the activist's political intent, as they often merely reflect the integrity and consistency of the protester's democratic convictions.

Sentencing, in short, should neither trivialize unlawful protest nor suppress its expressive dimension. Instead, it should locate it within a broader normative framework that recognizes both the activist's message and the state's culpable failure. Only then can punishment in liberal democracies remain both just and legitimate in the face of the urgent challenge of climate injustice.

References

Bergelson, Vera. 'The State Fault and the Right to Mitigation of Punishment.' In *Responding to the Culpable State. Is Sentence Mitigation Appropriate?*, edited by Leo Zaibert, Julian V. Roberts, and Jesper Ryberg, pp. 43–60. Oxford: Hart Publishing, 2025.

Binder, Guyora. 'The Rhetoric of Motive and Intent'. *Buffalo Criminal Law Review* 6, no. 1 (2002): 1–96.

Brinkmann, Matthias. 'Degrees of Legitimacy'. *Res Publica* 31 (2024): 145–167 https://doi.org/10.1007/s11158-024-09675-x.

Busche, Daniel. 'Verfassungsrechtliche Vorgaben für die strafrechtliche Bewertung der Sitzblockaden von Klimaaktivisten'. *Klima und Recht* 2, no. 4, (2023): 103–107.

Cammiss, Steven, Hayes, Graeme and Doherty, Brian. 'Defending the Integrity Principle: Necessity, Remorse and Moral Consistency in the Protest Trial'. *Oxford Journal of Legal Studies* 45, no. 2 (2025): 329–357 https://doi.org/10.1093/ojls/gqaf003.

Chrisman, Matthew and Hubbs, Graham, 'Protests'. In *The Routledge Handbook of Social and Political Philosophy of Language*, edited by Justin Khoo and Rachel Katherine Sterken, pp. 379–401. New York: Routledge, 2021a.

Chrisman, Matthew and Hubbs, Graham, '"The Language of the Unheard": Rioting as a Speech Act'. *Philosophy & Public Affairs*, 49, no. 4 (2021b): 379–401 https://doi.org/10.1111/papa.12201.

Coca-Vila, Ivó, 'Our "Barbarians" at the Gate: On the Undercriminalized Citizenship Deprivation as a Counterterrorism Tool'. *Criminal Law and Philosophy* 14, no. 2 (2020): 149–167 https://doi.org/10.1007/s11572-019-09517-5.

Coca-Vila, Ivó, 'Punishing the Last Citizens? On the Climate Necessity Defence'. *Res Publica* 30, no. 3 (2024): 567–587 https://doi.org/10.1007/s11158-023-09642-y.

Coca-Vila, Ivó and Irarrázaval, Cristián, 'A Criminal Law for Semicitizens'. *Journal of Applied Philosophy* 39, no. 1 (2022): 56–72 https://doi.org/10.1111/japp.12534.

Coca-Vila, Ivó, Feldman, David, and Lefkowitz, David, 'Civil Disobedience on Trial: A Comparative Criminal Law Perspective'. In *Core Concepts in Criminal Law and Criminal Justice*, edited by Matthew Dyson, Stefanie Bock, Julian V. Roberts, Jenia Turner, and Alec Walen. Bloomsbury: Bloomsbury Publishing, 2026 https://www.bloomsbury.com/ca/fundamental-concepts-in-criminal-law-and-criminal-justice-9781509967056/.

Demay, Clémence, 'Is Political Disobedience an Honourable Motive?'. This volume.

Douglas, Roger, 'Sentencing Political Offenders'. *Australian Journal of Human Rights* 1, no. 1 (1994): 86–116 https://doi.org/10.1080/1323238X.1994.11910904.

Duff, R. Antony, 'Principle and Contradiction in the Criminal Law: Motives and Criminal Liability'. In *Philosophy and the Criminal Law*, edited by Antony R. Duff, pp. 156–204. Cambridge: Cambridge University Press, 1998.

Duus-Otterstrom, Göran. 'State Illegitimacy and Punishment: Examining the Case for Discounts'. In *Responding to the Culpable State. Is Sentence Mitigation Appropriate?*, edited by Leo Zaibert, Julian V. Roberts, and Jesper Ryberg, pp. 7–24. London: Hart Publishing, 2025.

Dworkin, Ronald. 'Civil Disobedience and Nuclear Protest'. In *A Matter of Principle*, pp. 104–116. Harvard MA: Harvard University Press, 1985.

Eldar, Shachar and Laist, Elkana, 'The Irrelevance of Motive and the Rule of Law'. *New Criminal Law Review: An International and Interdisciplinary Journal* 20, no. 3 (2017): 433–464.

Fernández Perales, Francisco, 'La colisión de derechos en la dogmática jurídico-penal'. *Anuario de Derecho Penal y Ciencias Penales* 75, no. 1 (2022): 753–802. https://doi.org/10.53054/adpcp.v75i1.9704.

Fortas, Abe, *Concerning Dissent and Civil Disobedience*. New York: New American Library, 1968.

Frisch, Wolfgang, 'Unrecht und Schuld im Verbrechensbetriff und in der Strafzumessung'. In *Grundfragen staatlichen Strafens. Festschrift für Hein Müller-Dietz*, edited by Guido Britz, pp. 237–260. München: Beck, 2001.

Groß, Thomas. 'Das Staatsversagen angesichts der Klimakatastrophe'. *Juristen Zeitung* 79, no. 20 (2024): 893–944 https://doi.org/10.1628/jz-2024-0276.

Günther, Hans-Ludwig, 'Verwerflichkeit von Nötigungen trotz Rechtfertigungsnähe? – Zugleich ein Beitrag zur Sitzblockadeproblematik'. In *Festschrift für Jürgen Baumann zum 70. Geburtstag*, edited by Gunther Arzt, pp. 213–225. Bielefeld: Gieseking, 1992.

Günther, Klaus, 'Criminal Law, Crime and Punishment as Communication'. *Normative Orders Working Paper: Normative Orders, Cluster of Excellence at Goethe University Frankfurt* 2 (2014): 1–22.

Greenawalt, Kent, *Conflicts of Law and Morality*. New York: Oxford University Press, 1987.

Hall, Matthew R. 'Guilty but Civilly Disobedient: Reconciling Civil Disobedience and the Rule of Law'. *Cardozo Law Review* 28, no. 5 (2007): 2083–2131.

Hampton, Jean, 'Correcting Harms versus Righting Wrongs: The Goal of Retribution'. *UCLA Law Review* 39 (1992): 1659–702.

Hessick, Carissa Byrne, 'Motive's Role in Criminal Punishment'. *Southern California Law Review* 80, no. 1 (2006): 89–150.
Hörnle, Tatjana, 'Die Grenzen für politische Proteste'. *Jahrbuch für Recht und Ethik/ Annual Review of Law and Ethics* 31, no. 1 (2024): 15–39 https://doi.org/10.3790/jre.2023.337799.
Hurd, Heidi M. and Moore, Michael S., 'Punishing Hatred and Prejudice'. *Stanford Law Review,* 56, no. 4 (2004): 1081–1147.
Husak, Douglas, 'Motive and Criminal Liability.' In *The Philosophy of Criminal Law: Selected Essays,* edited by Douglas Husak, pp. 53–68. Oxford: Oxford University Press, 2010 https://doi.org/10.1093/acprof:oso/9780199585038.003.0003.
Kahan, Dan M., 'Two Liberal Fallacies in the Hate Crimes Debate'. *Law and Philosophy* 20 (2001): 175–193.
Kahan, Dan M. and Nussbaum, Martha C., 'Two Conceptions of Emotion in Criminal Law'. *Columbia Law Review* 96, no. 2 (1996): 269–374.
Kubiciel, Michael, 'Der Kampf ums Strafrecht'. *JuristenZeitung* 79, no. 5 (2024): 167–174.
Kyoto Protocol to the United Nations Framework Convention on Climate Change (adopted 11 December 1997, entered into force 16 February 2005) 2303 UNTS 162.
Lefkowitz, David, 'On a Moral Right to Civil Disobedience'. *Ethics* 117, no. 2 (2007): 202–233 https://doi.org/10.1086/510694.
Lefkowitz, David, 'Defense of Penalizing (But Not Punishing) Civil Disobedience.' *Res Publica* 24, no. 3 (2018): 273–289 https://doi.org/10.1007/s11158-017-9362-5.
Lessig, Lawrence, 'The Regulation of Social Meaning'. *University of Chicago Law Review* 62, no. 3 (1995): 943–1045.
Magnus, Dorothea, 'Notstandsrechtfertigung für Klimaaktivisten?' *Juristische Rundschau* 1 (2024): 9–17 https://doi.org/10.1515/juru-2023-2111.
Manikis, Marie, 'Recognising State Blame in Sentencing: A Communicative and Relational Framework'. *Cambridge Law Journal* 81, no. 2 (2022): 294–322 https://doi.org/10.1017/S0008197322000198.
Martí, José Luis, 'Sources and the Legitimate Authority of International Law: Democratic Legitimacy and the Sources of International Law'. *The Oxford Handbook of the Sources of International Law,* edited by Samantha Besson and Jean d'Aspremont, pp. 724–746. Oxford: Oxford University Press, 2017.
Martin, Richard, 'Convicting Peaceful Protesters: Proportionality's Proper Place at Criminal Trial'. *Oxford Journal of Legal Studies* 44, no. 2 (2024): 342–375 https://doi.org/10.1093/ojls/gqae009.
McEwen, Stephen J., 'The Protester: A Sentencing Dilemma'. *Notre Dame Journal of Law,Ethics & Public Policy* 5, no. 4 (2012): 987–993.
Monaghan, Jake, 'Policing Disobedient Demonstrations'. *Criminal Law and Philosophy* 17, no. 3 (2023): 653–668 https://doi.org/10.1007/s11572-023-09653-z.
Montenegro, Lucas, 'Töten mit gutem Gewissen. Weshalb politische Beweggründe als niedrig i.S.v. § 211 II StGB einzustufen sind'. *Goltdammer's Archiv für Strafrecht* 168, no. 2 (2021): 101–113.
Moraro, Piero, 'On (Not) Accepting the Punishment for Civil Disobedience'. *The Philosophical Quarterly* 68, no. 272 (2018): 503–520 https://doi.org/10.1093/pq/pqx058.
Norrie, Alan, *Crime, Reason and History: A Critical Introduction to Criminal Law.* London: Weidenfeld & Nicolson, 1993.
Nussbaum, Martha, 'Civil Disobedience and Free Speech in the Academy'. *Academic Freedom,* edited by Jennifer Lackey, pp. 170–185. Oxford: Oxford University Press, 2018 https://doi.org/10.1093/oso/9780198791508.003.0010.

Paris Agreement (adopted 12 December 2015, entered into force 4 November 2016) 3156 UNTS 79.

Pasternak, Avia, 'Political Rioting: A Moral Assessment'. *Philosophy & Public Affairs* 46, no. 4 (2018): 384–418.

Payer, Andrés, 'Klimaprotest als achtenswerter Beweggrund? Besprechung von BGE 149 IV 217'. *forumpoenale* 4 (2024): 285–292.

Peralta, José Milton, Motivos reprochables. *Una investigación acerca de la relevancia de las motivaciones individuales para el Derecho penal liberal.* Madrid: Marcial Pons, 2012.

Radbruch, Gustav, 'Der Überzeugungsverbrecher'. *Zeitschrift für die gesamte Strafrechtswissenschaft* 44 (1924): 34–38 https://doi.org/10.1515/zstw.1924.44.1.34.

Rajamani, Lavanya, 'Interpreting the Paris Agreement in its Normative Environment'. *Current Legal Problems* 77, no. 1 (2024): 167–200. https://doi.org/10.1093/clp/cuae011.

Rawls, John, *A Theory of Justice*. Harvard MA: The Belknap Press of Harvard University Press, 1971.

Rönnau, Thomas, 'Grundwissen – Strafrecht: Klimaaktivismus und ziviler Ungehorsam'. *Juristische Schulung* 63, no. 2 (2023): 112–115.

Ryberg, Jesper, 'Standing to Punish, Sentence Mitigation and the Applicability Challenge'. In *Responding to the Culpable State. Is Sentence Mitigation Appropriate?*, edited by Leo Zaibert, Julian V. Roberts, and Jesper Ryberg, pp. 61–78. Oxford: Hart Publishing, 2025.

Ryberg, Jesper (2026). 'Sentencing Honourable Offenders: On the Complexities of Assessing Human Motives', Chapter 3 of this volume.

Silva Sánchez, Jesús María, *Derecho Penal. Parte General.* Madrid: Civitas, 2025.

Smith, William, *Civil Disobedience and Deliberative Democracy.* New York: Routledge, 2013.

Sunstein, Cass R. 'On the Expressive Function of Law'. University of Pennsylvania Law Review 144 (1995): 2021–2053.Tadros, Victor, 'Poverty and Criminal Responsibility'. *Journal of Value Inquiry* 43, no. 3 (2009): 391–413 https://doi.org/10.1007/s10790-009-9180-x.

Timm, Frauke, *Gesinnung und Straftat. Besinnung auf ein rechtsstaatliches Strafrecht.* Berlin: Duncker & Humblot, 2012.

Wringe, Bill (2026). *Denunciatory Punishment of Criminal Protest.* Chapter 8 of this volume.

Zimmermann, Till, 'Ziviler Ungehorsam als Strafunrechtsausschließungsgrund'. *Kriminalpolitische Zeitschrift* 10, no. 2 (2025): 1–7.

5

Sentencing Rebels with a Cause

Should Ethically-Motivated Offenders Receive Mitigation?

Netanel Dagan and Julian V. Roberts

1. Introduction

For millennia, debates have focused on the appropriate moral response towards ethically-motivated crimes.[1] Despite this long-standing interest, the sentencing for such offences remains an under-theorized area of penal theory. With a few exceptions (e.g., terrorism offences), modern criminal law evinces little interest in the offender's motive for the crime. At trial, the law assumes free, rational agents who chose to offend, and whose motives are largely irrelevant.[2] However, motivation is clearly relevant to sentencing. For example, racist or hate-based motivations are common aggravating sentencing factors. The criminal law considers that such crimes bespeak higher *culpability* and cause greater *harm* compared to more common criminal motivations.[3] If malign motivations can aggravate sentence, should not ethical motivation result in mitigation? But why, and are there normative limits to such mitigation?

A criminal offence normally assumes that the act is a moral public wrong, yet motives are not always malign. Offences can be motivated by ethical, even virtuous intentions.[4] Offences arise from diverse and highly complex socio-legal and political contexts, as penal theorists, psychologists, and criminologists

[1] For example, in the Old Testament, Malachi 1:13: '"*and you bring what was taken by robbery*... this you bring as an offering? Should I receive it with pleasure from your hand?" says the Lord'; *The Jerusalem Talmud* (Tractate Challah 1:6) observed during the second century AD that 'no sin can be a good deed... no good deed can be a sin...'.

[2] For a critique of this 'division of labour', see Eldar and Laist (2017).

[3] See Norrie (2014: 42); Racially-motivated offending impugns the victim's identity and carries a threat to the victim's community, not simply the individual victim. As a result, the hate-motivated offender is also deemed more culpable. Most common law jurisdictions have created specific aggravated forms of offending or have codified an aggravating factor of hate motivation.

[4] Norrie (2014: 42) writes, 'a crime may be committed from the best of motives and yet remain a crime'.

Netanel Dagan and Julian V. Roberts, *Sentencing Rebels with a Cause* In: *Sentencing the Ethically-Motivated Offender*. Edited by: Julian V. Roberts, Leo Zaibert, and Jesper Ryberg, Oxford University Press. © Netanel Dagan and Julian V. Roberts 2026. DOI: 10.1093/9780198993025.003.0006

have all recognized.[5] Ethically-motivated offending comes in many forms, ranging from vigilantes who victimize unprosecuted perpetrators,[6] through to a poor person who steals medicine to save the life of his wife.[7] Some sentencing regimes—Italy for example—officially recognize mitigation for some forms of such offending. Bondi (this volume) notes that the Italian Criminal Code provides for a sentencing reduction of up to one third for any criminal offence if the offender 'acted for reasons of particular moral or social value'. In contrast, other jurisdictions, including some Australian states, are unsympathetic: ethically-motivated offenders (EMOs) are seen to require strongly censuring and deterrent sentences.[8]

In this chapter, we discuss the sentencing of ethically-motivated offending. We illustrate, as a case study, the challenges of justifying mitigation using the increasingly common example of activists committing offences for what they assert is a noble cause. Consider these recent examples relating to climate change: in 2022, 'Just Stop Oil' protesters climbed gantries over the M25 (an English motorway) thereby disrupting traffic for hours; in London, other members of the organization threw soup at van Gogh's 'Sunflowers' painting in the National Gallery, causing criminal damage.[9] In 2024, the climate group 'Last Generation', seeking to convince the German government to pursue an international agreement to exit coal, oil, and gas, broke onto the Cologne/Bonn airport's runway and glued themselves to the ground.[10]

2. Overview

Section 3 of the chapter explores the potential justifications for sentence mitigation in cases of ethically-motivated offending (EMO). To anticipate the discussion, we see principled and practical objections to the justifications for mitigation in these cases. Section 4 considers how courts should sentence these offenders. Here we advocate the application of conventional aggravating and mitigating factors. We conclude that there are only limited grounds for mitigation for positive motives. Beyond a reduction for first-time offenders, there are principled arguments against awarding significant sentence reductions. In

[5] See Fleetwood and Sandberg (2021).
[6] See Robinson (2013: 454–457).
[7] See Kohlberg (1981).
[8] See Walvisch (2018: 428).
[9] See Gayle (2022).
[10] See *Deutsche Welle* (2024).

addition, there are insuperable practical objections to implementing such a practice in a principled sentencing framework.

3. Justifying Sentence Mitigation for Ethically-Motivated Offending

3.1. Instrumental Justifications

On an instrumental level, sentence mitigation may be justified because ethically-motivated EMOs are less dangerous, have a heightened social conscience (at least compared to most other offenders) and may be more easily rehabilitated.[11] Thus, courts sometimes recognize that protesters and other EMOs are otherwise law-abiding people for whom deterrent sentencing is unnecessary.[12] Additionally, mitigating sentences for such offenders could be justified as a form of dialogue between the community and the EMOs regarding the duty to obey the law, even by those resisting it. As one English court noted, 'it is more likely to be effective where authorities (including judicial authorities) show restraint in anticipation that the defendant will respond by desisting from further breaches' and 'appreciates the reasons why in a democratic society responsible citizens must obey the law and respect the rights of others, even where the law or other people's lawful activities are contrary to the protestor's own moral convictions'.[13]

Courts have proved sceptical about this claim for mitigation, as seen in the US Federal Sentencing Guidelines which recognize deterrence as a valid consideration for ethical offenders who oppose government policies.[14] From the perspective of general deterrence, the power of the criminal law derives, at least to some degree, from its certainty. There is a need to deter, especially people

[11] As one Australian court observed: 'I consider that there is a low likelihood the offender will re-offend by committing an offence similar in nature and scale to the present. He is not a criminal in the classic sense of one who needs rehabilitation, although I consider that there is some likelihood that he may continue to engage in what might be regarded as minor breaches of the law as acts of disobedience to further his beliefs and purposes. The sentence needs to have regard to that matter.' *R. v Moylan* [2014] NSWSC 944 at [100] (Davies J).

[12] See *Cuadrilla Bowland Ltd & Ors v Lawrie & Ors* [2020] EWCA Civ 9 at [98]: '... the fact that such a protestor is generally – apart from their protest activity – a law-abiding citizen, there is reason to expect that less severe punishment is necessary to deter such a person from further lawbreaking'.

[13] *Cuadrilla Bowland Ltd & Ors v Lawrie & Ors* at [98].

[14] 'Where the interest in punishment or deterrence is not reduced, a reduction in sentence is not warranted. For example, providing defence secrets to a hostile power should receive no lesser punishment simply because the defendant believed that the government's policies were misdirected': United States Sentencing Commission, 2023, §5K2.11.

who have strong ideological resistance to legal norms.[15] Even from a communicative perspective, penal censure is appropriate irrespective of the offender's attitude after censure or their change of moral stance following the sentence.[16]

Furthermore, there are reasons for deterring EMOs in particular. Protesters need to be deterred because—unlike other offenders—they instrumentalize the criminal law for the purpose of drawing attention to their cause. Ethically-motivated defendants are overtly public in their offending.[17] Rather than seeking to break the law without attracting arrest, prosecution, or punishment, they actively seek public attention, even if accompanied by state action. Climate change and other activists strive for the public attention and media coverage that conventional offenders such as drug dealers and fraudsters shun. This being the case, protesters cannot legitimately complain about being instrumentalized for the purpose of general deterrence since they deliberately seek publicity through their offending (see Wringe, this volume). This reality may strengthen the case for imposing a deterrent sentence towards the public.[18]

Furthermore, and still from a deterrence perspective, if courts reward ethical offending with generously mitigated sentences, they send a mixed message that the law is discretionary. This undermines the rule of law as equally applied to all citizens regardless of their political or moral motivations. It creates a status of 'first-class' offenders or offences (Jacobs, this volume). In the case of repeat offending, a harsher sentence is appropriate as their moral position remains unaltered by the court's repeated sentencing communications.[19] (We discuss repeat offenders in more detail later in the chapter.) Finally, if the court awards a generous mitigation, for example, for offenders who vandalize a petroleum multinational, this may confer a degree of judicial approval, at least implicitly, both of the cause for which the offence was committed, and the offending itself.

Deterrence theorists would see a need to *aggravate* rather than mitigate sentences for EMO. Psychological studies demonstrate that strongly-held moral convictions are associated with greater intolerance of attitudinally

[15] See *R. v Hallam and Others* [2025] EWCA Crim 199 at [14]: 'The court may temper the sanction imposed because there is a realistic prospect that it will deter further law-breaking and encourage the offender to appreciate why in a democratic society it is the duty of responsible citizens to obey the law and respect the rights of others, even where the law is contrary to the protesters' own moral convictions.'

[16] See Brownlee (2007: 179).

[17] See *Cuadrilla Bowland Ltd & Ors v Lawrie & Ors* at [87]: 'The public nature of the act – in contrast to the actions of other law-breakers who generally seek to avoid detection – is a demonstration of the protestor's sincerity and willingness to accept the legal consequences of their actions'.

[18] See Chow (2023: 938).

[19] See Brownlee (2007).

dissimilar others and an inability to accept solutions to resolve disagreements.[20] Ideologically-motivated individuals (e.g., terrorists or hate-motivated offenders) are usually harder to deter,[21] something that some courts accept in the context of climate protesters.[22] Other empirical evidence, however, suggests that even ideologically-motivated offenders engage in rational decision-making, weighing potential material, political, or symbolic rewards against the potential risks.[23]

Finally, rehabilitation may be less relevant to such offenders. Social activists usually do not need to be reintegrated into the community—it is the community that has motivated their offending. Furthermore, seeking their rehabilitation might be viewed as coercive 'brain-washing' by the state against resisting minorities, forcing them to express remorse for something they believe is not only not wrong, but a virtue. In any case, the utility of rehabilitating such EMOs requires empirical support as much as the use of sentencing mitigation for promoting their rehabilitation.

To summarize, preventive theories allow no room for sentence mitigation in cases of ethical offending.

3.2. Retributive Considerations

From a retributive perspective, the principal purpose of a sentence is to deliver proportionate censure for the crime, commensurate with the harm and culpability caused or threatened. Mitigation for such offenders could be justified on three main grounds: positive moral character, culpability, and unfair advantage.

a) Positive moral character

Some retributivists support character-based mitigation. The crime is seen as 'out-of-character', an act unrepresentative of the defendant's moral 'core'.[24] Consequently, some courts regard ethical offenders as fundamentally good (even virtuous) people who are worthy of respect; some courts view their

[20] See Skitka, Bauman, and Sargis (2005); Hoskins, this volume.

[21] 'The concept of deterrence is both too limiting and too naïve to be applicable to the war on terrorism': Davis and Jenkins (2002: xviii); see Miller (2013: 132).

[22] See *R. v Hallam and Others* at [20]: 'The strength of the protesters' beliefs was on any view material to the question of rehabilitation'.

[23] '. . . even seemingly fanatical terrorists, intensely motivated by religious beliefs, are not irrational in a sense that makes them impossible to deter': Trager and Zagorcheva (2005: 88); Perry and Hasisi (2015: 53).

[24] See Murphy (2011).

motives positively, while disagreeing with their methods.[25] However, here too, the case of ethically motivated offending may lead in the opposite direction. Unlike most other offenders, ethical offenders assert that their offence derives strongly from their (real or believed) core ethical character rather than other, less honourable 'external' motivations. This sets them apart from other defendants, who may claim that their crime was caused by poor life circumstances.[26] Furthermore, character-based mitigation for EMO raises several problems for principled, consistent, and just sentencing that is based on a liberal retributive theory.

First, character-based mitigation requires the judge to assume the role of moral assessor. Themis' blindfolded eyes represent the principle of equality before the rule of law. Judging an offender's character requires judges to unveil their eyes. Yet the sentencing judge is neither a moral arbiter nor a democratically-elected legislator. Questions of politics and moral principle are controversial and should be resolved by the legislature and not judges in individual cases. Allowing judges to determine what constitutes ethical behaviour and which motivations are morally superior, potentially turns courts into 'political theatres'.[27]

Secondly, it is unclear how a judge can evaluate the ethics of offenders' motivations fairly and consistently, and without transforming herself into a political actor. After all, as one court put it: 'It is no part of the judicial function to evaluate (or comment on) the validity or merit of the cause(s) in support of which a protest is made'.[28] In addition, it is unclear how such an assessment would operate in practice. In Italy, for example, to receive mitigation, good motives must be 'particular' (i.e., especially relevant), 'non-egoistic', useful for the common good, and congruent with the act. The motive must be the main driver, not just coexist with other motives (Bondi, this volume). However, the very motivation for ethically-motivated offending is that it does *not* align with what the public views as the 'common good', which needs to be shocked,

[25] In *Neal v The Queen* [1982] 149 CLR 305 at [10], Murphy J noted: 'That Mr. Neal was an "agitator" or stirrer in the magistrate's view obviously contributed to the severe penalty. If he is an agitator, he is in good company. Many of the great religious and political figures of history have been agitators, and human progress owes much to the efforts of these and the many who are unknown. As Wilde aptly pointed out in "The Soul of Man under Socialism", "Agitators are a set of interfering, meddling people, who come down to some perfectly contented class of the community and sow the seeds of discontent amongst them. That is the reason why agitators are so absolutely necessary. Without them, in our incomplete state, there would be no advance towards civilisation." Mr. Neal is entitled to be an agitator.'

[26] For example: 'As the character evidence indicates, and as I learned for myself during the trial, you are an intelligent and well-educated young woman. Neither immaturity nor personal disadvantage has driven you to crime; your own conscious choices have.' (*R. v Hallam and Others* [78].)

[27] See Jacobs, this volume.

[28] *R. v Trowland* [2023] EWCA Crim 919 [50].

mobilized, and changed towards the protesters' views. Activists offend to jolt public opinion out of its alleged complacency with respect to some issue. It is also unclear how exactly a judge should determine that the EMOs' offences reflect 'non-egoistic' reasons. People often have multiple (even contradictory or self-deceiving) motivations: some good, some bad, some conscious, some unconscious; some are clear now, and some will only become clear years later, or may remain unclear for ever.[29]

Thirdly, a liberal state is reluctant to promote specific ethical beliefs and remains morally neutral lest it be criticized for policing citizens' ethical lives.[30]

Questions of ethics belong in the private realm and, thus, the criminal law is seldom involved in 'rewarding' citizens for their ethical conduct (Jacobs, this volume). Furthermore, for the liberal criminal law, the most important thing is to *do* the right moral thing (avoiding criminal wrongdoing), not to do the right thing for the *right moral reasons.*[31] This normative distinction is also reflected at the empirical level: public opinion research suggests that an offender's overall good deeds or positive character have little influence over people's attitudes to sentencing.[32]

Finally, the assessment of a genuine ethical motivation seems to be a challenge even for the most committed judge. Offenders often rationalize and justify their acts by appealing to higher moral authorities.[33] In some cases, offenders' motivations are mixed (in different ways), and in such cases, it is unclear why only one motive should count as mitigation, and what the 'real' motivation may be (see Ryberg, this volume). In addition, as the same *intention* (e.g., causing harm to property) can be based on very different *motivations* (and possibly more than one), it is unclear how a judge distinguishes between good and bad motives in a way that goes beyond personal preferences or political sympathies.[34] Even if we can identify benign motives, ranking them (determining which is 'better') is likely to be extremely difficult.

[29] See Freud [1916] (2001).

[30] see Jacobs, this volume, and Berlin (2014: 231).

[31] We thank Shmuel Baron for bringing this point to our attention.

[32] Only 15 per cent of respondents found any sentence reduction warranted when such factors were at issue (Robinson, Jackowitz, and Bartels 2012).

[33] See Sykes and Matza (1957): 'Offenders neutralize internal and external controls by claiming that their behaviors are consistent with the moral obligations of a specific group to which they belong.' See Maruna and Copes (2005: 233).

[34] See, for example in the Australian case of *Dixon-Jenkins v The Queen* [1991] 55 A Crim R 308: 'Whether the [offender's criminal] activity is for well-meant purposes or is merely self-indulgent seeking of attention and enjoyment of power, it is unnecessary to decide. The latter view, however, is certainly open', cited in Walvisch (2018: 448).

b) Promoting the community's 'real' values

Legal and community values seldom overlap fully. The criminal law is slow to evolve and often outdated. There are many examples of the law failing to punish crimes severely enough to reflect their actual harm, or severely enough to reflect societal disapproval.[35] On this ground, an EMO may claim mitigation for moving the 'law' closer to what the community values are (or should be); they bridge the gap between what the criminal justice system should do and what it is actually doing. Here, the analogy could be made to acts of vigilantism that seek to implement the real or imagined values of public opinion. Vigilantes act, they claim, to achieve a just outcome which the criminal justice system has singularly failed to secure. For example, the state's failure to prosecute a 'known' sex offender justifies, in the vigilante's mind, the infliction of rogue justice. Activist protesters follow the same logic: the state has failed, and they are nobly sacrificing themselves to alert the public to this culpable failure.[36]

However, the criminal law discourages private citizens from enforcing public laws. Members of the public who witness a crime are normally expected to call the police rather than take the law into their own hands. Private prosecutions are possible in most jurisdictions, but the state normally assumes carriage of the case early in the criminal process. In general, the use of force by individuals to prevent crime is strongly discouraged.[37] The criminal law requires victims to relinquish their private justice interests in order to avoid the risk of victims or others inflicting disproportionate punishment in pursuit of 'justice'.[38] The state's near-monopoly on the use of force represents the social contract by which citizens relinquish their right to use force and cede this authority to the criminal justice system. EMOs' acts conflict with such principles. Furthermore, someone who violates the law lacks the legitimacy to criticize the violation of norms by others. The protesters who cause harm to property or life assume they are exceptions to the rule of law.[39]

Finally, offenders are bound to obey the law that expresses the shared values of a political community. Generous sentencing mitigation for ethical offenders risks fragmenting and politicizing the criminal law into an infinite number of

[35] Such crimes might include environmental offences, domestic violence or abuse, and prior to codification of hate crime statutes, offences motivated by bias or hate.

[36] See Tonry (2025).

[37] See *R. (on the application of DPP) v Stratford Magistrates' Court* [2017] EWHC 1794 (Admin) [18].

[38] See Robinson (2015).

[39] As the court noted in *R. v Hallam and Others*, at [173]: 'You two simply had no right to do what you did to Sunflowers, and your arrogance in thinking otherwise deserves the strongest condemnation. The pair of you came within the thickness of a pane of glass of irreparably damaging or even destroying this priceless treasure. That must be reflected in the sentences I pass.' (Citing the sentencing court.)

'mini' criminal laws, one for each group (or sub-group). This undermines criminal law's role in reinforcing solidarity; the criminal law ceases to reflect the community's shared values and its collective judgment about wrongdoing.[40]

c) 'Nothing in it for me'

Unlike other offenders, ethically motivated offenders do not personally benefit from the offence. Is this a justification for mitigating their sentences? Unlike fraudsters or drug importers, they gain no 'unfair advantage' by breaking the law. The ethical offender stands apart from the offence: she is responsible for the offence but is not a beneficiary. As a result, severe punishment (and even punishment at all) may be less justified to restore the moral equilibrium. However, as before, the logic of unfair advantage may lead to a paradoxical result when applied to EMOs. If protesters find it hard to restrain themselves from acting according to their strong moral convictions, by their offence they free themselves from a greater burden of self-restraint than offenders acting from non-moral motives, and thus they warrant more, rather than less punishment to remove that advantage (Hoskins, this volume). EMOs 'release' themselves from the burden of complying with the law. As such, they secure a greater moral advantage compared to other offenders who do not resist the law so strongly. Ethically-motivated offenders are therefore 'enjoying' greater benefits from the offence (in a sense of a greater amount of freedom from the restraint of the legal burden of criminal law). They have less financial gain but more illegal freedom, and therefore are undeserving of motive-based mitigation.

d) Reduced culpability

A more plausible claim for mitigation for EMOs relates to the offender's level of culpability. Some courts have recognized this argument as a reason for mitigation.[41] What makes an act a criminal offence is the offender's culpable mental state at the time of the crime. The reduced culpability argument could be based on several grounds. First, these offenders deserve less censure as their level of culpability is lower than non-ethically motivated offenders. Protesters' offences reflect moral grounds rather than merely 'criminal' motivations such as greed or aggression. Thus, such EMOs are morally closer to the community than 'ordinary' offenders. According to this argument, the actions of EMOs

[40] See Duff (2013).

[41] See *Cuadrilla Bowland Ltd & Ors v Lawrie & Ors*, at [87]: 'The fact that acts of deliberate disobedience to the law were committed as part of a peaceful protest will seldom provide a defence to a criminal charge. But it is well established that it is a relevant factor in assessing culpability for the purpose of sentencing in a criminal case.'

are not considered to be as wrongful, or to carry the same stigma, as offenders who break the law for selfish reasons.[42] In *Jones*, the English court shows some respect to EMOs, something that should result in reduced sentences as it is connected with what could be honourable acts of civil disobedience in a civilized society: 'It is the mark of a civilised community that it can accommodate protests and demonstrations of this kind'.[43]

A second reason for reduced culpability for EMO is to respect citizens who assume the burden of a legal sentence in order to further social causes.[44] Mitigation for EMOs also recognizes that for such offenders, adherence to the law may be more than onerous than for other citizens. In England and Wales (and other systems), sentencing guidelines consider culpability-based mitigation in cases where the offence was committed out of mercy,[45] or as the offender felt obliged, distressed, and forced to do the act. The reduced culpability argument is supported by courts in this system, one without special guidelines for such cases.[46]

4. State Misconduct as a Source of Mitigation

There has been a surge of recent interest in state misconduct mitigation.[47] If the state acts unlawfully, it lacks the full moral standing to punish the offender.

[42] See Walvisch (2018: 439).

[43] *R. v Jones (Margaret)* [2007] 1 AC 161 [89]: 'My Lords, civil disobedience on conscientious grounds has a long and honourable history in this country. People who break the law to affirm their belief in the injustice of a law or government action are sometimes vindicated by history. The suffragettes are an example which comes immediately to mind. It is the mark of a civilised community that it can accommodate protests and demonstrations of this kind . . . . The police and prosecutors, on the other hand, behave with restraint and the magistrates impose sentences which take the conscientious motives of the protesters into account. The conditional discharges ordered by the magistrates in the cases which came before them exemplifies their sensitivity to these conventions.'

[44] See Brownlee (2007: 183); Chow (2023: 932).

[45] *R. v Latimer* [2001] 1 SCR 3 (Canada).

[46] e.g., *R. v Trowland*, at [50] ('Where conscientious motive on the part of a protester is a relevant consideration for sentencing purposes, as submitted for the protesters and accepted by the respondent, it falls most logically to be factored into the assessment of culpability'); see *R. v Roberts (Richard)* [2018] WL 06345027 [6] ('it is well established that committing crimes, at least non-violent crimes, in the course of peaceful protest does not generally impute high levels of culpability'); in Australia, see *Avery & Ors v Queensland Police Service* [2019] QDC 21 [78]–[81] ('The motivation of an offender can go to increase or diminish culpability. It forms no part of a court's function to adjudicate, even sub silencio, on the merits of controversial issues but it is well established that committing crimes, at least non-violent crimes, in the course of peaceful protest does not generally impute high levels of culpability . . . whilst offending committed in the course of a peaceful protest would not generally impute a high level of culpability, and while the conscientious motives of protestors are to be taken into account, whether the protestors have behaved with a sense of proportion by not causing excessive loss, damage or inconvenience by their protest actions will be an important consideration in assessing the objective seriousness of the offending and the culpability of the offenders involved').

[47] See Zaibert, Roberts, and Ryberg (2025) for a collection of perspectives on this issue.

The individual who has been assaulted by police on arrest, or in pre-trial detention while awaiting trial, may claim mitigation for this reason. 'Activist' offenders claim that the state is acting unlawfully, for example by breaching climate control conventions or selling arms to countries who then deploy them against civilians in violation of the Geneva Convention.

We have argued elsewhere against sentence mitigation to reflect state misconduct, unless the state's actions contributed to the crime.[48] However, even if there is a principled justification arising from state misconduct, the unlawful actions need to be evidenced in submissions by counsel and subsequently acknowledged by the court. If the police assaulted the offender on arrest, the defence must provide evidence to support the allegation (unless it is conceded by the prosecution). This evidence will be subject to adversarial scrutiny. This is a relatively straightforward exercise involving evidence and testimony from the offender, the alleged perpetrator and other witnesses. However, this adversarial requirement creates insuperable practical difficulties in the context of social or politically-motivated offences.

It is hard to see how the activist defendant can adduce evidence that state armaments were unlawfully deployed against civilian targets, or that specific state actions are in breach of international law. Documenting unlawful state actions with respect to environmental issues will be particularly challenging and would consume considerable time in court. In a criminal proceeding, it is the defendant and not the prosecuting authority who is on trial. Other fora as well as legal mechanisms and institutions exist to hold the state accountable for any unlawful acts. Even if a court agreed to entertain submissions on the state's misconduct, how would it proceed? An adjudication is required to establish whether, for example, the state has violated some international treaty, law, or convention. A busy trial court lacks the jurisdiction to adjudicate such disputes and would be unable to determine the veracity of claims in this regard.

5. The Limits on Mitigation for Ethically-Motivated Offenders

Many politically-motivated offenders cite their commitment as evidence of good character and therefore as a reason for mitigation. If some mitigation

[48] We argue that this practice undermines the integrity of the sentencing process, and results in one wrong (state misconduct) justifying a second (a disproportionately lenient sentence). In addition, there are more effective and appropriate remedies for misconduct by the state or its representatives, see Roberts and Dagan (2025).

is appropriate, the level should not depend on the offender's degree of commitment to his or her cause. The mitigation must be justified for all forms of offending, although there are grounds to reduce the mitigation as the offending becomes more serious. It may suggested that the offences committed by climate change civil disobedients are relatively minor. Two objections may be raised. First, some climate and political protest offending is manifestly anything but minor. Even apparently minor acts of vandalism can trigger longer-term costs resulting in losses which would justify imprisonment if they arose from a fraud or other crime. Soup can be readily wiped from a picture frame, but the costs of closing the gallery, increasing the number of security guards present and expanding the level of surveillance cameras is far from trivial. Ask the patients who missed medical appointments, or mourners who missed funerals as a result of the M25 motorway closure. Similarly with respect to the destruction of property, the offenders who spray-painted Royal Air Force jets to protest the UK involvement in the conflict in Gaza caused millions of pounds worth of damage. Second, ethical motives either should or should not mitigate—the motive does not become more or less compelling as the seriousness of the crime changes.

There is a clear challenge in determining the exact level of mitigation appropriate for ethically-motivated offending.[49] As in other cases of mitigation or aggravation in sentencing, it is hard to be precise. As a general approach, the principle of proportionality is of particular importance for sentencing of EMOs both for aggravation and mitigation. In ensuring that the sentence is proportionate in such cases, the court ensures that the state is not attempting to regulate or punish the protesters for their *conscience* but for their *offences against the criminal law*.[50] At the same time, ordinal proportionality places limits on the degree of mitigation awarded EMOs. Generous sentence reductions would send confusing messages regarding the real moral value of the offence; politicized sentencing and undermines the rule of law as binding on all citizens. The two basic retributive components are culpability and harm.

[49] ibid., para. 26 ('as a general proposition, a sentencing judge is not obliged to attribute specific percentage values or figures to individual factors which have been taken into account in the sentencing exercise ... *that includes not only aggravating and mitigating factors, but also factors, such as conscientious motivation, going to the assessment of culpability*. There is no parallel to be drawn with the approach to discounts for guilty pleas, for which a quantified reduction in sentence is made at a discrete stage in the sentencing process').

[50] See Chow (2023: 944).

5.1. Culpability

The moral justification for mitigation in the context of ethical offending stems, at least partly, from the wrongfulness of their offences or their reduced culpability.[51] In *Hallam*, the Court of Appeal determined that sentencing of non-violent protests is to be guided by normal sentencing principles. The court noted that the sentencing judge 'took no account at all of the appellant's conscientious motivation. Whilst he was right that conscientious motivation is not a matter of mitigation, it is a factor which may reduce culpability',[52] but 'conscientious motivation did not preclude a finding that any appellant's culpability was still high'.[53] The Court ruled that the offenders who threw soup over van Gogh's 'Sunflowers' painting saw no reduction in their sentence of two years and 20 months, respectively. Hallam was originally jailed for five years for conspiring to disrupt traffic. His sentence was reduced to four years. Other protesters originally received four-year prison terms for their involvement in the same protest, reduced to three years and 30 months, respectively, all being 'manifestly excessive'.[54] This approach suggests that the degree of mitigation for serious EMOs should be modest, and custodial sentences could be imposed in such cases.

a) Harm

The reduced culpability argument is connected to the proportionality of the harm caused by the offence: 'the more disproportionate or extreme the action taken by the protester, the less obvious is the justification for reduced culpability and more lenient sentencing'.[55] The connection between the harm caused by EMO and the degree of mitigation reflects for courts the notion that there is, in essence, '*a bargain* . . . operating in such cases. A sense of proportion on the part of the offenders in avoiding excessive damage or inconvenience is matched by a relatively benign approach to sentencing'.[56] When EMOs cause significant harm to people or property, the justification for mitigation is even less convincing. First, there may be doubts about the sincerity and the validity of their ethical motivations. The more severe the harm caused or intended to be caused, the harder it is to view the act as merely

[51] See Brownlee (2007: 184).
[52] *R. v Hallam and Others* [81].
[53] ibid. [26].
[54] ibid. [85].
[55] *R. v Trowland*, at [50].
[56] *R. v Roberts (Richard)* [2018] WL 06345027, at [9].

political protest rather than a criminally-motivated act (e.g., motivated by aggression).[57]

This implies that the court should determine whether there was any evidence on the EMOs' part (e.g., they could make their aim public in a lesser disruption or act lawfully) or were completely indifferent to the consequences of their acts in order to cause maximum disruption.[58] Australian courts require a 'nexus or proportionality or close or direct causal link between this crime and the alleged political objectives'.[59] That is, since 'The political nature of the offence is also more difficult to accept if it involves acts of an atrocious nature'.[60] For these reasons, victims who are political or judicial actors or innocent parties increase both harm and culpability. Second, intentional harm to life or limb minimizes the moral difference between EMOs and that of ordinary lawbreakers.[61] Third, in cases of grave harm, the EMOs do not try to persuade public opinion but coerce it through illegal acts and threats. At this point we move from the theory to the practice of sentencing ethical criminality.

6. Sentencing the Ethically-Motivated Offender

Ethically-motivated offenders use their crimes to communicate with society and the government. The same cannot be said for most other forms of offending; people who steal phones, rob banks, or defraud the public do so for personal gain or some other benefit. At sentencing, a court communicates a message of censure, with the stringency of the sanction reflecting the degree of harm and making allowance for any diminished culpability such as drug addiction. The state should respond differently—initially at least—to the ethical offender. The court's initial communication to the ethical offender is two-fold. First, to recognize the ethical nature of their offence which may distinguish

[57] See *Cuadrilla Bowland Ltd & Ors v Lawrie & Ors*, at [97]: '. . . the means of protest adopted transgress the law, the protestor is engaged in a form of political action undertaken on moral grounds rather than in mere criminality'.

[58] See *R. v Hallam and Others*, at [21].

[59] See *Minister for Immigration and Multicultural Affairs v Singh* [2002] HCA 7, [40], [46]: '. . . it must be, that political purpose is the defining feature of a political crime, references to "proportionality", "nexus" or "causal link", as made by the Tribunal, assume legal significance. A crime is unlikely to have a political purpose if it has no relevant connection with the political aims of those involved in its commission. So, too, as has been explained in other legal contexts, "proportionality" is a useful indicator of purpose. The true purpose of actions which are unnecessary or disproportionate to the end which is said to justify those actions is unlikely to be the achieving of that end but is likely to be the satisfaction of some other and different purpose.'

[60] Cited in *Singh* at [21].

[61] Cited in *R. v Hallam and Others*, at [107].

them from other offenders, and second that there are morally superior (lawful) means for them to express their views.

Translated into practice, the sentence of the court could include requirements which focus on reminding the offender about legal avenues of protest, or it may highlight the adverse consequences of the offending on innocent victims and the public. The offender may not have been fully aware of either at the time of the offending, especially if this was her first crime. Offenders might be required to engage with members of the public affected by the protest offending. As a consequence, the first conviction should result in a mitigated sentence, to see how the offender responds to the state's appeal to move to more socially-acceptable means of protesting. However, the most committed activist is likely to reject the message in favour of further offending. Many examples of such recalcitrance exist. The offender who spray-painted a painting was subsequently charged with the same conduct involving airport departure boards—before being sentenced for the previous crime. In the language of communicative sentencing, the recipient of the penal message (the offender) didn't even wait for the communicator (the court) to finish speaking before responding with another act of defiance. There seems no reason to mitigate sentence or modify the court's message thereafter: none so deaf as those who will not hear.

Prior to awarding mitigation for 'ethical' offending, courts should ask a series of questions. These pertain to the individual and not the relative merits of their cause. First, was there an alternate lawful means for achieving the offender's objective of raising public or official awareness of the cause? Secondly, if so, did the offenders decline the opportunity to pursue these lawful avenues of protest prior to breaking the law? Thirdly, has the offender previously been granted mitigation in recognition of their 'honourable intentions'? Fourthly, might the offender have been unable to predict the full consequences of the acts committed? If, for example, closing a runway had unforeseen or unforeseeable harmful consequences, this might justify some mitigation. Affirmative answers to these questions would disentitle the offender to mitigation for the current crime.

6.1. Lawful Alternatives and the Offender's History

The first two questions can be addressed by considering the level of political freedom and the offender's history involving lawful means of protest. The offending may be interpreted as a mild version of a defence of necessity. The merciful murderer is an analogy. Such a murderer may argue that all legal avenues to relieve suffering had been foreclosed by the irreversible and irremediable medical condition from which the victim is suffering. Necessity exculpates because the offender was deprived of the full agency to act in a lawful manner. At sentencing the activist offender may claim diminished agency, as a result of a pressing emergency. Some external influence (or actor) has constrained their potential range of lawful responses. As a result, the offender is compelled, or at least pressured, to act unlawfully. Much will depend on the range of lawful options open to the offender to express their views. Throwing paint at an artwork of inestimable importance, obstructing a busy motorway, or closing an airport runway are clearly not the only ways of attracting the public's attention to the climate crisis or influencing government policy.

To varying degrees (depending on the country and the constitutional framework), citizens in liberal democracies generally enjoy the freedom to protest. Climate protesters in the UK and other western democracies have many legitimate avenues to exploit before they are required to break the law. For example, a public space directly in front of the UK Parliament is regularly (and lawfully) occupied by individuals and groups protesting against a wide variety of state actions and policies. This freedom to lawfully protest undermines claims for mitigation.

Protesters who break the law undermine the legitimate avenues of protest. Their message is that these forms of dissent—mass marches, encampments near the legislature, media campaigns, and so forth, are either ineffective or inappropriate. If closing Gatwick airport for two hours attracts immediate and widespread media coverage, why would other protesters bother holding a rally in Trafalgar Square? Freedom of speech exists to facilitate persuasion by words and reason in the marketplace of ideas.

For these reasons, mitigation in these cases should be modest and time-limited. In a dictatorship, however, citizens' freedom to protest is rather different. Courts should be more sympathetic to political protesters in a society in which the freedom to express their views has been significantly compromised or removed entirely. In contrast, pro-democracy protesters in China, for example, deserve mitigation for unlawful acts as they have fewer lawful opportunities to express their views. Such demonstrators have a stronger case for sentence reduction (assuming they can find a court sufficiently independent to consider such a plea in mitigation). As for the third question, a court should consider whether the offender had previously received mitigation for similar offending. If this is the first occasion on which they appear for sentencing, mitigation is surely appropriate. (We explore the sentencing of repeat activist offenders in more detail later in the chapter.)

There are clear limits on the mitigating power of ethical motives. First, motives only affect the culpability branch of a proportional sentence; crime seriousness is unaffected. Second, unlike some other mitigating factors, mitigation for an ethical motive often runs contrary to the interests of the crime victim. The store owner whose stock has been stolen for distribution to the poor, and the passenger whose flight was cancelled thanks to an environmental protest, will be unlikely to see any justification for mitigation. Other grounds for mitigation—for example, when the offender harms himself in committing the crime—do not infringe the interests of the crime victim and often actually attract some sympathy from the victim.

Determining the degree of mitigation is challenging and may be culturally determined. Societies will differ in the extent to which they tolerate disruption caused by political or environmental protests. The Swiss, for example, appear relatively forgiving with respect to the inconveniences and disruption occasioned by political or environmental protesters (Demay, this volume). A considerable degree of social tolerance will presumably explain why some jurisdictions (including Italy) have codified a mitigating factor to reflect ethical offending.

Potential mitigating factors include: the absence of lawful opportunities for legitimate protest; evidence of community support or consensus regarding the cause; the existence of steps taken to minimize the harm or impact on property or personal victims; the personal relevance of the cause. Young adults protesting the US involvement in Vietnam during the 1960s faced the draft and a trip to the battlefields themselves—the state whose war was the cause of their protest required them to enlist. This sets them apart from, say, protesters in another country not subject to being drafted into the US army. The age of the offender has been overlooked in some judgments. In *Hallam*, for example, one of the defendants was a young adult aged 20 yet the court stated that her 'relative youth' provided no mitigation.[62] An offender of this age is always entitled to some young adult mitigation and politically-motivated offenders are no exception.

a) Aggravating factors and in particular prior convictions

For fairness and consistency, all relevant aggravating factors should apply to activist offenders, but one deserves additional discussion. After the seriousness of the crime, an offender's criminal history is the most significant predictor of sentencing outcomes.[63] Guidelines across the United States formally

[62] See *R. v Hallam and Others*, at [78].
[63] See Roberts (2008).

incorporate prior convictions as one of the two axes of the two-dimensional sentencing grid. Jurisdictions without such guidelines, or indeed without any form of guidelines, also take an offender's criminal history into account.[64] Almost all jurisdictions, both common law and civil law, impose harsher penalties on repeat offenders and mitigate sentence for first offenders. The general pattern is often cumulative, with sentence severity increasing in direct proportion to the seriousness of the criminal record. How then should sentencing courts approach the sentencing of a repeat offender convicted of crimes committed for some political or social cause?

For many defendants, the first sentencing hearing will also be the last. They may not return to court because their offence was out of character, the individual was youthful, or the crime was triggered by exceptional circumstances or temporary economic pressures. Or the experience of arrest, prosecution, trial and punishment may have achieved a permanent return to a law-abiding life. Activists differ from this profile. The cause of the offending is internal rather than external; it reflects a conscious decision to act, rather than a response to personal difficulties or criminogenic influences. By definition, the word 'activism' implies an ongoing commitment to a cause. Environmental protesters don't close an airport terminal one weekend and then return to board a long-haul flight the next. The persistence of their offending reflects (and substantiates) their commitment to the cause. As a consequence, repeat offending is common among such individuals. This raises the question of how the sentencing process should take persistent 'activist offending' into account.

Preventive theories are clear on this issue: repeat offenders represent a higher risk of re-offending and accordingly should be punished more harshly. Preventive theories would disregard the offender's motivation for the crime; the only consideration would be their likelihood of reoffending. Activist offenders are by their own words high-risk; they often proclaim their intention to reoffend before sentencing for their current offence. As noted, many environmental protesters have been arrested for further crimes while on bail awaiting sentencing for previous convictions. General deterrence has clear limits as a crime prevention strategy. Nevertheless, to the extent that it is effective, deterrence advocates would see harsher sentences as justified in the case of social activists and courts have adopted general deterrence as a means to prevent further offending by associates of convicted activists. Advocates of individual deterrence would also support progressively harsher punishments to deter the specific offender. And for offenders convicted of the most serious

[64] See Frase and Roberts (2019).

forms of offending, incapacitation would require significant prison terms subject to an individualized risk assessment.

How should repeat activist offenders be punished under a retributive rationale? Retributivists place limits on the degree of aggravation for prior crimes and recognize the need for a significant first offender discount.[65] In daily life we express less blame when a person transgresses for the first time. We give first offenders the benefit of the doubt because we are more willing to accept innocent explanations for the breach—a colleague who thoughtlessly delays the departmental staff meeting for half an hour is blamed less on the first occasion than when it becomes a monthly occurrence. In each case he might have been unavoidably delayed for a number of reasons. However, his lack of punctuality on a third consecutive occasion is harder to ascribe to transportation delays, and more likely reflects a culpable indifference to the interests of colleagues.

Andrew von Hirsch's approach to prior convictions supports multiple, declining mitigations for first offenders or those with modest criminal histories. This influential model reflects the well-established principle of progressive loss of mitigation. On this account, mitigation is awarded to all first offenders, and then repeatedly extended, albeit to a diminishing degree, for recidivists with few priors. At its heart, this approach justifies mitigation for first offenders on the basis that their offending constituted a 'lapse'. Von Hirsch draws upon everyday moral judgments to justify the need to show understanding, tolerance, and sympathy for 'the all-too-human fallibility that can lead to a first offence'.[66] He argues that: 'Our everyday moral judgments include the notion of a *lapse*. A transgression (even one of a substantial nature) is judged less stringently when it occurs against a background of prior compliance . . . even an ordinarily well-behaved person can have his or her moral inhibitions fail in a moment of weakness or willfulness'.[67]

The sentencing process should mitigate sentence in recognition that many people lapse occasionally into criminality. However, once the individual has accumulated multiple convictions, further mitigation on this account becomes implausible: a sixth conviction cannot be described as a lapse. As a result, the fully proportionate sentence should be imposed. Thereafter sentence severity should remain at that level for each further offence, with no additional increments in severity. This pattern respects the position that the focus at sentencing is on the current and not previous offences.

[65] See Frase and Roberts (2019).
[66] See von Hirsch (2017: 75).
[67] ibid: 76.

The justifications for regarding first offenders as being less blameworthy invoke considerations such as the absence of formal censure and warnings, the greater possibility of innocent explanations for the offence, incomplete awareness of the consequences of the crime (see earlier discussion), and the lack of the possibility to formally rehabilitate after conviction. None of these arguments are plausible in the context of activist offenders. Their offending does not represent an inadvertent lapse. Indeed, most would strongly reject any such imputation. They act intentionally and deliberately out of their strongly-held ethical beliefs. First offenders are treated with leniency to reflect their claim that the offence was out of character. Again, the activist would reject any suggestion that their offending was out of character; it was wholly aligned with their personal values. To summarize, whether from a preventive or a retributive perspective, first offender mitigation should exhaust more rapidly for recidivists since their repeated offending in no way represents an unrepresentative lapse.

7. Conclusion

As noted in the introduction to this volume, a wide range of offenders claim an ethical motive for their crimes. Setting aside crimes of 'merciful intention' murder which constitute an exceptional case, we see very limited grounds for mitigation for positive motives in a principled sentencing framework. Beyond a limited reduction for first offenders, there are principled arguments against awarding significant sentence reductions. In addition, there are insuperable practical objections that derive from the exceptional nature of ethically-motivated offending in terms of both retributive and instrumental sentencing rationales.

References

Berlin, Isaiah. 'Two Concepts of Liberty'. In *Reading Political Philosophy: Machiavelli to Mill,* edited by Warburton, N., Matravers, D., and Pike, J.E., pp. 231–237. New York: Routledge, 2014.

Brownlee, Kimberley. 'The Communicative Aspects of Civil Disobedience and Lawful Punishment'. *Criminal Law and Philosophy* 1, no. 2 (2007): 179–192 doi: https://doi.org/10.1007/s11572-006-9015-9.

Chow, Pok Yin S. 'The Change in Judicial Practice in Cases Concerning Civil Disobedience Protests and its Constitutional Significance'. *The Modern Law Review* 86, no. 4 (2023): 927–950 doi: https://doi.org/10.1111/1468-2230.12787.

Davis, Paul and Jenkins, Michael. *Deterrence & Influence in Counterterrorism: A Component in the War on Al Qaeda*. Santa Monica: Rand, 2002. Available at: https://www.rand.org/content/dam/rand/pubs/monograph_reports/2005/MR1619.pdf (accessed: 18 July 2025).

Deutsche Welle. 'Germany: Climate protesters block Cologne/Bonn airport'. 24 July 2024. Available at: https://www.dw.com/en/germany-climate-protesters-block-cologne-bonn-airport/a-69749119 (accessed: 18 July 2025).

Duff, R.A. 'Relational Reasons and the Criminal Law'. In *Oxford Studies in Philosophy of Law, Volume* 2, edited by Green, L. and Leiter, B., pp. 175–208. Oxford: Oxford University Press, 2013 doi: https://doi.org/10.1093/acprof:oso/9780199679829.003.0006.

Eldar, Shachar, and Elkana Laist. 'The Irrelevance of Motive and the Rule of Law'. *New Criminal Law Review: An International and Interdisciplinary Journal* 20, no. 3 (2017): 433–464.

Fleetwood, Jennifer, and Sveinung Sandberg. 'Narrative Criminology and Ethnography'. In *The Oxford Handbook of Ethnographies of Crime and Criminal Justice*, edited by Sandra M. Bucerius, Luca Berardi, and Kevin D. Haggerty, pp. 246–268. Oxford University Press, 2021 doi: https://doi.org/10.1093/oxfordhb/9780190904500.013.12.

Frase, Richard S. and Roberts, Julian V. *Paying for the Past: The Case Against Prior Record Sentence Enhancements*. Oxford: Oxford University Press, 2019.

Freud, Sigmund. 'Some Character Types Met with in Psycho-Analytic Work'. In *The Standard Edition of the Complete Psychological Works of Sigmund Freud, Volume XIV: (1914–1916), On the History of the Psychoanalytic Movement, Papers on Metapsychology and Other Works*, pp. 309–333. London: Vintage, [1916] 2001.

Gayle, Damien. 'Just Stop Oil activists throw soup at Van Gogh's Sunflowers'. *The Guardian*, 14 October 2022. Available at: https://www.theguardian.com/environment/2022/oct/14/just-stop-oil-activists-throw-soup-at-van-goghs-sunflowers (accessed: 18 July 2025).

Kohlberg, Lawrence. *The Philosophy of Moral Development: Moral Stages and the Idea of Justice*. San Francisco CA: Harper & Row, 1981.

Maruna, Shadd, and Heith Copes. 'What Have We Learned from Five Decades of Neutralization Research?'. *Crime and Justice* 32 (2005): 221–320 doi: https://doi.org/10.1086/655355.

Miller, Gregory D. 'Terrorist Decision Making and the Deterrence Problem'. *Studies in Conflict & Terrorism* 36, no. 2 (2013): 132–151 doi: https://doi.org/10.1080/1057610x.2013.747075.

Murphy, Jeffrie G. 'Some Second Thoughts on Retributivism'. In *Retributivism: Essays on Theory and Policy*, edited by White, M.D., pp. 93–106. Oxford: Oxford University Press, 2011 doi: https://doi.org/10.1093/acprof:oso/9780199752232.003.0006.

Norrie, Alan W. *Crime, Reason and History: A Critical Introduction to Criminal Law* (3rd edn). Cambridge: Cambridge University Press, 2014.

Perry, Simon and Hasisi, Badi. 'Rational Choice Rewards and the Jihadist Suicide Bomber'. *Terrorism and Political Violence* 27, no. 1 (2015): 53–80 doi: https://doi.org/10.1080/09546553.2014.962991.

Roberts, Julian V. *Punishing Persistent Offenders: Exploring Community and Offender Perspectives*. Oxford: Oxford University Press, 2008.

Roberts, Julian V. and Dagan, Netanel. "'One Wrong Treads upon the Heels of Another'": Mitigating Sentence in Response to State Misconduct'. In *Responding to the Culpable State: Is Sentence Mitigation Appropriate?*, edited by Zaibert, L., Roberts, J.V., and Ryberg, J., pp. 79–96. Oxford: Hart Publishing, 2025 doi: https://doi.org/10.5040/9781509975686.ch-006.

Robinson, Paul H. 'The Moral Vigilante and Her Cousins in the Shadows'. *University of Illinois Law Review*, no. 2 (2013): 401–478 doi: https://doi.org/10.2139/ssrn.2360303.

Robinson, Paul H., Sean E. Jackowitz, and Daniel M. Bartels. 'Extralegal Punishment Factors: A Study of Forgiveness, Hardship, Good Deeds, Apology, Remorse, and Other Such Discretionary Factors in Assessing Criminal Punishment'. *Vanderbilt Law Review* 65, no. 3 (2012): 737–826.

Skitka, Linda J., Christopher W. Bauman, and Edward G. Sargis. 'Moral Conviction: Another Contributor to Attitude Strength or Something More?'. *Journal of Personality and Social Psychology* 88, no. 6 (2005): 895–917 doi: https://doi.org/10.1037/0022-3514.88.6.895.

Sykes, Gresham M., and David Matza. 'Techniques of Neutralization: A Theory of Delinquency'. *American Sociological Review* 22, no. 6 (1957): 664–670 doi: https://doi.org/10.2307/2089195.

Tonry, Michael. 'Vigilantism and "Public Confidence": The Pertinence of Public Opinion to Sentencing'. In *Sentencing, Public Opinion, and Criminal Justice*, edited by Watson, G. and Manikis, M., pp. 247–264. Oxford: Oxford University Press, 2025 doi: https://doi.org/10.1093/9780191991936.003.0019.

Trager, Robert F., and Dessislava P. Zagorcheva. 'Deterring Terrorism: It Can Be Done'. *International Security* 30, no. 3 (2005): 87–123 doi: https://doi.org/10.1162/016228805775969564.

United States Sentencing Commission. *Federal Sentencing Guidelines Manual*. Washington DC: US Government Publishing Office. Available at: https://www.ussc.gov/sites/default/files/pdf/guidelines-manual/2023/GLMFull.pdf (accessed: 18 July 2025).

von Hirsch, Andreas. *Deserved Criminal Sentences: An Overview*. Oxford: Hart Publishing, 2017.

Walvisch, Jamie. 'Lone Anarchists and Peace Pilgrims: The Relevance of Political Motivations to Sentencing'. *Monash University Law Review* 44, no. 2 (2018): 428–457 doi: https://doi.org/10.2139/ssrn.3394600.

Zaibert, Leo, Roberts, Julian V. and Ryberg, Jesper. (eds.) *Responding to the Culpable State: Is Sentence Mitigation Appropriate?* London: Hart Publishing, 2025.

6

Moral Motives and Criminal Sentencing

Zachary Hoskins

1. Introduction

When five members of the 'Just Stop Oil' protest group were each sentenced in 2024 by a UK court to four years (or for the group's leader, five years) in prison for conspiring to cause gridlock on London's motorways, many people criticized the sentences as excessively harsh, in part because the defendants acted from laudable moral motives: namely, drawing attention to the climate crisis and persuading the UK government to end new oil and gas licensing and production. The Court of Appeal in 2025 reduced the protesters' sentences, explaining that the sentencing judge had erred in taking 'no account at all of the appellants' conscientious motivation' (*R. v Hallam and Others* [2025] EWCA Crim 199, 81). Also in 2025, Lisa Davenport, who pleaded guilty to manslaughter by diminished capacity after smothering her terminally ill, 88-year-old father, was sentenced by a UK court to a two-year suspended sentence. The judge explained that he had 'taken a merciful course', as Davenport's 'sole motivation was to bring your father's suffering to an end' (Grierson 2025).

What role, if any, should moral motivations play as a consideration in criminal sentencing? As the courts' decisions in these two cases reflect, there is intuitive plausibility to the notion that, other things being equal, a defendant who was motivated by her moral convictions should receive a somewhat less severe sentence than a defendant acting from some other motive. Interestingly, this idea is not clearly supported by prominent theories of punishment.

In section 2, I examine the relevance of moral motives for sentencing according to deterrence theory, moral education theory, fair play retributivism, and communicative retributivism. I consider three defendants in a public protest case, where the facts for each remain the same except for their motives, to examine what the theories would imply about whether different sentences are warranted in each case. As we will see, some theories are ambiguous about, or possibly even in tension with, the idea that a moral motivation should count

Zachary Hoskins, *Moral Motives and Criminal Sentencing* In: *Sentencing the Ethically-Motivated Offender*.
Edited by: Julian V. Roberts, Leo Zaibert, and Jesper Ryberg, Oxford University Press.
DOI: 10.1093/9780198993025.003.0007

toward a reduced sentence. If the issue of moral motives and sentencing raises questions for this or that consequentialist or retributivist theory of punishment, it appears to present a particularly sharp challenge to some versions of pluralist theory—which seek to incorporate elements of deterrence, retribution, and other considerations—as it highlights unhelpful ambiguities, or even internal incoherence, within such accounts. In section 3, after fleshing out the challenge moral motive sentencing presents for pluralist accounts, I articulate a version of a pluralist theory that can make sense of the relevance of moral motives in sentencing without falling into ambiguity or incoherence.

Two points are worth highlighting here at the outset. First, we can distinguish two senses in which one's motivations might be characterized as 'moral'. One sense of moral motivations contrasts with non-moral motivations, as when we say a person was motivated by some moral concern rather than by self-interest or some other non-moral considerations. I sometimes refer to this sense of moral motivation as being motivated by one's moral convictions. Another sense of moral motivations contrasts with immoral motivations, as when we say the reasons motivating a person were morally good ones (or, as in the Italian Criminal Code, were reasons of 'moral or social value': see Bondi, this volume). As will become clear, a key question is whether someone motivated by her moral convictions but whose convictions are misguided should be treated differently in sentencing from the person who is motivated by appropriately aligned moral convictions, or the person who is motivated by non-moral considerations.

Second, I should acknowledge that there are a number of practical challenges with taking moral motivations into account in sentencing decisions: challenges arising from mixed motives, over-determined motives, and so on (see Ryberg, this volume). The challenges are important; if they cannot be met, then this is a significant point against considering motivations in sentencing. That said, my starting point is that there is something intuitively plausible about the notion that a person who commits a crime motivated by his moral convictions should, as in the cases I highlighted earlier, receive a somewhat reduced sentence. My central interest is in assessing whether we receive support for this intuitively plausible idea from various prominent theories of punishment.

2. Motivations and Theories of Punishment

Consider a public protest case in which three defendants are among the participants in a group activity to cause gridlock on a busy London motorway with the stated aim of raising public awareness about climate change. All that differs among the three defendants' situations are their motivations for participating. The first defendant, Kristen, believes it is her moral duty to help raise awareness about environmental degradation, and this moral conviction motivates her to participate in the protest. The second defendant, Louis, is also motivated to participate by his moral convictions. Louis believes that London has become a hub for the spread of utilitarianism in the United Kingdom, and because he regards utilitarianism as a morally pernicious theory, he regards it as his moral duty to disrupt the city's workings at any opportunity he gets. He does not particularly care about climate change, but he is happy for the opportunity the protest provides him to participate in the disruption of one of the city's major motorways. Here I just stipulate that whereas Kristen and Louis are both motivated by their moral convictions, Kristen's moral concerns are legitimate ones, but Louis's are not. The third defendant, Mark, is motivated to participate by non-moral reasons. He is not interested in the environment and doubts that the protest will achieve its stated aims anyway, but he is attracted to Kristen, and he thinks participating in the protest might help to spur her interest in him. Mark believes the disruptive protest is wrong, but he does not care.

Let us stipulate that none of the defendants have justifying or excusing defences for their criminal actions; they are all criminally liable. There remains a question of appropriate sentencing. Specifically, how, if at all, should the various defendants' motivations factor into sentencing decisions? Here I consider what guidance we can glean from four prominent accounts of punishment: deterrence, moral education, fair play, and communicative retributivism. There are obviously many other theories of punishment available, but space prevents my considering them all, and these four are sufficient to highlight my point that prominent theories do not provide clear, uniform support for moral motivation sentence mitigation.

2.1. Deterrence

Standard deterrence theory is a species of consequentialist account, which holds that the institution of punishment is justified insofar as, on balance, it contributes to better consequences than not maintaining such an institution, and its benefits outweigh its costs. The most commonly cited benefit to which punishment is thought to contribute is crime reduction, and deterrence is often cited as a key means of reducing crime. Specifically, the state threatens burdensome consequences for criminal conduct in order to dissuade potential offenders, and then it carries out punishment on those who do commit crimes to maintain the credibility of the deterrent threat. The threat of punishment might dissuade members of the public generally from committing crimes they would otherwise have committed (general deterrence); or, for those who have committed crimes and been punished, the threat of undergoing punishment again might serve as a disincentive to committing future crimes (specific deterrence).

Empirical research about punishment's deterrent effects tends to suggest that the likelihood of punishment has a greater deterrent effect than the severity of punishment (see Nagin 2013). But suppose, as seems plausible, that sentence severity does have some non-negligible deterrent effect.[1] If so, then this is because the motivation to avoid burdensome punitive treatment is sufficient to outweigh whatever motivations potential offenders might have to commit crimes. On the logic of deterrence, then, the severity of punishment should vary according to the strength of the counter-motivations to offend. As Jeremy Bentham, perhaps the most famous philosophical proponent of deterrence theory, wrote:

> The strength of the temptation, *ceteris paribus,* is as the profit of the offense: the quantum of the punishment must rise with the profit of the offense: *ceteris paribus,* it must therefore rise with the strength of the temptation. (Bentham 1789, ch. XIV, § IX)

In the cases we are considering, deterrence theory asks us to consider what severity of punishment is sufficient to dissuade Kristen, Louis, and Mark, as well as similarly motivated members of the public, from disrupting motorways in the future. Psychological research supports the intuitively plausible idea that moral convictions tend to be especially strong motivations compared to other sorts of motivations (see, e.g., Skitka 2010: 268; Skitka and Mullen 2002). Thus, people motivated by moral convictions will tend to be more difficult to dissuade than those who are motivated by other concerns. Kristen and Louis acted from moral motivations, whereas Mark acted from non-moral motivations. This suggests that, for deterrence, Kristen and Louis should receive somewhat more severe sentences than Mark for participating in the disruption.

[1] A deterrence theorist must hold that sentence severity matters at least to some extent, or else the theory would offer no basis for sentencing any offender to more than the least severe sentence possible.

The point I have just raised seems most salient with respect to specific deterrence: if Kristen's and Louis's motivations are stronger than Mark's, then it appears that, other things being equal, a more severe punishment would be needed to dissuade Kristen and Louis from reoffending than to dissuade Mark. As we will see, other things may not be equal, so even with specific deterrence it may be unclear whether moral motivations should count in favour of sentence mitigation. But if we focus instead on general deterrence, things may seem even less clear, insofar as members of the general public may not tend to be aware of, or pay much attention to, differences in individual sentence levels.

It is also important to note that, for deterrence theory, sentencing should be responsive not only to motivation strength but also to the seriousness of the crime. As Bentham put it, 'The greater the mischief of the offense, the greater is the expense which it may be worth while to be at, in the way of punishment' (Bentham 1789, ch. XIV, § X). In the cases we are considering, the defendants all participated in the same crime. But perhaps a deterrence theorist might hold that disrupting motorways from a non-moral motive, as in Mark's case, is worse—and thus warrants more severe deterrence—than disrupting them from moral motives, as in the other two cases. The question is why this would be so. Because all three are participating in the same group activity, it follows that the effects—the disruption to motorists and any indirect consequences, whether this be raised awareness about climate change or, conversely, backlash and resentment toward environmental activists—are the same.

A deterrence theorist might respond that disrupting traffic from non-moral motives is *inherently* a greater wrong, and thus warrants more severe deterrence, than doing so from moral motives.[2] This would be a distinctly non-standard deterrence account, although there is nothing about deterrence per se that precludes a concern for reducing wrongs as well as (or instead of) reducing harms. One problem with such a strategy, however, is that even if we accept that an agent's motives are relevant to the evaluation of the rightness or wrongness of his action, it is implausible that actions done from non-moral motives are always worse than actions done from moral motives (I return to this point later). Another problem is that deterrence theory traditionally accepts the notion that punishment can only be justified if the bad consequences it prevents outweigh the bad consequences it causes. As Bentham wrote:

[2] Many deontological views imply that an agent's motives matter in our assessment of her actions: perhaps most famously, Kant (1785, ch. 1) wrote that only acts from the motive of duty have moral worth. Some consequentialists also contend that motives are relevant to the rightness or wrongness of actions (see, e.g., Sverdlik 2011).

> [A]ll punishment is mischief: all punishment in itself is evil. Upon the principle of utility, if it ought at all to be admitted, it ought only to be admitted in as far as it promises to exclude some greater evil. (Bentham 1789, ch. XIII, §1)

For the utilitarian Bentham, the basis for assessing the 'evil' done or prevented by punishment was suffering. Making assessments of whether some severity of punishment would cause more suffering than it would prevent is no doubt a formidable challenge. But at least Bentham was working with a common currency. It is much less clear how a deterrence theorist should weigh potential wrongs to be prevented against the harms caused by punishment. Things are even more difficult than this, though: Suppose a deterrence theorist could provide a plausible account of (a) how crimes committed from non-moral motives are worse wrongs than the same crimes committed from moral motives, and (b) how the prevention of these wrongs should be weighed against the harms caused by punishment. This account would still need to be balanced somehow with the fact that, as discussed, moral convictions are especially strong motivations and thus appear to require greater deterrence than non-moral motivations. It is not obvious how a deterrence theory should reconcile these apparently conflicting considerations.

All of this is not to say that deterrence theory definitely cannot support sentence mitigation for offences committed from moral motivations. My aim has been more modest: I have discussed one consideration that is relevant for deterrence theory—the strength of motivations—and suggested that this consideration appears to count against sentence mitigation for moral motivations and may even count in favour of more severe sentences for those who acted from their moral convictions. I acknowledged that other considerations are relevant for deterrence theory, such as the seriousness of the crime, but I have tried to show that analysing this consideration only muddies the waters further. I conclude, then, that we do not find clear support in deterrence theory for moral motivation sentencing mitigation.

2.2. Moral Education

Whereas the logic of deterrence involves reducing crime by providing potential offenders with prudential reasons not to (re)offend—namely, a desire to avoid some burdensome treatment—we might instead hold that punishment is justified insofar as it aims to persuade people not to commit crimes for moral reasons: namely, that criminal conduct is morally wrong. In an influential articulation of the moral education theory, Jean Hampton accepts 'the deterrence theorist's contention that the justification of punishment is connected with the fact that it is a necessary tool for preventing future crime and promoting the public's well-being' (1984: 211). But Hampton likens crime prevention solely through deterrence to the conditioning of animals through painful stimuli; such treatment, she argues, is not appropriate for autonomous moral agents.

> Thus, according to the moral education theory, punishment is not intended as a way of conditioning a human being to do what society wants her to do (in the way that an animal is conditioned by an electrified fence to stay within a pasture); rather, the theory maintains that punishment is intended as a way of teaching the wrongdoer that the action she did (or wants to do) is forbidden because it is morally wrong and should not be done for that reason. (1984: 212)

As with deterrence theory, for moral education theory we can distinguish two potential audiences for the message conveyed by punishment: the offenders themselves (call this specific moral education) and the general public (call this general moral education). Hampton makes clear that she regards the primary intended audience for the moral lesson conveyed by punishment to be offenders themselves, but she acknowledges that punishment can also convey the moral message to the public.

So, what would a moral education account imply for Kristen's, Louis's, and Mark's sentencing, and in particular for whether Kristen's or Louis's moral motivations should count toward a reduction in their sentences compared with Mark's? Because Hampton states that the offenders themselves are the primary audience of punishment's moral message, we can focus on what specific moral education requires. Kristen and Louis were each motivated by their moral convictions; they believed their actions were morally right (albeit for different reasons). Insofar as the rationale of punishment is, as Hampton puts it, to teach 'the wrongdoer that the action she did . . . is forbidden because it is morally wrong', it appears that there is, in Kristen's and Louis's cases, educative work for punishment to do. After all, both Kristen and Louis acted from their moral convictions; they believed they were doing their moral duty. Kristen's concern for the environment is at least a morally legitimate motivation, even if it does not justify or excuse her criminal behaviour. She might thus require somewhat less moral education than Louis, whose actions were motivated by misguided moral convictions about combating the spread of utilitarianism. Even this is not entirely clear, though, because Louis might hold his misguided moral convictions more lightly than Kristen holds her well-attuned concerns; Louis, then, might be more easily persuaded that his moral convictions did not justify his criminal behaviour.

Mark, by contrast, recognized that what he was did was wrong; he just did not care. It is thus not clear what moral lesson Mark's sentence should aim to teach him. If we focus on moral education as correcting moral ignorance, it looks as though Mark, who acted from non-moral motives but understood that his action was wrong, warrants less of a sentence than either Kristen or Louis, who were each motivated by moral concerns that they believed, incorrectly, justified their criminal behaviour. Rather than indicating a lower sentence for moral motivations than for non-moral motivations, this construal of moral education would seem to indicate the opposite.

Perhaps an education theorist might respond that Mark is still in need of education, just of a different sort: he does not need to be taught that what he did was wrong, but rather needs to be taught to care about this. This is a fair response, although I agree with Antony Duff that we should be wary of making it a 'definitional truth that all wrongdoing shows the wrongdoer to be in need of moral (re-)education' (Duff 2001: 212, n. 13). At any rate, if we adopt this more expansive notion of moral education as correcting moral ignorance and, when needed, teaching offenders to care about, and be motivated by, their moral beliefs, then the theory's sentencing implications become deeply unclear. We would need some account not only of what degree and mode of punishment are needed to correct moral ignorance, but also what degree and mode of punishment are needed to bring offenders sufficiently to care about their moral beliefs. Since we are here focused on specific moral education, we would also need to account for the likelihood that some offenders are more responsive than others to moral education in either of these senses (see, e.g., Shafer-Landau 1991: 211).

Hampton would deny that moral education theory implies these sorts of sentencing complexities. She acknowledges at several points how difficult it would be to make predictions about the efficacy of a given sentence in morally educating a given offender. Central to the moral education view, she explains, is a concern to respect offenders as autonomous moral agents who are free to accept or reject the moral lesson the state aims to teach through punishment. She writes, 'the choice of whether to reform or not is a free one, and hence one the state cannot hope to predict' (Hampton 1984: 2011). Thus, in its criminal sentencing, the state should attempt to convey to offenders—and, secondarily, to the general public—the wrongness of their conduct, but it is entirely up to the intended recipients of the message, and entirely unpredictable by the state, whether they learn the lesson it aims to teach.

I do not think that the moral education view can so easily avoid the concerns about tailoring sentence severities based on their likelihood of teaching the moral lesson. As I mentioned, Hampton begins by accepting the deterrent theorist's claim that the justification of punishment is tied to its role as a necessary tool in reducing crime and ensuring public safety. This is to adopt a consequentialist framing: what justifies punishment is its contribution to crime reduction, and the appropriate way for it to make this contribution is by morally educating offenders (and the general public). But if what justifies the practice is the contribution it makes to crime reduction through moral education, then surely it is relevant whether, and to what extent, it is effective at promoting this end. It seems, therefore, that on the moral education view, the state must concern itself with what sorts of sentences are likely to be effective in teaching offenders (and potential offenders) about the moral wrongness of various forms of criminal conduct. The claim to be attempting to teach a lesson can ring hollow if it is not accompanied by some attempt to discern whether the methods of teaching are likely to be effective.

So, I think Hampton should acknowledge that although people are free to accept or reject the moral message being conveyed by punishment, her moral education theory requires the state to make some efforts to tailor sentences based on its best assessments (imperfect though these will be) of their likelihood of teaching the desired lesson. As I discussed before, if we take moral education to be a matter of correcting moral ignorance, then it looks as though Kristen and Louis, both of whom believed their actions were morally right, are more in need of educative punishment than is Mark, who already believes his actions were wrong. If instead we understand moral education to be about bringing offenders to care about the moral wrongness of their actions as well as simply recognizing that they were wrong, then the question of sentencing guidance in the three cases becomes extremely complicated.

2.3. Fair Play

Deterrence theory and moral education theory each aim to justify punishment in virtue of its contribution to crime prevention. Suppose, instead, we consider the sentencing guidance offered by retributivist accounts, which hold that punishment is inherently justified as a deserved response to crime. Here

I consider fair play retributivism, then in section 2.4, I examine communicative retributivism.

Fair play theory began as an account of people's obligation to obey the law. The theory casts society as a cooperative venture in which each of us benefits from general compliance with the rules of the venture. Sometimes the rules require people to constrain their behaviour when they do not want to do so. Those who accept the benefits made possible by others' compliance with the rules have an obligation of fairness to comply as well. Those who break the law are essentially free riders: they enjoy the benefits of others' compliance with the law, but then they violate the law when it suits them. Although it was initially offered as a theory of political obligation, some scholars have extended the theory to offer a justification of punishment. On these accounts, punishment is justified as the deserved removal of the unfair advantage that an offender gains, relative to other members of society, when he commits a crime. As Herbert Morris puts it, 'Justice — that is, punishing such individuals — restores the equilibrium of benefits and burdens by taking from the individual what he owes, that is, exacting the debt' (Morris 1968: 478).

What does fair play retributivism imply for sentencing? This depends on how we construe the unfair advantage that an offender gains relative to the rest of the society, the advantage that punishment is meant to remove. The most prominent answer, offered by Morris, is that an offender gains the advantage of freedom from the burden of self-constraint, a burden that other members of the community have accepted (1968: 477). It follows that if compliance with some law is generally regarded as very burdensome, then the person who violates that law gains a significant advantage relative to everyone else, and a more severe sentence is required to remove that advantage. If compliance with a law, however, is generally regarded as a relatively small burden, then the advantage gained from violating that law is low, and a less severe sentenced is warranted.

I discussed earlier that moral motivations tend to be stronger than non-moral motivations. This suggests that, in general, constraining one's behaviour to comply with the law when one has moral motivations to violate it will be more difficult, a bigger burden, than constraining one's behaviour to comply when one's motivations to violate it are non-moral. In turn, it follows that when people do violate the law from moral motivations, as Kristen and Louis did, they free themselves from a greater burden—and thus gain a greater unfair advantage relative to law abiders—than do people who violate the law from non-moral motivations, such as Mark. Because the role of punishment is to remove the offender's unfair advantage, it appears that Kristen and Louis each warrant a more severe sentence than does Mark.

Other fair play accounts offer different characterizations of the unfair advantage an offender gains, which punishment aims to remove. Richard Dagger, for example, contends that offenders gain freedom from the burden of compliance not with the particular law violated, but rather with the law in general. This general compliance, Dagger writes, is a genuine burden: 'there are times for almost all of us when we would like to have the best of both worlds — that is, the freedom we enjoy under the rule of law plus freedom from the burden of obeying laws' (Dagger 1993: 483). One challenge for this type of fair play view, however, is that it appears to suggest that all offences are, for the purposes of sentencing, the same offence. Every offender—the murderer, the tax cheat, the shoplifter—frees himself from the burden of general compliance with the law, and it is this advantage that punishment removes. This formulation of the fair play view thus appears to generate its own counter-intuitive sentencing guidance. For our purposes, however, we only need to note that this account does not provide a basis for moral motivation sentence mitigation. Kristen, Louis, and Mark all committed the same type of offence, and in doing so they freed themselves from the burden of general compliance with the law. It does not appear that their different motivations are relevant to sentencing on this version of fair play theory.

To sum up to this point, the idea that moral motivations should count as mitigating factors in sentencing, which I have suggested is an intuitively plausible idea, does not receive clear support from deterrence theory, moral education theory, or fair play theory. I turn now to a theory that I argue does provide support for this sentencing practice.

2.4. Communicative Retributivism

Arguably the most influential version of retributivism in recent decades holds that punishment is justified insofar as it conveys deserved public condemnation, or censure, of the offender's wrongdoing. On some versions, the primary intended recipient of the message is the offender herself (e.g., Duff 2001); on others, punishment expresses to the community generally the state's denunciation of the crime (e.g., Wringe 2016; Bennett 2016). Like the moral education theory, communicative retributivism regards punishment's moral message as central to its justification. But whereas for moral education theory, punishment's justification depends on its effectiveness in conveying the message and, in turn, contributing to crime reduction, communicative retributivism holds that it is inherently appropriate for the state to condemn the wrongdoing. Regardless of whether it contributes to crime reduction or some other socially valuable goal, the public condemnation is a deserved response to the crime.

On a communicative retributivist account, Kristen's, Louis's, and Mark's sentences should reflect the degree of condemnation they each deserve; that is, their sentences should reflect how blameworthy they each are for what they have done. Here I think we have a clear grounding for the idea that moral motivations should count at least somewhat in favour of reduced sentences. We generally think that a person's motives matter in assessing how blameworthy she is for her actions. A person such as Kristen, who commits a crime from her moral conviction that raising awareness about the environment is the right thing to do, is less blameworthy than Mark, who commits the same type of crime not from any moral conviction but just from his self-interested motivation of winning Kristen's interest. Thus I think we should say, with the communicative retributivist, that Kristen deserves a somewhat reduced sentence compared to Mark's.

But what about Louis? Like Kristen, he acted from his moral convictions, but unlike Kristen, his moral convictions were misguided. Fighting the rise of utilitarianism in the United Kingdom is not a legitimate moral concern. It might seem that Louis is at least as blameworthy as Mark, perhaps more so. And this might seem to suggest that communicative retributivism, like the other views we have considered, does not clearly support the notion that moral motivations should always count in favour of reduced sentences. We can put the point even more sharply. People can be motivated by their moral convictions to do truly reprehensible things. Why should we think, then, that we can draw any general conclusions about the relative blameworthiness of committing crimes from moral motives as compared with non-moral motives? As Julia Markovits writes: '[T]he fact that Göbbels was driven by his conscience to persecute the Jews does not exonerate him, much less endow his acts with moral worth' (Markovits 2010: 224).[3]

Here I think we should distinguish different respects in which we can assess a person as more or less blameworthy for some criminal action: in addition to evaluating the action itself and evaluating his motivation, we can also regard

[3] Markovits makes this point in the context of her argument that whereas what philosophers term *de re* moral motivation is praiseworthy, *de dicto* moral motivation is not. Briefly, *de dicto* moral motivation is motivation to do the right thing in a somewhat abstract sense; that is, a motivation to do one's duty or do what is right whatever that might amount to in particular circumstances. Contrast this with someone who is *de re* motivated by the considerations that actually make an action the right thing to do in the given circumstances. I do not wade into the *de dicto-de re* debate in this chapter, as I believe there is less to the distinction than has been suggested (on this, I follow Johnson King (2020)).

him as blameworthy for his unreasonable (or even, as with Göbbels, abhorrent) moral values or beliefs. He may still be deeply blameworthy in virtue of his action and his unreasonable moral values, but somewhat less blameworthy all things considered because he was acting from moral conviction. Thus, in response to Markovits's point, Zoë A. Johnson King writes:

> [W]e can compare a clueless Göbbels who sincerely believes that what he is doing is morally right with a knowing Göbbels who is fully aware that what he is doing is deeply wrong but just doesn't care. I am inclined to think that the former Göbbels is slightly better than the latter. If so, this is presumably because his intentions are good. (Johnson King 2020: 423)

I think we should similarly say that Louis, who was motivated by his moral convictions, is therefore somewhat less blameworthy in that respect than Mark, whose motives were non-moral. Louis might still be more blameworthy for his action all things considered, however, in virtue of his unreasonable moral values or beliefs (I think we would need to flesh out the cases more than I have done here to make a full assessment). Another way to see that moral motivations can mitigate blameworthiness even in a case such as Louis's is to compare Louis with Louise, another participant in the motorway disruption who was motivated by a concern to disrupt utilitarian hotbed London at any opportunity, but who, unlike Louis, knew her actions were wrong and just did not care. It seems to me that Louis is less blameworthy than Louise and thus warrants a comparatively lighter sentence on communicative retributivist grounds, because unlike Louise, Louis acted from his moral convictions.

I contend, then, that of the theories I have considered, communicative retributivism provides the most plausible grounding for the intuitively compelling notion that the fact that a crime was motivated by moral convictions should count as a mitigating factor in sentencing. I take this to be a fairly modest conclusion in at least two respects: First, as I wrote earlier, there are of course other theories of punishment available; my aim here was not to do a full accounting. Second, suppose I am right that moral motivation sentence mitigation is an intuitively appealing practice, and that there is a lack of clear support for this practice from deterrence theory, moral education theory, and fair play retributivism. This would count as a point, but only one point, against these theories as accounts of sentencing; defenders of any of these theories might respond that all things considered, the virtues of their preferred theory outweigh the virtues of communicative retributivism or other theories.

3. Hybrid Theories

In the remainder of this essay, I want to consider what a hybrid theorist should say about moral motivation sentence reductions. Hybrid theories, which typically aim to incorporate consequentialist and retributivist concerns into their accounts of punishment's justification, became prevalent among philosophers of punishment in the early and middle twentieth century. The most influential hybrid account was offered by H.L.A. Hart (1960), although punishment theorists had for decades been working to develop accounts that cobbled consequentialist aims together with retributivist constraints (see, e.g., Ewing 1927; Ross 1930: 56–64; Quinton 1954). Although the popularity of hybrid philosophical accounts receded in the latter part of the twentieth century, as retributivist theories of one form or another predominated, recent years have seen something of a resurgence of the hybrid approach by philosophers and legal scholars.

The central challenge for theorists attracted to the hybrid strategy is how the consequentialist and retributivist elements should be incorporated into a coherent theory of punishment. The question of how to treat moral motivations at sentencing is just one illustrative example, I think, of the extent of the challenge of developing a principled hybrid theory. In the previous section, I contended that different prominent theories of punishment offer different guidance about sentence mitigation for moral motivations. Some theories may even have internal tensions on this issue. But hybrid views attempt to integrate considerations from multiple theories: most commonly, deterrence and retribution, but also often considerations of offender reform similar to those motivating moral education theory. How should a hybrid theorist deal with conflicting sentencing guidance offered by different theories (or even the tensions within certain theories)?

David Wood (2002) usefully distinguishes three types of hybrid view, which he terms 'split-level dualism', 'integrated dualism', and 'mere conjunction dualism'. Briefly, split-level dualism distinguishes the issue of punishment's justification into multiple levels, with distinct considerations relevant at each level. Hart (1960), for example, distinguished the question of punishment's general justifying aim from the question of its proper distribution. Ross (1930) distinguished the question for lawmakers of why certain types of conduct should be criminalized and warrant punishment from the question for judges of what sentences are appropriate in particular cases.[4] Integrated dualism,

[4] John Rawls (1955) employed a similar strategy to Ross's in his well-known discussion of punishment. Unlike Ross, however, Rawls is defending a rule utilitarian approach (the retributivist constraints

rather than distinguishing separate questions, attempts (as the name suggests) to integrate consequentialist and retributivist considerations: essentially, although neither crime reduction nor retributivism on its own is sufficient to justify punishment, the combination of these considerations provides sufficient justification (cf. Boonin 2008: 208, who terms this a 'conjunctive hybrid' approach). Mere conjunction dualism, by contrast, holds that 'penal measures and their use in individual sentences must be justified both of grounds of retribution and crime reduction', but that no clear structure or integration of these considerations can be provided (Wood 2002: 318).

Wood ultimately rejects split-level dualism and integrated dualism and thus accepts mere conjunction dualism, which he calls a 'pessimistic conclusion' (ibid.).[5] More recently, however, Douglas Husak has argued in favour of what I take to be the mere conjunction hybrid strategy (although he does not use Wood's term). Husak offers seven normative desiderata that he believes are relevant to justifying punishment:

> [T]he state should aspire to: (1) promote justice by treating offenders as they deserve; (2) enhance public safety; (3) use resources efficiently; (4) express and communicate the appropriate values to offenders and communities; (5) minimize opportunities for abuse by legal officials; (6) provide those accused with an opportunity to answer; and (7) gain the confidence and support of the citizens in the jurisdiction where the punishment takes place. (Husak 2025: 77)

Husak contends that 'the inability to merge these criteria into a uniquely coherent whole should not be taken as a refutation of pluralism, as some commentators have alleged' (ibid.: 78). In particular, he is critical of split-level accounts such as Hart's. He writes, 'more plausible versions, I submit, offer multiple answers to single questions about the justification of punishment' (ibid.: 80).[6]

on sentencing are only justified insofar as a system with such constraints will have better consequences overall than an alternative system). Thus I do not discuss Rawls's account here.

[5] Antony Duff seems to have something like mere conjunction dualism in mind when he asks whether we must 'recognise that we can never achieve more than an unstable compromise — that we will always face conflicts, which cannot be confidently or readily resolved, between the demands of justice and those of crime prevention'. (Duff 1996: 8).

[6] Husak cites me as a defender of 'the particular hybrid theory of Hart and Rawls' (2025: 80), which is odd given that, in the article he cites (Hoskins 2020), I discuss that Hart's and Rawls's theories are not the same and that Rawls's is in fact not best construed as a hybrid theory at all (but rather a rule utilitarian theory). Also, I do not endorse either Hart's or Rawls's theories in the article, although as I discuss below, I think Hart was in the right ballpark.

What would a mere conjunction hybrid account tell us about Kristen's and Mark's sentences? Louis is, in my view, the most difficult case, so I leave him out here to give the mere conjunction approach the best chance at providing some useful guidance. As I have discussed, the aim of enhancing public safety (Husak's desideratum 2) through deterrence would suggest that somewhat more severe sentences may be needed to deter morally motivated offenders, such as Kristen, than non-morally motivated offenders, such as Mark. But if we accept, as I have suggested we should, that Kristen's moral convictions make her somewhat less blameworthy than Mark, then considerations of treating offenders as they deserve (1) and also conveying the appropriate values (4) seem to suggest that Kristen's sentence should be somewhat less severe than Mark's. However, if we believe treating offenders as they deserve (1) is a matter of removing their unfair advantage, then this would indicate that Kristen's sentence should be somewhat more severe than Mark's. Alternatively, if efficient use of resources is our concern (3), then insofar as ascertaining defendants' genuine motivations may not be a straightforward matter, perhaps we should just give Kristen and Mark the same sentence as they committed the same crime. As far as I can tell, Husak's account offers no answer to how his various desiderata should be structured into a framework that would provide genuine guidance in cases such as Kristen's and Mark's.

The point generalizes: mere conjunction hybrid accounts do not provide sufficient clarity about how the various considerations should be structured or weighted relative to each other. One problem with the mere conjunction approach is that the lack of guidance risks reducing consistency across sentencing decisions, which would in turn risk undermining public confidence and support (thus violating Husak's desideratum 7).

Can a hybrid view do better? I think so. I conclude by sketching the sort of hybrid approach I favour, which I contend can provide comparatively clear, intuitively plausible guidance about moral motivation sentence mitigation. I begin with what I take to be the crucial insight from Hart's hybrid account of punishment, namely that 'in relation to any social institution, after stating what general aim or value its maintenance fosters we should enquire whether there are any and if so what principles limiting the unqualified pursuit of that aim or value' (Hart 1960: 9–10). This should, I think, be a fairly uncontroversial claim. Consider another social institution, taxation: we can ask what the compelling rationale is for maintaining a system of taxation, and presumably the answer will cite the roads, healthcare, or other public goods that taxes support. But we can also sensibly ask what considerations should govern how taxes are levied: whether we should rely on income tax or sales tax, whether we should tax in proportion to wealth or use a flat tax, and so on. And it should not be surprising if the considerations relevant to taxation's rationale are not the only considerations relevant to how taxes should be levied. This same goes for punishment: we can ask what compelling rationale there is to maintain an institution of punishment, but we should not be surprised if our answer to this question does not exhaust the considerations relevant to answering how the institution should be administered.

I agree with deterrence theorists and with Jean Hampton that the compelling rationale for the institution of punishment is its contribution to reducing crime. One of a state's central obligations to its citizens is to protect and promote their safety and security. If our best empirical evidence demonstrated that punishment had no effect on crime levels, then I do not believe the institution could be justified. Note that punishment is just one of the ways that a state can pursue the goal of reducing crime: It might invest more in early childhood education or poverty relief, as some empirical research indicates that doing so can help to lower crime levels. It might invest in so-called situational crime prevention tools: speed bumps to reduce speeding, employment restrictions to keep people believed to be dangerous away from vulnerable populations, or fences to reduce trespassing. Punishment is, in this respect, one of the tools in the state's crime reduction toolkit.

Punishment, though, is a distinctive crime reduction tool. It has an expressive function: part of punishment's social meaning is that it conveys the political community's condemnation of the offender for her offence (see Feinberg 1965).[7] So, if the state is going to choose this particular crime reductive tool from among those in its toolkit, it must be careful to use it in ways that convey the condemnatory message appropriately. This means that sentencing must be guided by considerations of desert. As von Hirsch and Ashworth explain:

> Once one has created an institution with the condemnatory implications that punishment has, then it is a requirement of justice, not merely of efficient crime prevention, to punish offenders according to the degree of reprehensibleness of their conduct. Disproportionate punishments are unjust not because they possibly may be ineffective or counterproductive, but because they purport to condemn the actor for his conduct and yet visit more or less censure on him than the degree of blameworthiness of that conduct would warrant. (von Hirsch and Ashworth 2005: 134)

[7] Philosophers have debated whether this expressive function is an essential feature of punishment or merely a conventional one. For my purposes, it is enough to acknowledge that punishment, in our society, does convey the condemnation of the offender for her crime.

Other considerations, such as crime reduction through deterrence or moral education, should not feature in sentencing. If the sentencing guidance they offer aligns with the guidance of desert, then they are redundant anyway. If, however, they offer sentencing guidance that conflicts with what desert requires, then desert should be the governing consideration.

How is this consistent with claiming that crime reduction is the compelling rationale of punishment? Shouldn't the aim of crime reduction indicate that considerations of crime reduction should factor into sentencing determinations? The aim of crime reduction does imply a type of constraint on punishment: namely, the state's use of punishment can only be justified if it serves the crime reductive rationale. If punishing offenders proportionately with the degree of censure their criminal conduct deserves does not adequately serve this rationale, then the state should look to its other tools for reducing crime. It should not adjust sentencing levels out of proportion with offenders' blameworthiness in order to serve crime reductive rationales. If, however, punishing offenders consistently with their level of desert does contribute to reducing crime, then there is a compelling rationale for the state to maintain such a system.

So, what should we say about Kristen's, Louis's, and Mark's sentencing? The communicative retributivist is right: the governing consideration in their sentencing should be their blameworthiness, the degree of censure that each deserves. Moral motivation should count as a mitigating factor, as an offender who acts from a moral motivation is in that regard less blameworthy than an offender who acts from a non-moral motivation. Kristen should thus receive a somewhat lower sentence than Mark. But if one's moral convictions are based on unreasonable, even repugnant, values or beliefs, then one may be blameworthy in this regard as well. Thus, even though Louis is somewhat less blameworthy in virtue of acting on moral convictions, in my view the unreasonable content of his convictions is sufficiently blameworthy that, all things considered, he not only deserves a more severe sentence than Kristen but also a somewhat more severe sentence than Mark.

4. Conclusion

I have contended that whether offenders who were motivated by their moral convictions should receive sentence mitigation depends on which theory of punishment we endorse. Of the theories I considered, communicative retributivism provides the clearest basis for the notion that moral motivation should count as a mitigating factor in sentencing. As I take this to be an intuitively plausible idea, I take this to count as a point in favour of communicative retributivism, or at least its sentencing guidance. I also examined what hybrid theories might say about moral motivation sentence mitigation. I contended that the issue illustrates serious challenges faced by mere conjunction hybrid theories, which seek to avoid offering an account of how the different considerations relevant to punishment should be structured or weighted relative to each other. I ended, however, by sketching a hybrid account that I take to be plausible in its own right and can offer relatively clear sentencing guidance, including support for moral motive sentence mitigation.

References

Bennett, Christopher. 'Punishment as an Apology Ritual'. In *The New Philosophy of Criminal Law*, edited by Chad Flanders and Zachary Hoskins, pp. 213–230. London: Rowman Littlefield, 2016.

Bentham, Jeremy. *An Introduction to the Principles of Morals and Legislation.* Reprinted in *The Collected Works of Jeremy Bentham: An Introduction to the Principles of Morals and Legislation*, edited by J.H. Burns and H.L.A. Hart. Oxford: Clarendon Press, [1789] 1996.

Boonin, David. *The Problem of Punishment.* New York: Cambridge University Press, 2008.

Dagger, Richard. 'Playing Fair with Punishment'. *Ethics* 103 (1993): 473–488.

Duff, R.A. 'Penal Communications: Recent Work in the Philosophy of Punishment'. *Crime and Justice* 20 (1996): 1–97.

Duff, R.A. *Punishment, Communication, and Community.* Oxford: Oxford University Press, 2001.

Ewing, A.C. 'Punishment as Moral Agency: An Attempt to Reconcile the Retributive and the Utilitarian View'. *Mind* 36, no. 143 (1927): 297–305.

Feinberg, Joel. 'The Expressive Function of Punishment'. *The Monist* 49, no. 3 (1965): 397–423.

Grierson, Jamie. 'Woman who killed her terminally ill father walks free from court'. *The Guardian* (11 April 2025). https://www.theguardian.com/uk-news/2025/apr/11/lisa-davenport-who-killed-terminally-ill-father-free-from-court.

Hampton, Jean. 'The Moral Education Theory of Punishment'. *Philosophy & Public Affairs* 13, no. 3 (1984): 208–238.

Hart, H.L.A. 'Prolegomenon to the Principles of Punishment'. *Proceedings of the Aristotelian Society* 60 (1960): 1–26.

Hoskins, Zachary. 'Hybrid Theories of Punishment'. In *The Routledge Handbook of the Philosophy and Science of Punishment*, edited by Bruce Waller, Elizabeth Shaw, and Farah Focquaert, 37–48. London: Routledge, 2020.

Husak, Douglas. 'Pluralistic Theory'. In *The Oxford Handbook of the Philosophy of Punishment*, edited by Jesper Ryberg, pp. 76–89. Oxford: Oxford University Press, 2025.

Johnson King, Zoë A. 'Praiseworthy Motivations'. *Nous* 54, no. 2 (2020): 408–430.

Kant, Immanuel. *Groundwork of the Metaphysics of Morals.* In *The Cambridge Edition of the Works of Immanuel Kant: Practical Philosophy*, translated and edited by Mary J. Gregor, pp. 37–108. Cambridge: Cambridge University Press, [1785] 1996.

Markovits, Julia. 'Acting for the Right Reasons'. *Philosophical Review* 119, no. 2 (2010): 201–242.
Morris, Herbert. 'Persons and Punishment'. *Monist* 52 (1968): 475–501.
Nagin, Daniel S. 'Deterrence in the Twenty-First Century'. *Crime and Justice* 42, no. 1 (2013): 199–263.
Quinton, A.M. 'On Punishment'. *Analysis* 14, no. 6 (1954): 133–142.
Rawls, John. 'Two Concepts of Rules'. *The Philosophical Review* 64, no. 1 (1955): 3–32.
Ross, W.D. *The Right and the Good*. Oxford: Oxford University Press, 1930.
Shafer-Landau, Russ. 'Can Punishment Morally Educate'. *Law and Philosophy* 10, no. 2 (1991): 189–219.
Skitka, Linda J. and Elizabeth Mullen. 'The Dark Side of Moral Conviction'. *Analyses of Social Issues and Public Policy* 2, no. 1 (2002): 35–41.
Skitka, Linda J. 'The Psychology of Moral Conviction'. *Social and Personality Psychology Compass* 4, no. 4 (2010): 267–281.
Sverdlik, Steven. *Motive and Rightness*. Oxford: Oxford University Press, 2011.
von Hirsch, Andrew and Andrew Ashworth. *Proportionate Sentencing: Exploring the Principles*. Oxford: Oxford University Press, 2005.
Wood, David. 'Retribution, Crime Reduction and the Justification of Punishment'. *Oxford Journal of Legal Studies* 22, no. 2 (2002): 301–321.
Wringe, Bill. *An Expressive Theory of Punishment*. London: Palgrave Macmillan, 2016.

7

Are Disadvantaged Offenders Ethically Motivated? A Critique of Christopher Lewis

*Benjamin Ewing**

1. Introduction

Robin Hood and the mercy killer embody one paradigm of the ethically motivated offender: a person who breaks the law to ameliorate the suffering of someone who is in urgent need but lacks good lawful means of helping herself. Typically, we assume that this suffering person is someone other than the offender. But if socially disadvantaged offenders' own unmet needs and unrealized capabilities are great, and their lawful opportunities are poor, might there be an ethical motivation behind even their seemingly self-interested crimes? In recent work supportive of such a thought, Christopher Lewis contends that because disadvantaged offenders generally will have had greater 'incentives' to offend, presumptively the state has weaker evidence of bad motivation and blameworthiness on their part and should mitigate their punishment. In this chapter, I show that Lewis's analysis is more transparent and plausible if reframed as an argument that disadvantaged offenders' crimes are presumptively less negative in their overall expected impact on society (and in that sense more 'ethical'), because meeting disadvantaged offenders' basic needs has a moral priority over satisfying non-disadvantaged offenders' less important interests. Even when reframed in that way, however, the argument is ultimately unconvincing. I doubt that the criminal law should presume disadvantaged offenders have stronger incentives to offend, or more ethical motivations for offending, than non-disadvantaged offenders.

* For helpful feedback on earlier drafts of this chapter, I thank the other contributors to this volume and all three editors of it, especially Leo Zaibert, who gave me detailed written comments.

Benjamin Ewing, *Are Disadvantaged Offenders Ethically Motivated? A Critique of Christopher Lewis* In: *Sentencing the Ethically-Motivated Offender*. Edited by: Julian V. Roberts, Leo Zaibert, and Jesper Ryberg, Oxford University Press.
 DOI: 10.1093/9780198993025.003.0008

2. Overview

In section 3 of the chapter, I reconstruct Lewis's argument that owing to stronger incentives to offend, disadvantaged offenders presumptively have better motivations for their crimes than non-disadvantaged perpetrators of them and merit mitigated criminal sentences on that account. In section 4, I consider how variance in the probability and magnitude of expected punishment can lead to differences in people's incentives to offend. I suggest that this poses a problem for Lewis's argument about the evidentiary significance of incentives to offend by complicating two key relationships: those between (a) social disadvantage and incentives to offend, and (b) incentives to offend and ethical motivations for offending. In section 5, I entertain a potentially principled reason for Lewis's apparent choice to abstract from expected punishment when assessing offenders' incentives to offend as evidence of the ethical character of their motivations for offending. But I contend that Lewis's decision to exclude expected costs of offending to offenders, when weighing their incentives as evidence of their motives, is inconsistent with his underlying theory of why we have weaker evidence of culpability when it comes to offenders who had stronger incentives to offend. Lewis's selective concern about certain incentives but not others shows that incentives to offend are not, as such, good evidence of the ethical quality of offenders' motives.

In section 6, I submit that the important difference between the disadvantaged and non-disadvantaged offenders in the hypothetical cases of interest to Lewis is not that the disadvantaged offenders expect to gain more from their crimes, per se. Rather, because their unmet basic needs have a moral priority over non-disadvantaged offenders' less important interests, disadvantaged offenders' crimes can arguably produce surplus gains for them (relative to non-disadvantaged perpetrators of the same crimes) that come at no one else's expense, thus making the aggregate impact of their crimes somewhat less negative when their own interests are taken into account. However, suppose that crime is generally bad, on net, for those who commit it, and that any given setback to a person's interests is morally worse when that person is disadvantaged. Then as I observe, even if disadvantaged offenders will tend to have had less to lose by their crimes, disadvantaged offenders' crimes should not necessarily be presumed less bad overall, precisely because it is more morally important to avoid any given setback to a person's interests if that person is disadvantaged. Moreover, in section 7, I offer reasons for thinking that even if a crime is *in some sense* less negative in its overall effects, that does not necessarily mean that it should be viewed as such from the standpoint of a criminal justice system and its distinctive values.

3. Lewis on Disadvantage, Incentives, and Culpability

Lewis (2016: 161–170), (2021: 1240–1259) contends that disadvantaged offenders presumptively merit lesser sentences than non-disadvantaged offenders for many crimes. He believes that the disadvantaged typically have greater incentives to offend, and that this diminishes the degree of ill will or disregard for other people's interests—and thus culpability—that we have the evidential warrant to infer from disadvantaged offenders' crimes. Lewis's argument, as best I can reconstruct it in premise–conclusion form, relies upon at least two novel, contestable assumptions about offenders' incentives:

(P1) Disadvantaged offenders should be presumed to have had objectively greater 'incentives' than non-disadvantaged offenders to commit various crimes, including economic offences and many violent crimes.

(P2) As between two perpetrators of the same crime, if one had an objectively greater 'incentive' to commit it, then his crime presumptively evinces less ill will or insufficient concern for others' interests than does the other offender's crime.

Lewis's argument also requires two additional premises that are comparatively familiar and relatively uncontroversial:

(P3) The perpetrator of a crime is less culpable or blameworthy for it if her commission of it shows less ill will or less insufficient concern for others' interests.

(P4) If members of a group of offenders are presumptively less culpable or blameworthy than non-members, members of that group presumptively have a *pro tanto* claim to mitigation at sentencing relative to non-members.

From those four premises Lewis draws the following conclusion:

(C) Disadvantaged offenders presumptively have a *pro tanto* claim to mitigated sentences (relative to those of non-disadvantaged offenders) for various crimes, including economic offences and many violent crimes.[1]

[1] Strictly speaking, Lewis (2016: 169–170) is 'agnostic' about whether 'disadvantage ought to be taken as a kind of mitigating factor with respect to civic blame or . . . advantage should be taken as a kind

Lewis (2016: 161) recognizes at the outset of his discussion that '[n]ot all incentives to break the law, or to do wrong, are relevant to the morality of blame.' Sensibly, Lewis makes clear, for instance, that he is concerned with *objective* incentives to offend, rather than with the *subjective* allure or appeal of a crime to an offender. To measure incentives to offend in an objective way without presupposing a thick, controversial conception of well-being and the good life, Lewis (2016: 162) proposes that we measure one's incentive to commit an offence by the degree to which doing so can be expected to contribute to one's Rawlsian 'primary goods' (i.e. goods such as fundamental rights and liberties, income, wealth, and the 'social bases of self-respect,' which are valuable on any reasonable conception of a good life) (see Rawls 2001: 58–61) or one's 'capabilities', in the sense of interest to Sen (1980) and Nussbaum (2000)—which Lewis glosses as '(roughly) one's opportunities to live a life that one has good reason to value'.

Though Lewis's reasons for endorsing P1 differ somewhat for economic and violent offences, the plausibility of P1 appears to depend on the idea that because the disadvantaged have fewer resources and poorer lawful opportunities, any given earnings or achievement through crime can bring about a greater marginal enhancement of primary goods or capabilities for disadvantaged offenders than for non-disadvantaged offenders (see Lewis 2016: 165–166, 2021: 1249–1252). And the basic idea behind P2 seems to be that, as Lewis (2021: 1252) puts it:

> If the offender has weaker incentives to commit the crime—measured in terms of primary goods or capabilities—they need to weigh their own interests more heavily relative to the interests of the victim in order to go through with the crime. Someone with strong incentives to commit the crime need not place as heavy a weight on their own interests relative to the interests of the victim, compared to an offender whose incentives are weaker.

For example, Lewis (2016: 165–166) compares hypothetical drug dealers 'Arthur and Brandon', the former of whom is disadvantaged and the latter of whom is comparatively advantaged, and notes that Arthur 'could certainly be motivated to sell drugs by a number of relatively basic wants', whereas Brandon presumably has less important motivations, such as funding 'expensive nights

of aggravating factor'. But there is no harm in framing his argument as a defence of sentence *mitigation* for disadvantaged offenders, provided we remember that it is a defence of mitigated sentences for disadvantaged offenders *relative* to non-disadvantaged offenders.

out and weekends away'. And Lewis (2021: 1249) asks us to imagine two different 'stickup artists': one an indigent 'day labourer' living out of his van and the other a 'mid-career law professor who makes a six-figure salary'. In Lewis's view, 'absent some special explanation, it seems [the law professor] must have weighted an extremely trivial interest of his own over the much more fundamental interests of his victims'. By contrast, we need not presume that the day labourer put so low a value on his victims' interests, given that the day labourer 'has no money and is afraid of being homeless' (Lewis 2021: 1250).[2]

4. Expected Costs of Offending and their Impact on Incentives to Offend

An initial worry about Lewis's argument is that he motivates P1—i.e. the premise that disadvantaged offenders will tend to have had greater incentives to commit their crimes—by emphasizing one reason, in particular, why it is likely to be true: any given payoff of crime is likely to bring about a greater marginal enhancement of primary goods or capabilities for disadvantaged offenders than for non-disadvantaged offenders because disadvantaged offenders have greater unmet basic needs and vulnerabilities that their crimes can help to address (e.g. financial or physical security, or Rawlsian 'social bases of self-respect'), and poorer lawful alternative means of addressing them (see e.g. Lewis 2016: 162–163, 165–167). Yet there are many other variables that affect people's incentives to commit, or refrain from committing, crimes. Most obviously, punishment is intended to disincentivize offending. Increases in the expected magnitude or probability of punishment reduce a person's incentive to offend. As Lewis himself recognizes, however, it seems difficult to tell a

[2] Lewis's way of analysing examples such as these implies that what ultimately matters in assessing offenders' culpability is the ulterior motives on which they act. It is questionable, however, whether the best version of Lewis's argument would treat incentives merely as a *predictor* of better ulterior aims that subjectively motivated an offender, as opposed to a *determinant* of objectively better immediate reasons an offender had for offending, whatever his actual motivations may have been. I do not believe that my critiques of Lewis's argument depend on which of these formulations we choose or emphasize. But suppose that, as seems to be the case, Lewis presumes that the disadvantaged have objectively greater incentives to offend than the advantaged largely for the following reason: any given payoff of crime will be objectively more significant for disadvantaged offenders, because they have greater unmet needs and poorer means of satisfying them. It seems to me that neither the truth nor the importance of that idea is hostage to the further (potentially naïve) assumption that disadvantaged offenders will tend to put the payoffs of their crimes to better uses than non-disadvantaged offenders. Formulating Lewis's argument in a way that stresses the moral priority of payoffs to the disadvantaged as opposed to the advantaged—irrespective of the purposes to which they might put their payoffs—would also enable us to avoid epistemic difficulties and moral controversies surrounding uncertain or mixed motives, or motivational overdetermination. For discussion of such issues, see Ryberg (this volume).

simple story about how the expected magnitude or probability of punishment may differ for disadvantaged offenders as compared with non-disadvantaged ones. On the one hand, criminal convictions and punishments may be objectively worse for the 'white-collar professional' with more to lose than for a member of 'the ghetto poor' (see Lewis 2016: 163–164), and it may be easier to commit violence with impunity in a ghetto than in a privileged neighbourhood. On the other hand, perhaps concentrated policing in ghettos and structural disadvantages that ghetto denizens face in the criminal process make the likelihood and magnitude of their punishment greater (see Lewis 2016: 164). It would be perilous to generalize without careful analysis of many different variables and the best available empirical evidence of their effects.

In his first article arguing that greater incentives to offend should presumptively be a mitigating factor for disadvantaged offenders, Lewis leaves the reader with the impression that although in principle differential deterrents can create differences in people's incentives to offend, he simply does not want for P1 (i.e. the premise that disadvantaged offenders will generally have had greater incentives to offend) to be thought dependent on the assumption that disadvantaged offenders are likely to have faced weaker deterrents to committing crimes. After all, the evidence for that hypothesis is mixed and debatable. As Lewis (2016: 163–164) puts it: 'We should be wary of the idea that the disadvantaged have stronger incentives to commit crime than the well-off because they face weaker deterrents. . . . it isn't obvious whether the disadvantaged face relatively stronger or weaker deterrents to crime, all things considered.' If costs of offending were irrelevant to incentives to offend or should be ignored or discounted as a matter of principle in assessing the strength of incentives to offend and their impact on offenders' presumptive culpability, we would expect Lewis to say so. Instead, he writes: 'The strength of a person's incentives to commit any given crime depends in part on the objective costs and benefits associated with both the crime in question and the available alternatives' (Lewis 2016: 161). And he sketches empirical evidence for and against 'the idea that the disadvantaged have stronger incentives to commit crime than the well-off because they face weaker deterrents' (Lewis 2016: 163).

Yet in a subsequent article arguing for the counter-intuitive idea that recidivists should receive a sentencing *discount* (rather than a premium)—on the grounds that the collateral consequences of prior convictions leave ex-offenders with poorer lawful opportunities and thus greater incentives to offend—Lewis (2021: 1213) suggests that his argument is limited to 'the strength of the offender's "incentives" to commit [his] crime, measured in terms of the extent to which *getting away with* that crime would foreseeably add to the offender's [primary goods or capabilities]' (emphasis in original). Here, it seems, Lewis does not merely want to be agnostic about whether differences in expected punishment may lead recidivists to have greater or weaker incentives to offend. Instead, he wants to claim that, as a matter of principle, greater incentives to offend are appropriately mitigating only when they arise from greater 'payoffs' from 'getting away with' crime. Lewis (2021: 1248–1249) contends that while in one sense an offender who reasonably perceived a lower likelihood of being punished had a greater incentive to offend, this 'does not excuse or justify the crime even partially. So, incentives related to the expected *costs* of committing a crime should not figure into how we calculate our moral response to crime either' (emphasis in original). By contrast, Lewis (2021: 1249) tells us: 'Incentives related to the objective *benefits* or payoffs of committing crime are a different story' (emphasis in original).

What Lewis perhaps senses at this point, but still does not make explicit, is that uncertainty about differences in policing and punishment for disadvantaged and non-disadvantaged offenders calls both P1 and P2 into serious question. Even if we grant Lewis that any given payoff of crime typically means objectively more to a disadvantaged person than to a non-disadvantaged one, we cannot endorse P1—i.e. Lewis's generalization that disadvantaged offenders will have had greater incentives to commit their crimes—merely on the grounds that there is *one respect* in which disadvantaged offenders can be expected to have had greater incentives to offend. If the disadvantaged face greater expected punishment for any given crime than the non-disadvantaged, then to that extent the disadvantaged have *weaker* incentives to offend, not stronger ones. Acknowledging that differences in expected punishment affect people's incentives to offend also calls into question P2—i.e. Lewis's supposition that when an offender had a greater incentive to offend, we presumptively have evidence only of lesser culpability on his part. For if an offender had a greater incentive to offend merely because he was more likely to 'get away with' his crime, that does not seem like a good reason for us to see in his crime weaker evidence of inadequate regard for other people. Given that the impact of people's differing prospects of punishment on their incentives to offend threatens both key premises of Lewis's argument, it is unsurprising that he wishes to exclude the incentive effects of punishment from that argument.

The problem, however, is that when Lewis (2021: 1249) justifies excluding 'incentives related to the expected *costs* of committing a crime' (emphasis in original) from his analysis merely on the ground that differences in offenders' expected punishment do not seem to mitigate their culpability for their crimes, he does not merely qualify, or limit the scope of, his original argument. Rather, he installs a brace on his edifice that mars its façade and suggests a problem with its foundation. To flesh out the metaphor, excluding costs of offending in measuring offenders' incentives to offend creates at least two problems. First, it makes misleading Lewis's frequent talk of the mitigating force of objectively greater 'incentives' to offend, because his argument is only that a very specific subset of objectively greater incentives to offend should be mitigating factors. And that casts doubt on the idea that objectively greater incentives, as such, are what matter. Second, excluding the expected costs of offending to offenders when measuring their incentives to offend appears inconsistent with—and thus casts doubt on—the normative core of Lewis's argument.

The core, distinctive normative premise of his argument is P2—i.e. that when an offender had a greater incentive to offend, to that extent we have less evidence of her ill will or inadequate regard for others. And what explains and justifies P2? As we have seen, it is precisely this thought: if an offender had a weaker incentive to offend, she was willing to disregard her victims' interests for less of a potential enhancement of her own; hence, she implicitly put a lower value on her victims' interests, demonstrating a greater deficiency of adequate regard for them (see Lewis 2021: 1252). Variance in people's expected punishment for a crime thus creates a dilemma for Lewis. Given the underlying premise that undergirds P2, he faces theoretical pressure to accept, as a counter-intuitive implication of his argument, that greater expected costs of offending (potentially including greater expected punishment) reduce people's incentives to offend and presumptively enhance their culpability for their crimes. Accepting that implication would be doubly difficult for Lewis because it would also threaten P1—i.e. Lewis's generalization that disadvantaged offenders will have had greater incentives to offend. But without a principled reason for refusing to bite these bullets, Lewis courts the charge that he has placed an ad hoc limitation on the scope of his argument to keep it from unravelling.

Let us illustrate this with a concrete example. Suppose, for instance, that one person kills for $250,000, knowing that he is likely to get away with it, whereas an otherwise equally situated person does the same deed for the same pay but knows that there is a high likelihood that he will be identified and incarcerated for the rest of his life. The normative core of Lewis's argument would seem to suggest that the killer who is more likely to get away with the crime is presumptively less culpable because he has not revealed as low an implicit valuation of his victim's life as the other killer, whose objective expected payoff was greatly diminished by being paired with a high likelihood of life imprisonment.

Though there is something superficially attractive about that line of reasoning, its conclusion is ultimately untenable, and Lewis (2021: 1248–1249) recognizes this. We should not presume an offender had better motives, or is less worthy of blame or punishment, merely because he was more likely to get away with his crime. However, to protect his argument from counter-intuitively imputing less culpability to those who were more likely to get away with their crimes, Lewis cannot simply ignore, or stipulate away, the following reality: expected costs of offending for offenders *are* relevant to offenders' incentives to offend and, more specifically, relevant to how offenders implicitly weigh their victims' interests against their own, in choosing to offend. Being more likely to get away with a crime *does* increase what one can reasonably expect to gain from the crime yet *does not* intuitively weaken other people's evidence of one's bad motivations or blameworthiness. And that undercuts the idea that the more an offender can reasonably expect to gain by committing a crime, the less ill will or disregard for other people his crime manifests, such that we have evidence only of lesser culpability on his part.

5. Incentives to Offend as Net Payoffs in Abstraction from Punishment?

We might try to improve Lewis's argument, however, by a friendly amendment. Lewis (2021: 1249–1250) tells us that 'incentives related to the expected *costs* of committing a crime should not figure into how we calculate our moral response to crime', and that the morally significant difference between two offenders' incentives to commit a crime 'does not stem from their respective personalities, values, or assessments of the risks or expected costs of committing that crime'. Yet Lewis makes these claims immediately after rejecting the idea that there is even partially exculpatory force to having reasonably expected lesser punishment or lower odds of punishment. What if, in assessing people's incentives to offend, we were simply to abstract from the expected costs of *punishment*, specifically, and not from other expected costs (such as expected expenditures or risks of injuries or other losses in carrying out a crime)?

One reason not to let *expected* punishment affect offenders' presumptive culpability and *appropriate* punishment is that this has the potential to create a self-perpetuating cycle. For instance, if acted upon by the state, Lewis's prescription of reduced punishment for disadvantaged offenders who had greater incentives to offend would exacerbate the very problem of disadvantaged individuals having greater incentives to offend. And that would appear to create a feedback loop wherein advanced notice of mitigation at sentencing for disadvantaged offenders would reduce their presumptive culpability, thereby justifying further planned mitigation at sentencing that would further reduce their presumptive culpability, and so on.[3]

Such a problem would not result, however, merely from recognizing how incentives to offend are impacted by expected costs (other than punishment) of crimes to their perpetrators—e.g. expenditures required for their preparation, planning, and execution, or injuries likely to occur during their commission. And it seems not merely unmotivated but incoherent to assess incentives to offend in abstraction from *all* costs of crime to its perpetrators. For instance, suppose a bank robbery promises to yield $500,000 in revenue, but the cost of necessary equipment is $200,000. Clearly in such a case we should say that the incentive to offend is $300,000, not $500,000. Likewise, surely the contribution to one's primary goods or capabilities that is promised by selling illegal drugs is not meaningfully measured by reference to one's expected gross revenue from dealing but only by reference to one's expected net profit from it. And the same point holds for non-economic benefits and costs. Suppose that a young man living in a dangerous neighbourhood has been spat on and shoved by a tough guy in front of many other people. To stem at the outset the potential for an escalating cycle of violence toward him that could arise were he to gain a reputation for weakness or cowardice, this young man is contemplating assaulting the other man who has just disrespected him. Should we say that his incentive to do so depends only on how much he stands to gain (in security and respect from his peers) if things go well, in abstraction from how much he stands to lose if things go wrong? Would it really make no difference to his incentive if he knew that fighting back would likely be counter-productive?

Charity would therefore seem to counsel us to revise what Lewis explicitly says and, instead, at most to exclude expected costs associated with

[3] Allowing *expected* punishment to affect offenders' presumptive culpability and *appropriate* punishment would also create a problem for Lewis's argument that recidivists ought presumptively to receive reduced sentences on account of their (supposedly) stronger incentives to commit their crimes. As Lewis (2021: 1240–1245) contends, collateral consequences of criminal conviction and incarceration can worsen ex-offenders' alternatives to crime and thereby increase their incentives to offend. This effect might be counterbalanced, however, if expected punishment were allowed to factor into our assessment of ex-offenders' incentives for the purposes of Lewis's argument. For it might turn out that people with prior convictions are (justifiably) subject to greater and more effective law enforcement, which increases the likelihood that they will be punished for future crimes they commit and to that extent reduces their incentives to offend. Interestingly, when critiquing the idea that a recidivist premium might be justified on grounds of deterrence, Lewis (2021: 1226) writes: 'Repeat offenders are more likely to get caught than first-time lawbreakers; and the probability of detection drives decisions about whether or not to commit crime much more than the anticipated severity of punishment conditional on being detected.'

punishment, but not other expected costs of offending, when assessing people's incentives to offend. This would not eliminate the tension, however, between the normative core of Lewis's argument and his insistence that we must ignore expected punishment in assessing the incentives to offend that offenders weigh against their victims' interests. Nor would it entirely rid Lewis's argument of counter-intuitive implications.

6. What Justifies Mitigation: How a Crime Impacts an Offender, or Everyone Affected?

Let us consider another such counter-intuitive implication of Lewis's argument, which remains even if, when assessing offenders' incentives to offend, we ignore expected punishment (or, for that matter, *all* expected costs of crimes to their perpetrators).

Imagine two different hitmen for whom all else is equal except that one hitman's client pays him \$100,000, whereas the other hitman's client pays him only \$1,000.[4] The bigger of the two paydays would do an awful lot more to bolster an offender's primary goods (which include, among other things, income, wealth, and the social bases of self-respect) or capabilities. Hence, by the logic of the core normative idea on which Lewis's argument rests, it would seem as though the hitman willing to kill for less money puts a lower value on his victim's life (and is therefore presumptively more culpable) because he implicitly values that life below \$1,000, whereas the higher-paid hitman implicitly values his own victim's life only below \$100,000 (and is therefore presumptively less culpable). But that strikes me as a misguided analysis of the cases.

From the standpoint of *everyone* in society affected by his crime—including the person who hires him as well as the victim he kills—the higher-paid hitman's greater payoff is merely the result of a greater voluntary transfer of primary goods (namely, wealth) from one person (the client) to another (the hitman). And if we allow a greater voluntary, zero-sum redistribution of resources from others to the offender to enhance the overall weight of what the offender implicitly took to be more important than his victim's rights and interests, then we perversely privilege a crime as less worthy of blame and

[4] If one offender expects to accrue greater benefits from his crime (than another perpetrator of an otherwise comparable offence) by inflicting greater wrongful losses on his victim, this ought to be *aggravating* rather than *mitigating*. But then we are not comparing two otherwise morally equal crimes that happen to be committed by offenders with differing incentives. The offender with a greater incentive to offend is also causing greater wrongful harm.

punishment merely because it is *better for the offender* to precisely the extent that it is *worse for third-parties*. Even if offenders tend, as a matter of fact, to ignore or discount the impacts of their crimes on third parties, we should sit in judgment of offenders from a standpoint of impartial concern for *everyone's* interests. And from that perspective, it makes no sense to view an offender as having any better a motive or reason to commit her crime merely because it will better promote *her* objective interests while setting back another person's interests to an equal corresponding extent.[5]

Lewis could argue that a higher-paid hit would be less culpable if all else were equal, but that all else is not equal, morally speaking: the higher-paid hitman's greater payoff comes at the equally greater corresponding expense of the client, who has to pay more for the killing, which counterbalances and thereby masks the intuition we would otherwise have—namely, that a greater payday from killing renders a hitman presumptively less culpable. For what it is worth, I think that is wrong. It seems to me that a higher-paid hit is neither presumptively worse because the client pays more money nor presumptively better because the hitman receives more money. The extent of the transfer of money simply does not seem relevant to the hitman's culpability one way or another. But in any case, even if a greater financial payoff for a contract crime were to be best understood as triggering aggravating and mitigating considerations that cancel each other out, that would not undercut the central point I have been bringing out here: we cannot necessarily presume that an offender's greater incentive to offend means we have evidence only of lesser culpability on his part. We can presume so, if at all, only in those special cases in which an offender's greater expected benefit from offending does not simply come at someone else's greater expected expense.

Hence, to make attractive Lewis's intuition that offenders with stronger incentives to offend presumptively show less disregard for their victims' rights and interests and therefore evince lesser culpability, I believe we must restrict our focus to offenders with a special set of stronger incentives to offend: ones that arise not merely from greater potential transfers of resources or value to them from other people but from aspects of their crimes that can be expected

[5] Shifting from the perspective of an offender and her incentives to that of society and its interests points to a promising explanation of why greater incentives to offend stemming from greater odds of 'getting away with' one's crime should not be mitigating. From the offender's standpoint, the expected payoff of a crime is greater if one expects to get away with it. But society usually has a strong interest in offenders being held accountable for their crimes. From the perspective of impartial concern for everyone affected by a crime—which is the standpoint we ought to adopt when standing in judgment of how much disregard for other people an offender manifested by his crime—an offender who is more likely to 'get away with it' is, if anything, doing something *worse*.

to make them more beneficial to the offenders without being correspondingly more detrimental to others. This makes such crimes less detrimental (than they otherwise would be) in their aggregate expected impact on the interests of everyone affected by them, when offenders' own interests are taken into account.

To see what I have in mind, we need only to consider Lewis's own hypothetical pairs of cases meant to illustrate the presumptively lesser culpability of disadvantaged offenders, who Lewis assumes have stronger incentives to offend. Contrasting hypotheticals can isolate our intuitions about the relevance of some difference between them only if the hypotheticals control for other potentially confounding variables. Yet Lewis repeatedly presents pairs of hypotheticals that ostensibly show the same crime committed in response to a greater or a weaker incentive, but which involve other morally significant differences between the perpetrators and between the crimes themselves. Lewis compares (a) individuals from relatively privileged backgrounds with lesser incentives to offend with (b) individuals from (potentially unfairly) disadvantaged backgrounds who have greater incentives to offend. And the disadvantaged individuals' greater incentives to offend do not reflect the possibility of greater zero-sum benefits to them at other people's expense but, rather, the possibility of value creation *ex nihilo*: a surplus that the disadvantaged can accrue by committing a crime (relative to non-disadvantaged perpetrators of it) that would not be merely counterbalanced by a greater loss for other people.

In Lewis's cases the disadvantaged economic offenders with greater incentives to commit their offences are not stipulated to be receiving more money from other people for their crimes. Instead, it is assumed that given disadvantaged offenders' greater unmet basic needs and poorer lawful opportunities, any given proceeds of crime can do more to enhance *their* primary goods or capabilities than such proceeds of crime would do to enhance the primary goods or capabilities of non-disadvantaged offenders (see Lewis 2016: 165–166, 2021: 1249–1252). Disadvantaged offenders have poorer lawful opportunities, including means of making money. Hence, any given criminal proceeds are likely to bring about more of an improvement upon lawful opportunities and income sources for disadvantaged offenders than for non-disadvantaged offenders. And disadvantaged offenders have greater unmet basic needs and unrealized capabilities. Thus, the same payoff in economic terms can contribute more to their primary goods or 'opportunities to live a life that one has good reason to value' (Lewis 2016: 162), thereby serving more morally important interests for disadvantaged offenders than for non-disadvantaged ones. As Lewis (2021: 1250) puts it: 'a few hundred extra dollars can make a huge difference in the life of someone who is destitute and without realistic hopes or plans to escape poverty'.

Lewis's disadvantaged violent offenders with greater incentives to commit their crimes have those incentives because their poverty confines them to dangerous neighbourhoods in which those who are disrespected must respond aggressively—perhaps even with violence—to avoid losing their street credibility and putting themselves at risk of future victimization (see Lewis 2016: 166–167, 2021: 1256–1257). Lewis's advantaged violent offenders with lesser incentives to commit their same acts of violence are people who have the privilege of living in comparatively safe neighbourhoods in which they need not worry about future reprisals for failing to protect their reputation in accordance with a 'code of the street'.[6] Again, the disadvantaged offenders and the non-disadvantaged offenders take equally from others (in this case, from the security and bodily integrity of those they assault), but the disadvantaged offenders can expect to get more in return—here, in terms of personal security and the social bases of self-respect.

We could attempt to shore up Lewis's argument about the presumptive partially exculpatory force of greater incentives to commit crimes by simply imposing yet a further stipulation on the meaning of incentives, or the type of incentives at play in Lewis's argument. We could shift our focus from 'incentives', as such, to potential improvements to an offender's primary goods or capabilities that would arise not from mere transfers of resources or value but from aspects of a crime that would make it less bad in its aggregate effects than it otherwise would be. But shifting our emphasis in that way would mean departing markedly from Lewis's argument as he has thus far framed it. Only a very small and unusual subset of enhanced incentives to offend would be mitigating, and it would not be offenders' greater incentives themselves but, rather, the overall expected impact of their crimes on everyone affected by them, that would be doing the important normative work.

Moreover, it is far from clear that any given crime is presumptively less negative in its aggregate effects when committed by a disadvantaged offender as opposed to a non-disadvantaged one. Suppose we make two very plausible assumptions: (1) the net expected gains from a crime to an offender are typically negative,[7] and (2) the interests of the disadvantaged have a moral priority over

[6] Lewis (2016: 166, 2021: 1257) cites Anderson (1999: 66–106) for the idea that acts of aggression by ghetto residents are often partly about protecting their status, to reduce their risk of future victimization.

[7] Lewis (2016: 164) seems to believe that this assumption is compatible with his argument, because as he stresses, his argument 'is comparative in nature'. He appears to think that what matters is that 'the

those of the non-disadvantaged, in the sense that any given setback to interest or well-being is worse when it occurs for a disadvantaged person.[8] It then follows that any given crime is typically in one respect *worse* when committed by a disadvantaged offender rather than a non-disadvantaged one: the setback to an offender's interest associated with any given crime is morally worse if the perpetrator is disadvantaged. Because a disadvantaged person's disadvantage makes setbacks to his interest or well-being morally worse, it is to that extent worse if he engages in self-sabotaging behaviour, which arguably includes most criminal offending. If that is correct, then even if Lewis is right that any given payoff of crime will do more to promote its perpetrator's primary goods or capabilities if that perpetrator is comparatively disadvantaged, the moral significance of that fact may be undercut or outweighed by the fact that a crime often sets back its perpetrator's interests on net, and any given setback to a disadvantaged person's interests is morally worse than an equivalent setback to a non-disadvantaged person's interests. Put differently, even if the disadvantaged have less to lose from offending than the advantaged (e.g. in primary goods or capabilities), it is quite plausible that any given losses suffered by the perpetrators of crime should be of greater concern to us when those perpetrators are disadvantaged.

disadvantaged still have much stronger incentives to break the law than the well-off' (Lewis 2016: 165), even if their 'incentives' to offend are negative such that what we really mean is that they have *weaker disincentives* to offend than the well-off. Lewis (2016: 164–165) gestures at the possibility that crimes may have negative expected value for offenders, whether because 'crime in general does not pay' or 'the moral wrongdoing that goes along with *malum in se* crime makes one intrinsically worse off.' I would stress a more obvious reason why the net expected gains from criminal offending are likely to be negative: a large amount of crime is committed under the influence of such forces as youth, stress, anger, temptation, and drugs or alcohol—any combination of which may strain a person's will-power and impair her cognitive functioning. For that reason and others, surely a great deal of crime reflects poor, impulsive judgment rather than instrumentally rational pursuit of self-interest.

[8] This assumption may be subtly but importantly different from the prioritization of disadvantaged offenders' interests that is implicit in Lewis's argument. The moral priority of satisfying disadvantaged offenders' unmet basic needs as compared with non-disadvantaged offenders' less important interests is at the heart of why Lewis believes that a theft of several hundred dollars by a disadvantaged offender could do more for her than such a theft by a non-disadvantaged offender would do for him. And that in turn explains why Lewis would presume that a disadvantaged offender's theft of several hundred dollars is less culpable than a non-disadvantaged offender's perpetration of the same crime (see Lewis 2021: 1249–1252). However, Lewis may be best interpreted as arguing merely that crimes can be expected to have a more positive impact on the primary goods or capabilities of disadvantaged offenders, and not that whatever positive impact crimes have on a person's primary goods or capabilities matters more for disadvantaged offenders because their interests have moral priority in principle. Nevertheless, there is considerable plausibility to the principle that the well-being of the disadvantaged has a moral priority over that of the non-disadvantaged. And that principle has an affinity with, and would offer further support for, Lewis's key idea that any given material payoff or achievement of crime is likely to translate into something objectively more important for disadvantaged offenders than for non-disadvantaged ones.

There may also be characteristic other-regarding reasons against socially disadvantaged offenders' crimes. Most saliently, offenders confined to worlds of social disadvantage might be more likely than non-disadvantaged offenders to take disadvantaged people as their victims—and, worse, more likely to get away with their crimes because legal actors implicitly devalue the interests of victims from disadvantaged backgrounds or because ghetto residents are less likely to cooperate with police investigations. Those are additional respects in which the crimes of the disadvantaged could turn out to be presumptively *worse*, and *more* culpable, than the crimes of non-disadvantaged offenders.

7. When is the Impact of a Crime Less Negative from the Criminal Law's Point of View?

Furthermore, my intuition is that even when a crime *is admittedly* less bad for society *in some sense*, sentence mitigation is most plausibly justified only when the crime is less bad by the lights of values comparable in kind and weight to the values that the crime is proscribed for undermining. If a crime is less costly than usual for society merely in terms of values much less morally significant than the values that the crime is wrong for setting back, then the way in which the crime is less bad might be irrelevant to how the criminal law should assess the offender's culpability and appropriate punishment.

It is one thing, for instance, to kill another person—even an innocent, unthreatening person—if this is necessary to save one's own life or limb. Even if we refuse to accept necessity or duress as a defence to murder, it does not seem unreasonable to say that intentionally killing another person shows less of a deficiency of adequate concern for other people when doing so is necessary to protect the killer's life or limb. In such a case, the killer has interests in protecting her bodily integrity that appropriately factor into her practical reasoning and make her crime somewhat less bad and unreasonable than it otherwise would be.

It is another thing, however, to kill a person to increase one's primary goods or capabilities—or even the overall primary goods and capabilities of members of society. It seems to be part of the very nature of the moral prohibition against murder that it calls upon us to exclude from our deliberations about whether to kill another person the degree to which doing so might increase people's resources or opportunities. And the same thing seems true of various other prohibitions, such as, for example, those against human trafficking, kidnapping, robbery, and other economically motivated acts of violence. To suppose that the reasonableness of committing such crimes depends on how they affect the 'primary goods' of their perpetrators may be to misunderstand, or to devalue inappropriately, the reasons not to commit such crimes. Even our reasons to avoid non-violent economic offences can have a moral significance qualitatively different from, and an order of magnitude greater than, the importance of enhancing people's resources or opportunities. It is therefore not obvious to me whether, from the criminal law's perspective, positive-sum improvements to an offender's primary goods should weigh in the balance against—and thereby make less unreasonable—even the mere violation of another person's legitimate, justly held property rights. Matters are different when an offender has committed a crime partly to avert a harm comparable in kind or magnitude to the harm that made his crime itself wrong and forbidden.

Lewis's use of effects on people's primary goods and capabilities to measure their incentives to offend may appear to mitigate the concern that not all senses in which a crime can be expected to be less bad for society are ones that the criminal law should recognize as grounds for mitigation at sentencing. Yet as we have seen, Rawlsian primary goods include income and wealth. Hence, measuring objectively greater incentives in terms of expected enhancements of primary goods does not protect Lewis's argument from, for example, the counter-intuitive implication that a crime that an offender reasonably expects to carry off more efficiently (and thus more cheaply) than another offender is on that account presumptively less culpable. To the extent that Lewis succeeds in protecting his argument from such a counter-intuitive implication, it is because he confines his argument (about the presumptively mitigating force of greater incentives to offend) to greater gross 'payoffs' of 'getting away with' crime, and he excludes greater incentives caused by lower expected costs of offending for the offender. Yet for reasons already discussed, that limitation on the scope of the argument is arguably incoherent. At best, it appears ad hoc and at odds with the central moral premise that underlies Lewis's argument.

Lewis (2016: 174) claims that his argument for mitigating the punishment of disadvantaged offenders has the virtue of not having 'relied on a background theory of social justice nor the assumption that socially stratified societies in the present-day developed world are unjust'. Yet his crucial premises P1 and P2—that disadvantaged offenders will tend to have had stronger incentives to offend, and that stronger incentives to offend reduce our evidence of an offender's ill will or insufficient concern for others—both seem dependent upon a single conceptually and morally contestable principle: the primacy of potential positive effects on offenders' primary goods or capabilities—if they 'get away with' their crimes—as a measure of the moral weight of offenders' incentives to offend. In Lewis's argument, that is central to explaining both why the disadvantaged are assumed to have greater incentives to offend and why greater incentives to offend are taken to constitute better reasons or motives for offending. Lewis also implicitly assumes that when a crime is committed by a disadvantaged offender, its negative expected overall impact is reduced in such a way that the offender should be presumed less blameworthy from the criminal law's point of view.

8. Conclusion

As the very existence of this book makes clear, even when an offender committed his crime in service of a putatively noble cause on behalf of other people (e.g. to show mercy to someone terminally ill and suffering, to advocate for morally important legal change through civil disobedience, or to redistribute wealth from the rich to the poor), whether this should be mitigating at sentencing may well be controversial. Yet Christopher Lewis has boldly contended that disadvantaged offenders presumptively merit reduced punishment merely on account of having objectively greater personal incentives to offend, which he believes make their crimes weaker evidence of bad motives or blameworthy attitudes on their part.

My effort to reconstruct and assess Lewis's argument has led me to conclude that it is misleading and ultimately unpersuasive. Stronger incentives, as such, do not diminish our evidence of bad motives or culpability on the part of an offender. As Lewis seems to recognize but not advertise, his claim about how disadvantaged offenders' incentives to offend affect our evidence of their culpability appears plausible only if restricted to a very specific subset of incentives: ones that are distinctive to disadvantaged offenders and depend for their existence as much on moral principle as on empirical generalization. Disadvantaged offenders' 'greater incentives' to offend are arguably mitigating insofar as they stem from the assumption that any given payoffs of crime can serve objectively more important interests when they accrue to disadvantaged offenders rather than non-disadvantaged ones. If that assumption is correct, then disadvantaged offenders' crimes may appear to be more 'ethical' in the following sense: at no one else's expense, they provide surplus expected benefits to their perpetrators relative to non-disadvantaged perpetrators of the same crimes, which makes disadvantaged offenders' crimes less negative in their aggregate expected effects on society, when offenders' own interests are considered.

I believe Lewis's argument is thus best reframed as a defence of the idea that disadvantaged offenders are presumptively more ethically motivated than non-disadvantaged perpetrators of their same crimes. Yet if understanding his analysis in that way renders it more transparent and plausible, it also shows it to be more dependent on undefended empirical assumptions and contestable normative judgments than Lewis acknowledges. Even when the aggregate expected impact of a crime on everyone affected by it is admittedly less negative *in some sense*, it remains a difficult further question whether it is less negative in the *right sense* to justify partially withholding legal blame or punishment. And in any case, it seems unwarranted to presume that any given crime will be less negative in its overall expected effects if perpetrated by someone who is disadvantaged as opposed to someone who is not. If the net expected benefits of crimes to their perpetrators are generally negative, and the interests of disadvantaged offenders have a moral priority over those of non-disadvantaged offenders, then there is at least one respect in which any given crime is presumptively *worse* for society overall when perpetrated by a disadvantaged person. Any given crime might also tend to be worse when perpetrated by a disadvantaged person if, owing to the local and interpersonal nature of much crime, the disadvantaged are more likely than the non-disadvantaged to take other disadvantaged people as their victims.

I have great sympathy for the idea that disadvantaged offenders have distinctive claims to reduced punishment for their crimes (see Ewing 2018, 2023, 2025; Ewing and Kerr 2024). But the question of this chapter has been whether Lewis has offered a clear, coherent, and compelling explanation of why that is so. And on that score, I am sceptical. I am not convinced that disadvantaged offenders presumptively merit mitigation on account of stronger incentives to offend or more ethical motivations for offending.

References

Anderson, Elijah. *Code of the Street: Decency, Violence, and the Moral Life of the Inner City*. New York: W.W. Norton & Co., 1999.

Ewing, Benjamin. 'Recent Work on Punishment and Criminogenic Disadvantage'. *Law and Philosophy* 37, no. 1 (2018): 29–68.

Ewing, Benjamin. 'Criminal Responsibility and Fair Moral Opportunity'. *Criminal Law and Philosophy* 17, no. 2 (2023): 291–316.

Ewing, Benjamin. 'Affirmative Action in Criminal Justice'. *Oxford Journal of Legal Studies* 45, no. 3 (2025): 702–726.

Ewing, Benjamin and Lisa Kerr. 'Reconstructing *Gladue*'. *University of Toronto Law Journal* 74, no. 2 (2024): 156–197.

Lewis, Christopher. 'Inequality, Incentives, Criminality, and Blame'. *Legal Theory* 22, no. 2 (2016): 153–180.

Lewis, Christopher. 'The Paradox of Recidivism'. *Emory Law Journal* 70, no. 6 (2021): 1209–1271.

Nussbaum, Martha C. *Women and Human Development: The Capabilities Approach.* Cambridge: Cambridge University Press, 2000.

Rawls, John. *Justice as Fairness: A Restatement*, edited by Erin Kelly. Cambridge MA: Harvard University Press, 2001.

Sen, Amartya. 'Equality of What?' In *The Tanner Lectures on Human Values*, vol. 1, edited by Sterling M. McMurrin, pp. 195–220. Salt Lake City UT: University of Utah Press, 1980.

8

Denunciatory Punishment of Criminal Protest

Bill Wringe

1. Introduction

Offenders can have many different motives for their crimes. States of all kinds have good reasons for paying attention to these motives (Husak 1989; Hessick 2006). Sometimes, as with hate crimes, a reference to motivation is written into the definition of a crime. And sometimes, motivation may be regarded as a mitigating or aggravating factor (as in the case of racially motivated crimes). It is less clear whether it is appropriate for states of any sort to choose a particular kind of rationale for determining a sentence on the basis of the motivation for the crime. In this chapter I shall argue that in at least one case it is: in particular, I shall argue that democratic republics should adopt a denunciatory rationale for punishing criminal protest. As I shall argue at the end of this chapter, the existence of this rationale has implications for the sentencing of those involved in criminal protest, though these implications may not be as easy to tease out.

Elsewhere I have argued in favour of a denunciatory account of all kinds of criminal punishment (Wringe 2016, 2017). Here, however, I am interested in the idea that a denunciatory rationale might be especially appropriate for cases of criminal protest. My argument is addressed particularly to those who are attracted to some form of expressivism, and so I shall start by saying something about why I take that to be an appropriate starting point.

2. Motivating an Expressive Conception of Punishment

I start from a point that is agreed in almost all discussions of (legal) punishment: in order for something to constitute punishment it should involve

Bill Wringe, *Denunciatory Punishment of Criminal Protest* In: *Sentencing the Ethically-Motivated Offender*.
Edited by: Julian V. Roberts, Leo Zaibert, and Jesper Ryberg, Oxford University Press.
DOI: 10.1093/9780198993025.003.0009

hard or burdensome treatment, imposed by an appropriate authority on an offender as a response to wrongdoing (Flew 1954; Benn 1958; Hart 1960).[1] However, it is widely agreed that there are kinds of treatment by the state which fall under this description but which are not forms of punishment. These include pre-trial detention, confinement of dangerous potential offenders on mental health grounds, and various kinds of collateral consequence of legal punishments (such as the obligation to disclose one's status as an ex-offender to a potential employer.) In order to distinguish between punishment properly so-called and other kinds of non-punitive burdens, some further condition needs to be identified (Boonin 2008; Hanna 2008, 2017, 2022; Wringe 2013, 2019, 2025).

One candidate for this further condition is that punishment involves an intention to inflict harm at least in part because it is harmful (Hanna 2022). A second is that the harm should have an expressive dimension (Feinberg 1965; Hampton 1991; Wringe 2013, 2016, 2019). One reason for preferring an expressive condition is that it can explain the kinds of proportionality constraint that apply to punishment, whereas the 'harm because harmful' approach cannot. Indeed, if we think there is something especially bad about intentions of this sort (as Hanna 2021 suggests), then we might think that the fact that punishment involves an intention to inflict harm because it is harmful gives rise to considerations that count against proportionality: for example, a reason to punish less rather than more whenever this is possible, whether or not this runs counter to proportionality considerations.[2]

It is important to distinguish here between proportionality constraints which apply to punishment in particular and constraints that apply to other forms of harm caused by the state which might also be called constraints of proportionality. Consider for example a state which imposes strict restrictions on the behaviour of young people during an outbreak of a serious disease. Someone might argue against such restrictions on the grounds that the benefit derived from them is too small to justify the restrictions involved. They might even use the language of proportionality in this context. But the kinds of constraint that are appealed to here differ from what we call proportionality constraints in the imposition of punishment in two ways. They involve a

[1] For a dissenting view see Zaibert (2006).

[2] One might think that proportionality constraints only ever establish upper bounds for permissible punishment, and that as a result they are compatible with a principle of minimizing punitiveness. However, I am not convinced that proportionality considerations only ever establish upper bounds. This is certainly not true where ordinal proportionality is concerned. Such considerations might demand that—relevant facts about the offenders being the same—murder committed by one offender should be punished at least as severely as wounding or attempted murder by another.

comparison of the costs of a measure with its supposed benefits. By contrast, constraints of proportionality in punishment involve either comparisons between measures inflicted on different individuals (in the case of ordinal proportionality) or (in the case of cardinal proportionality) between the level of harm inflicted and the previous behaviour of the individual on whom the harm is inflicted.[3]

The exact form that an explanation of proportionality principles will take will depend on the details of the expressive theory in question.[4] An audience-independent expressivist like Thad Metz holds that certain kinds of expressive response to wrongdoing are fitting (Metz 2007). If we find that plausible, we might also find it plausible that proportionality is a constraint on fittingness of emotional response not only in the case of punishment but more generally. A sigh or a momentary frown might be an appropriate response to a minor setback; something more might be called for in response to the destruction of one's life's work. On a view like Anthony Duff's, on which punishment is a way of communicating blame in such a way as to invite regret and remorse on the part of an offender, one might appeal to the principle that the severity of blame directed at an individual should be proportionate to their degree of wrongdoing (and might also appeal to the idea that proportionality in sentencing might play a role in enabling an offender to form a correct judgment of the degree to which they should feel remorse and regret) (Duff 2002).

Finally on a denunciatory view, on which punishment is intended to express condemnation to a wider political community, proportionality in punishment might play one of two roles. First, punishments which are disproportionate to the severity of offences may convey misleading denunciatory messages either about the comparative badness of different offences or the comparative badness of particular kinds of offence. Secondly, and perhaps more importantly, manifestly disproportionate punishments may undermine a state's capacity to convey condemnatory messages via the penal system at all: they may undermine a society's willingness to understand the imposition of punishments as a serious attempt to condemn crime.

Furthermore, a denunciatory account can explain why judgments of proportionality can only provide rough constraints on punishment, and why these

[3] Cf. Yaffe (2021).

[4] Although I have argued in Wringe (2016) and Wringe (2017) that denunciatory expressivism is superior to other expressivist views, I do not here attempt to defend the view that denunciatory expressivism provides a better explanation of proportionality constraints than other expressivist views. Elsewhere (Wringe forthcoming a) I have argued that the denunciatory view can explain better than its rivals how proportionality constraints apply in different ways to punishment and its collateral consequences.

constraints can easily be over-ridden (Von Hirsch 1992, 1996, 2014, 2017). If the level of hard treatment imposed on an offender is supposed to communicate a message to a political community about the seriousness of an offender's offence, there is little to be gained by making distinctions that are more fine-grained than the audience to whom this message is addressed is likely to appreciate.

3. Communicative Protest

In what follows I shall be arguing that a denunciatory rationale for the punishment of criminal protest is particularly appropriate, at least in certain kinds of states: namely those in which the laws can be seen as the laws of the citizens, not merely in the sense that they are the laws to which citizens are subject, but in the broader sense that the citizenry can be seen as the source or author of the laws.

As a first step, we need to disambiguate the term 'criminal protest'. We can distinguish at least three different kinds of offender. First, there are those who commit crimes in the course of protesting, as they might do in the course of any other kind of activity. (So, for example, someone might drive dangerously on their way to a protest, or shoplift spray cans and markers that are intended to be used for writing slogans.) Secondly, there are those who pursue means of protest which the state has chosen to make illegal: for example, by contravening regulations on where demonstration may take place; or defying the terms of a police order. A third kind of case, which is more useful for my purposes, involves the deliberate choice of illegal means, with the goal of exploiting the state's public response to the illegality of the means one has chosen as a way of communicating with and inviting a response from the public.

This third category includes many instances of civil disobedience, understood in the somewhat limited way that Anglo-American philosophers since Rawls have understood this term, but goes beyond it: it may include cases where there is no commitment to the use of peaceful means (including some cases of rioting); or where there is no commitment to accepting legally determined punishment; or where there is no appeal to a shared sense of justice. (Rawls 1977) In short, it includes cases of what Candice Delmas has memorably called 'uncivil disobedience' (Delmas 2018). One thing that unites them is their communicative aim: with that in mind I shall describe them as cases of communicative disobedience. (Some of the cases that I want to include here may fall under a broader and to that extent more satisfactory understanding of the term 'civil disobedience'. Nevertheless I choose to avoid the term here in order to avoid importing assumptions from a tradition of theorizing in which the Rawlsian conception has played a central role.) There are cases of disobedience which have a communicative aim which do not attempt to achieve that aim by exploiting the state's response to the illegality of the action. Some cases of whistleblowing fall into this category, although there may also be cases of whistle-blowing which do, at least in part, exploit the publicity of the judicial process as a way of making the information to which they seek to draw attention more widely known.

I use the term 'communicative disobedience' to pick out cases where the offenders' communication is aimed at the public. Why focus on such cases? Many kinds of protest, including disobedient protest, aim at changing the actions, laws or policies of the state. So we might wonder whether we should instead take our target to be cases where the offenders' communication is aimed at the state. There are three reasons why we should not.

First, many kinds of protest, including environmental protests, aim at changing the behaviour of agents other than the state. These may include collective agents, such as extractive corporations, and individual members of the public. Of course, it may be that one means by which the behaviour of these agents can be changed is by affecting the behaviour of states: certain kinds of actions might be made illegal, or encouraged or discouraged. Nevertheless, in many cases of this sort, state action may be only one of a variety of acceptable means by which the desired changes could in principle be brought about. Secondly, even in cases where what is aimed at is a change in state policy, the kind of cases I am interested in are ones where the point of the protest is not simply for the state's behaviour to change, but for it to change as a result of public pressure.

Still, one might wonder why one should be particularly interested in changes in state action brought about by one particular means—public pressure—rather than thinking that where the protest aims at changing the behaviour of agents other than the state, the means is irrelevant. There are three points to make in response. The first is that as a matter of fact, many kinds of protest involving criminal acts do aim at precisely this kind of change. Secondly, there is good reason for them to do so: it is reasonable to think that changes brought about in this way will be more securely grounded, harder to overturn and more difficult to evade than changes brought about in other kinds of way. And thirdly, as I shall be arguing in what follows, there is an interesting theoretical unity to these kind of cases: they are cases which ground a particular kind of rationale for punishment in an especially secure way.

4. Communicative Protest and Denunciatory Punishment

The kinds of case I am interested in should not be characterized as ones where protest is directed at the public *rather than* the state. In certain kinds of states—the ones in which we should hope to live—addressing the state will be one way in which one can address the public. This will be true in particular of states which fit a characterization of democratic republics offered by Antony Duff and Sandra Marshall (Duff and Marshall 2016): namely that they are states in which the laws are 'our laws', not simply in the sense that they are the laws which govern us but also that we are in some sense the source or co-author of the laws, and more generally the institutions of the state, including its judicial and punitive institutions, are our institutions. In a state of this sort, addressing the state is one way in which one might address the public.

There are at least two reasons independent of general considerations which may speak in favour of a denunciatory rationale when dealing with offenders engaged in communicative protest. We might think that for the citizens to be co-authors of the laws, it is sufficient that they have some input into the legislative process. But there are at least two kinds of reasons for thinking that in practice, in many actual states this will not be enough. One is theoretical, the other practical.

Part of the appeal of the idea of seeing the laws as the product of citizens' co-authorship is that when so seen they can be understood as in part the expression of the collective will of the citizenry. But for something to be properly seen as the expression of one's will, it is not enough that one have some kind of causal input into it. One has causal input into many slips, mistakes and misfires, none of which are properly so seen. The expression of one's will must allow for the possibility of revision and reconsideration.

We might suppose that this is ensured by periodical elections. But in practice this will not be the case. Elections provide opportunities for citizens to endorse or refrain from endorsing legislative programs, but once a decision to legislate is made there is little scope for reconsideration. For there to be the possibility of reconsideration, a state must allow for the possibility of contestation. Public protest is one form of contestation, though it need not be the only one. However, the possibility of contestation can only turn protest into something more than another way of exerting causal influence on the actions of legislators if it is seen as a forum in which reasons are presented to the state for consideration or rejection. In adopting a denunciatory rationale for punishing offenders the state does exactly that. It does so precisely by rejecting the reasons that protesters have and present for their actions and presenting those reasons to the public.

It is precisely because on the denunciatory rationale for punishment, this rejection is presented to the public, that it can be seen in this way. For even if in punishing the state rejects the protester's reasons, the public to whom they are presented need not. By contrast, if on a Duff-style communicative account the state provides the offender with the opportunity to express regret and remorse, it treats those reasons only as something to be repudiated, not as something whose rejection allows the possibility of future engagement.

These considerations provide reasons for thinking that many democratic states should allow for denunciatory punishment of communicative protest. As Avia Pasternak has recently argued, many states contain significant alienated minorities (Pasternak 2025). For such minorities, the idea that the electoral system puts them in a position where they can see themselves as co-authors of the laws under which they live seems implausible. In a world in which they could be seen as voting either for or against certain proposals which impact them, the notion of co-authorship via the ballot box might have some application. But as Pasternak notes, the problem that alienated citizens face is often not that when matters that affect them come up for public consideration, proposals that would benefit them or respond to their demands are outvoted. Such is the fate of anyone who lives in a democracy. The concern is rather that in many cases, the kinds of issues that might make significant differences to their lives simply do not find their way on to the political agenda in the first place.

Pasternak argues, in effect, that protest, including violent protest, may be one of the only means of political participation left open to alienated individuals, and that such protest can be defended morally on the basis of theories of defensive harm (Pasternak 2018, 2025). She also goes on to argue, on the basis of considerations which have something in common with those discussed in section 3 that because the state lacks standing to blame alienated protesters who commit crimes in the course of their violent protests, the state's response to such crimes should invoke processes of restorative justice (Pasternak 2025; Howard and Pasternak 2021).

Unsurprisingly, I reject Pasternak's arguments for restorative responses on two grounds. On the denunciatory account I favour, punishment involves censure rather than blame, and it is unclear that loss of standing to blame should entail loss of standing to censure. (One reason why one might think this, particularly in the context of Duff-style communicative theories of punishment, is that the importance of standing for the appropriateness of blame has something to do with the second-personal nature of blame—that is to say that blame is directed at the person blamed in particular, in a way that is not the case for denunciation.)[5]

However, there is room to go further than this, and argue that Pasternak's reasons for thinking of violent protest as a way of exercising a right to political participation also provide a positive rationale for denunciatory punishment. For one might think that in order for protest to secure the kinds of good that Pasternak takes it to secure—namely the good of democratic participation—it will not be enough that protest provides an avenue through which the views of alienated citizens can be expressed. Democratic participation requires not only avenues for the expression of views, but the possibility of uptake, where uptake is understood not necessarily as the accepting of views expressed, but their being considered as and responded to as the expression of political views. For the reasons that I have already suggested, denunciatory punishment can secure this in a way that restorative practices cannot. In restorative practices—at least as conceived of by Pasternak—the state endeavours to remove itself from the communication that the protesters initiate; whereas by engaging in denunciatory punishment it makes itself into a participant in the conversation.

Considerations about uptake also give rise to a third reason why states should adopt a denunciatory approach to punishing communicative criminal protest. Elsewhere I have argued that in a democratic state, the laws should be the laws 'of' citizens, but also of a significant class of non-citizens: resident non-nationals who lack the vote but who contribute significantly to the reproduction of social life (Wringe forthcoming b). The law cannot be the law 'of' such citizens in the same way that it is the law 'of' citizens. But I have argued that insofar as the state grants rights of address—including rights of protest—to non-citizens as well as citizens, there is a significant way in which the law can be their law as well. However, a right of address of this sort requires the possibility of uptake. Practices of denunciatory punishment can institutionalize the possibility of uptake for non-citizens in ways that are similar to the ways it can do so for alienated citizens.

[5] A further reason for rejecting Pasternak's view is that it is unclear to me that restorative processes are non-punitive. For arguments to suggest that they are see Brown Coverdale and Bill (2022).

5. Does Denunciatory Punishment of Criminal Protest Treat Protesters as a Mere Means?

Denunciatory accounts of punishment are sometimes attacked for instrumentalizing offenders. If the point of imposing punishments is to communicate with society at large, rather than with the offender in particular, it is natural to think that when punitive hardship is imposed on an offender they are treated as a means to an end. One might worry, not merely that they are treated as a means; but that they are treated merely as a means.[6]

However, as I shall now try to show, the arguments of the preceding section provide us with reasons for thinking that this will not apply to those who are engaged in communicative protest. Those who engage in communicative protest should be willing to accept a denunciatory rationale for the punishment of the offences that they commit as part of their protest. In particular they cannot fittingly complain that in so doing, the state treats them as a mere means, fails to respect their autonomy, or treats them as mere threats rather than as fellow citizens, or as those who are appropriately considered as mere subjects of the law rather than its joint authors.

It need not follow that such offenders should necessarily be willing—as some writers on civil disobedience have suggested—to accept punishment for their actions. My view is compatible with the idea that such protesters may be both zealous in their legal defence and take such actions as are necessary to avoid detection arrest trial and conviction, provided these actions are in other respects morally acceptable (though there may also be good strategic reasons for refusing to do these things.) The point is rather that if, as a result of legally appropriate arrest, trial and conviction, the state inflicts on them punishments which have a denunciatory rationale, that rationale does not provide the basis for a complaint that they are being treated as a means.

Some might find this counter-intuitive: they might think that whether or not someone is being treated as a mere means cannot depend on what kind of crime they have committed. But on many accounts of what is involved in being treated as a mere means, the question as to whether someone is being so treated will depend on whether it is possible for them to share the maxims of the individual treating them in that way.[7] The intentions of the

[6] For thoughtful discussion of what might be involved in avoiding treating an offender as a means, see Tadros (2011).

[7] I have in mind in particular influential accounts of Kant's 'Mere Means' principle advanced by O'Neill (1989) and Korsgaard (1996). For more detailed discussion of the 'Mere Means Principle', see Wringe (2014).

offender can clearly be relevant to that question: they may be such as to make it clear that they cannot reject the basis on which hard treatment is inflicted on them.

In saying that the protesters cannot fittingly complain that they are being treated as a mere means, I am not saying that they are indeed being treated as a mere means but that they have no right to complain about it, but that they are not being treated as a mere means and that for that reason whatever it is they have to complain about it cannot be treatment as a mere means. Those who engage in communicative protest aim to communicate dissent and disapproval and to provoke public reflection on actions policies and practices of which they disapprove. They do so with a view to helping the public to recognize the reasons against these policies, practices, and actions, and to act on those reasons.

While many protesters might think that it is in principle possible for private reflection on the part of individual citizens to lead them to a recognition of these reasons, in practice the existence or threatened imposition of these practices will be evidence that private reflection is insufficient to enable a shared appreciation of these reasons or the formulation and implementation of effective means of acting on these reasons. This will typically be because these effective means require co-ordinated collective action. All of which is to say that in addressing the public, those who engage in communicative protest aim to provoke public debate.

Insofar as the punishment of those who engage in communicative protest has a denunciatory role, it is one kind of contribution to that debate. It makes the position of the state—and thus, in a democratic republic, the position of the public—clear and unambiguous. The position thus made clear is a collective commitment. It is compatible with its being a collective commitment that individual members of the public should need it drawn to their attention: we don't always realize what we are publicly committed to. Furthermore, the actual imposition of penalties makes it clear that this is a genuine commitment on the part of the state in a way that a mere communication of what an appropriate sentence would be might not.[8]

On a denunciatory view, this communication is directed in precisely the direction that the individual engaged in communicative protest should want: that

[8] Expressivists are often challenged to explain why, on their view, the communication that the state needs to engage in response to criminal offences needs to involve hard treatment inflicted on offenders. In Wringe (2016) I argue that it is a contingent fact about societies like our own that this is needed for the state's communication to be understood as sincere. I take this explanation to apply both here and more generally.

is to say, it is aimed at the public, rather than at the protesting offender (except insofar as they are also a member of the public). It follows from this that the state's aim in punishing them—namely to engage in a denunciatory act—is far from being one that they cannot share. Indeed, in some forms of communicative protest, such as civil disobedience as conceived of by Rawls and others this is something that they must necessarily want.[9] (By contrast, it may well be that if the state has other rationales for punishment, this would indeed involve treating those whom they punish as a means.)

None of this entails that an individual who engages in communicative protest should want to be punished, or that they are obliged to accept the punishment. Nor does it entail that there are no constraints on the way in which states may treat protesting offenders (we shall consider this issue later). The point is rather that in imposing hard treatment with a view to expressing disapproval of the protesting offender, the state does not treat the offender in a way to which they cannot possibly consent. Rather it treats them in a way that they have good—though not necessarily conclusive—right to assent to. It does so by putting forward a counter-claim to the claim that the protesters are making in protesting. In doing so it does not treat them as mere threats: it engages, whether it wants to or not, and in ways that may be at odds with the wishes and intentions of the public officials involved in imposing the hard treatment in question.

6. May the State Adopt a Distinctive Rationale For Punishing Criminal Protest?

There are at least two potential objections to the idea of the state adopting a distinctive rationale for punishing crimes of a particular kind, especially when these crimes are distinguished from others on the basis of considerations about the motivations of the criminals. First, one might think that the adoption of such a policy conflicts with the requirement that citizens should be equal before the law. Second, one might worry that it is inappropriate for a liberal state to attempt to determine—and implicitly, to engage in moral judgment of the motivations of offenders. Even though neither objection seems particularly compelling, it may be worth articulating each of them.

[9] I take it that a necessary condition of a complaint's being fitting is that what is complained of is the case, and I thank Leo Zaibert for drawing my attention to the fact that in at least one sense of 'can' one can complain about both what is the case and what is not the case.

The ideal of equality before the law requires that those who have offended in appropriately similar ways should be treated by the law in similar ways. It certainly does not require that in considering how the law should treat protesters, no notice should be taken of factors that might mitigate or aggravate the seriousness of an offence. Instead, it requires that those reasons be taken to be applicable to all citizens rather than just to a favoured class. While there is room for discussion of what this ideal might require of our judicial and penal institutions in practice, it does not seem to rule out the possibility that reasons for the state to punish might be affected in various ways by the motivations of those involved in communicative protest. Consequently, it is hard to see in principle why the fact that an individual is involved in communicative protest could not, in principle, generate new kinds of reason to punish them, or render inoperative those that would otherwise apply.

Nor does there seem to be any reason to think that the state should not enquire into whether those who engage in what appears to be communicative protest have a genuinely communicative rationale for their offences. In most cases, those who are engaged in such protest will have reasons for wanting it to be known that their acts were engaged in with communicative intent. That being so, it is hard to see how taking this into account could constitute an unwarranted intrusion into the communicative protester's privacy. Or so one might initially think.

There are however, two considerations which might be urged against this. One is that some protesters may have reasons—or take themselves to have reasons—to deny having a communicative rationale for their offences. We might think that in requiring those who have a communicative rationale to make this rationale public, we are unduly constraining, in advance, the kinds of tactic that protesters might legitimately use.[10] This worry might be mitigated by requiring that communicative motivations should only be taken into account when these are explicitly avowed by protesters in the course of a trial, or where they are already part of the public record. (There will be reasons for disavowal if denunciatory rationales for punishment become reasons for exacerbating or enhancing the punitive hard treatment to which an offender

[10] One's actions might have a communicative rationale without one being willing to make the existence of that rationale public. One may for example, hope that one's actions of protest will be understood in a particular way while leaving it ambiguous as to whether one intends them to be understood in that way, or indeed any way at all. Consider for example the recent case of an individual arrested for bearing a T-shirt with the slogan 'I support Plasticine Action'. The individual in question denied wishing to support the proscribed group 'Palestine Action'. It may well be, however that his wearing of the T-shirt had a communicative rationale.

is subjected: we will consider how the extent to which this might be the case in due course.)

A further worry is that if questions of motivation are genuinely to be taken into account when determining whether and how an individual is punished, it will be difficult to avoid making the existence of such motivations a matter to be enquired into in a criminal trial. If so, the state will inevitably be involved in making judgments about the moral qualities manifested in individuals acts of protest. To this it is reasonable to respond that it is one thing to make the existence and genuineness of a communicative rationale into a matter for state enquiry, and another to require the state to pronounce on the validity of the communication involved. The idea that the state might have different kinds of reasons for punishing those involved in communicative protest from those which are applicable elsewhere only entails the first of these.

7. Sentencing

So far I have argued that a denunciatory approach to punishment is appropriate for crimes arising from communicative protest. What implications, if any, does this have for sentencing practices? I have already provided a partial answer to this question: if I am right, denunciatory rationales for punishment undermine arguments advanced by those attracted to expressive accounts of punishment for thinking that those engaged in communicative protest should either escape punishment altogether or be punished by restorative justice practices (Lefkowitz 2007, 2018; Brownlee 2012). Nevertheless, there may be more to be said.

One possibility to consider is that the existence of a denunciatory rationale for punishment provides us with a reason for sentencing offenders involved in communicative protest more severely than they would otherwise be punished. The rationale for this approach would be along the following lines. Suppose that there is some non-denunciatory rationale for punishing the communicatively protesting offender. We might think that this rationale provides a reason for a sentence of some particular level of severity. We might then think of the denunciatory rationale for punishment as providing reasons to add something to the punishment rationalized by the other operative rationales. We might, in other words, think of the denunciatory rationale as acting 'additively', as it were.

One natural drawback of this line of thinking is that it provides a reason for those engaged in communicative protest to attempt to conceal this fact at trial. For in avowing it, they would be making themselves liable to a more severe sentence than they would otherwise receive. It is true, of course, that defendants in criminal trials will often have reasons for not avowing facts about their motivation; and it is also true that some criminal protesters might take a strategic decision in the light of the goals of their communicative protest to avow a communicative motive in any case. Nevertheless, there seem to be two problems here. First, there seems to be something inappropriately manipulative about the state's providing offenders with an incentive to present themselves in a worse light than is warranted by the facts surrounding their offence. Secondly, by providing communicative protesters with an incentive to obscure the communicative nature of their offence, it undermines the rationale for denunciatory protest set out in the previous section.

Fortunately there is no reason for thinking that this additive conception of the denunciatory rationale for punishment is compulsory. One thing to note is that the same action may have two different rationales. I might make myself a coffee in the morning both to wake myself up and to provide myself with the opportunity of savouring its pleasant aroma. There is no need for me to make two cups of coffee. Similarly a single sentence might have two separate rationales. There would be no need to add something to the sentence that would otherwise be appropriate in order to make sure that the denunciatory rationale is satisfied.

One might then worry that this line of thought risks making the denunciatory rationale for punishment superfluous. But this need not be the case either. There are at least two other roles that a denunciatory rationale might play. First, it might undermine reasons against punishment or in favour of mitigating a sentence. Consider a case where a first time offence by an offender of otherwise good character might, in the absence of a communicative rationale for punishment attract a suspended sentence; or where a demonstration of remorse undermines a Duff-style communicative rationale for punishment. In such cases a denunciatory rationale might function, not as a reason for imposing additional punishment, but as undermining otherwise existing reasons in favour of mitigation.

Secondly, a denunciatory rationale for punishment might make a difference to the kind of punishment thought appropriate in cases of communicative protest. A denunciatory rationale for punishment appeals to the idea that punishment expresses a message to the political community. The appropriateness of a particular form of punishment will then depend on the extent to which it satisfies this rationale (Primoratz 1989; Dan-Cohen 1996). Suppose that community-based punishments are generally seen as being less arduous than sentences involving imprisonment; or suppose that sentences involving imprisonment generate different kinds of news coverage to community-based sentences (even when the available repertoire of community-based sentences includes measures are as severe or more severe than relatively short terms of imprisonment). To the extent that such sentences are less widely understood as being condemnatory, the existence of a denunciatory rationale for punishment provides a reason for avoiding them.

8. Conclusion

I have argued that democratic states have good reasons for adopting a denunciatory rationale for dealing with communicative criminal protest, and that those who engage in such protest can have no complaint if it does so (though they may, of course have complaints about the justice of the laws under which they are punished, the strategies the state employs in pursuing them and the sentences to which they are condemned). It is important that these conclusions apply only to the case of democratic states: those in which citizens are appropriately seen as co-authors of the laws which criminal protesters break.[11]

States in which citizens cannot appropriately be so seen cannot appeal to the role which an appropriate response to criminal protest might play in making protest into a scene of democratic contestation. But it is worth observing that even in states which are formally democratic, it may be inappropriate to see citizens as co-authors of the laws. This will be true if, for example, certain groups are so situated that in practice their electoral choices have no practical influence over the content of legislation. It may also be true in cases where the control of the legislature swings wildly from one party to another. In such cases, the appeal to the role that protests play in providing a forum for contesting the laws will be a mere sham. In such cases, it may be appropriate for states to mark their aspirations to be states in which citizens are co-authors by imposing denunciatory sentences, but marking their recognition of the ways in which this fails to be the case for groups engaged in communicative protest by engaging in a range of forms of sentence mitigation (up to and including the use of suspended sentences). Whether any actual states are capable of adopting such a policy is of course another matter.

[11] I discuss the relationship between non-citizens and the laws of a democratic state in Wringe (2020) and Wringe (forthcoming b). In the latter piece I argue in particular that non-citizens can be seen as co-authors of the laws under which they live provided they have rights of address to the state. These may include—but need necessarily not be limited to—rights to engage in political protest.

References

Benn, Stanley I. 'An Approach to the Problems of Punishment'. *Philosophy* 33 (1958): 325–341.

Boonin, David. *The Problem of Punishment.* Cambridge: Cambridge University Press, 2008.

Brown Coverdale, Helen and Wringe, Bill. 'Non-paradigmatic punishments'. *Philosophy Compass* 17, no. 5 (2022): e12824.

Brownlee, Kimberley. *Conscience and Conviction: The Case for Civil Disobedience* New York: Oxford University Press, 2012.

Delmas, Candice. *A Duty to Resist: When Disobedience Should Be Uncivil.* New York: Oxford University Press, 2018.

Duff, R. Anthony. *Punishment Communication and Community.* Cambridge: Cambridge University Press, 2002.

Duff R. Anthony and Sandra E. Marshall. 'Civic Wrongs'. In *Democratic Theory and Mass Incarceration*, edited by Albert Dzur, Ian Loader, and Richard Sparks, pp. 33–59. Oxford: Oxford University Press, 2016.

Feinberg, Joel. 'The Expressive Function of Punishment'. *The Monist* 49, no. 3 (1965): 397–423.

Flew, Antony. 'The Justification of Punishment'. *Philosophy* 29 (1954): 291–307.

Hampton, Jean. (1991) 'Correcting Harms Versus Righting Wrongs: The Goal of Retribution'. *UCLA Law Review* 39 (1991):1659–1685.

Hanna, Nathan. 'Say what? A Critique of Expressive Retributivism'. *Law and Philosophy* 27, no. 2 (2008): 123–150.

Hanna, Nathan. 'The Nature of Punishment: Reply to Wringe'. *Ethical Theory and Moral Practice* 20, no. 5 (2017): 969–976.

Hanna, Nathan 'Why Punitive Intent Matters'. *Analysis* 81, no 3 (2021): 426–435.

Hanna, Nathan. 'Punitive Intent'. *Philosophical Studies* 179, no. 2 (2022): 655–669.

Hart, Herbert L.A. 'Prolegomenon to the Principles of Punishment'. *Proceedings of the Aristotelian Society* 60, no 1 (1960): 1–26.

Hessick, Barbara. 'Motive's Role in Criminal Punishment'. *Southern California Law Review* 80 (2006): 89–151.

Howard, Jeff and Avia Pasternak. 'Criminal Wrongdoing, Restorative Justice, and the Moral Standing of Unjust States'. *Journal of Political Philosophy* 31, no. 1 (2021): 42–59.

Husak, Douglas N. 'Motive and Criminal Liability'. *Criminal Justice Ethics* 8, no. 1(1989): 3–14.

Kahan, Dan M. 'What Do Alternative Sanctions Mean?' *University of Chicago Law Review* 63 (1996): 591–653.

Korsgaard, Christine. *Creating the Kingdom of Ends.* Cambridge: Cambridge University Press, 1996.

Lefkowitz, David. 'On A Moral Right to Civil Disobedience'. *Ethics* 117, no. 2 (2007): 202–233.

Lefkowitz, David. 'In Defense of Penalizing (but not Punishing) Civil Disobedience'. *Res Publica* 24, no. 3 (2018): 273–289.

Metz, Thaddeus. 'How To Reconcile Liberal Politics with Retributive Punishment'. *Oxford Journal of Legal Studies* 27, no. 4 (2007): 683–705.

O'Neill, Onora. *Constructions of Reason.* Cambridge: Cambridge University Press, 1989.

Pasternak, Avia. 'Political Rioting: A Moral Assessment'. *Philosophy and Public Affairs* 46, no. 4 (2018): 384–418.

Pasternak, Avia. *No Justice, No Peace.* Oxford: Oxford University Press, 2025.

Primoratz, Igor. 'Punishment as Language'. *Philosophy* 64, no. 248 (1989): 187–205.
Rawls, John (1977). 'A Theory of Civil Disobedience'. In *The Philosophy of Law,* edited by Ronald Dworkin, pp. 89–11. New York: Oxford University Press, 1977.
Tadros, Victor. *The Ends of Harm: The Moral Foundations of Criminal Law.* New York: Oxford University Press, 2011.
Von Hirsch, Andreas/Andrew. 'Proportionality in the Philosophy of Punishment' *Crime and Justice* 16 (1992): 55–98.
Von Hirsch, Andrew. *Censure and Sanctions,* Oxford: Oxford University Press, 1996.
Von Hirsch, Andrew. 'Harm and Wrongdoing in Criminalisation Theory'. *Criminal Law and Philosophy* 8, no. 1 (2014): 245–256.
Von Hirsch, Andrew. *Deserved Criminal Sentences: An Overview.* Portland OR: Hart Publishing, 2017.
Wringe Bill. 'Must Punishment Be Intended to Cause Suffering?' *Ethical Theory and Moral Practice* 16, no. 4 (2013): 863–877.
Wringe, Bill. 'May I Treat A Collective As A Mere Means'. *American Philosophical Quarterly* 51, no. 3 (2014): 273–284.
Wringe, Bill. *An Expressive Theory of Punishment.* London: Palgrave, 2016.
Wringe, Bill. 'Rethinking Expressive Theories of Punishment: Why Denunciation is a Better Bet Than Communication or Pure Expression'. *Philosophical Studies* 174, no. 3 (2017): 681–708.
Wringe, Bill. 'Punishment, Jesters and Judges: a Response to Nathan Hanna'. *Ethical Theory and Moral Practice* 22, no. 1 (2019): 3–12.
Wringe, Bill. 'Punishing Noncitizens'. *Journal of Applied Philosophy* 38, no. 3 (2020): 384–400.
Wringe, Bill. 'Punishment: Who Says What To Whom?' in *Collective Action, Philosophy and Law,* edited by Teresa Marques and Chiara Valentini, pp. 228–246. London: Routledge, 2021.
Wringe, Bill. 'Expressive Theories of Punishment'. In *The Palgrave Handbook on the Philosophy of Punishment,* edited by Matthew C. Altman, pp. 245–265. London: Palgrave-Macmillan, 2022.
Wringe, Bill. 'Abolitionism'. In *The Oxford Handbook on Punishment Theory and Philosophy,* edited by Jesper Ryberg, pp. 173–188. Oxford: Oxford University Press, 2025.
Wringe, Bill. (forthcoming a) 'Deportation As Punishment', presentation at the Joint Session of the Aristotelian Society and Mind Association, Glasgow, July 2025.
Wringe, Bill (forthcoming b) 'Wer hat hier eigentlich Recht? (Wie) kann ein republikanisches Strafrecht Nichtbürger ansprechen bzw. vertreten?' In: *Bürgerstrafrecht in fragmentierten Gesellschaften*, edited by Valerij Zisman and Ivó Coca-Vila, Ivó, chapter 2. Tübingen: Mohr Siebeck.
Yaffe, Gideon. 'The Norm Shift Theory of Punishment'. *Ethics* 132, no. 2 (2021): 478–507.
Zaibert, Leo. *Punishment and Retribution.* London: Routledge, 2006.

9

Should Moral Motives Mitigate, and If So, When?

Jonathan A Jacobs

1. Introduction

The present discussion addresses some of the issues involved in the question of whether an ethical motivation can be a proper basis for mitigating sentence in modern constitutional democracies. I will argue that while sentencing should not be shaped by assessment of an offender's moral character there can be a place in sentencing for acknowledging moral features of motivation that are integral to the act that the offender performed. There is a place for motive-based mitigation, and it is clearest when the situation involves the direct involvement of the agent and there are no other ways of achieving the individual's objective. In such cases, disregarding the moral quality of motivation could result in misjudging blameworthiness. While the law is not a general guide for the enforcement of morality it can be responsive to the moral dimension of motives underlying actions. At the same time, we need to acknowledge respects in which such mitigation can be problematic, and perhaps even more problematic than grounds for aggravation of sentence for especially vicious motivation. The overall thrust of the discussion is to make a case for there being a role for justly mitigated sentence on grounds of moral motivation, but the kinds of cases appropriate for mitigation are fairly narrowly limited. Referring to the moral qualities of motivation might seem a way of introducing a troubling kind of subjectivity and undisciplined discretion. How that can be avoided is one of the concerns shaping the limitations of appropriate mitigation.

Jonathan A Jacobs, *Should Moral Motives Mitigate, and If So, When?* In: *Sentencing the Ethically-Motivated Offender*. Edited by: Julian V. Roberts, Leo Zaibert, and Jesper Ryberg, Oxford University Press.
DOI: 10.1093/9780198993025.003.0010

2. Basic Elements of the Issue

There is a vast literature on motives, intentions, and reasons for action; different philosophers and other theorists use the terms in a diversity of ways. The apparent fluency with which we use those concepts in the ordinary course of conversation and description does not reflect their considerable complexity and the ways in which they are disputed. Part of the difficulty is that neither a motive nor an intention has some distinguishing mark reliably picking it out as a particular mental state or episode. It is not as though careful introspection will disclose them accurately.

Motives and intentions are closely related to reasons for actions. To say that a person acted for a reason is to say that the act can be put under a specific type of description, one that shows that the actor regards some consideration as a basis for acting a specific way or was aiming at realizing some state of affairs. Sometimes the focus falls on a motive, as in: 'She was very grateful; that's why she organized the occasion to thank them.' Sometimes an intention is the focus, as in: 'He decided to take the train rather than driving himself so that he could work en route.' An action can be described in a number of ways, and the reason for it is not generally limited to just one description. Much can depend on what we want to know about the action or the agent, and that will influence whether we specify a motive or an intention. One's reason for acting is often the conclusion of deliberation and practical reasoning, and motives and intentions can be elements in such reasoning. There isn't a fixed codification about how motives and intentions are understood in the context of acting for reasons. Was her reason for taking an umbrella that (i) she thought it would rain, or that (ii) she wanted to stay dry if it rained, or that (iii) she intended to stay dry. Was wanting to stay dry her motive? Was believing that the umbrella would enable her to stay dry also part of her motive? My point is not that this is a hopelessly confusing matter. Rather, the concepts *motive*, *intention*, and *reason for an action* are all parts of a complex fabric of explicating rational activity and they figure in the answers to the numerous questions we can ask about an action. Clarity about how we are using them can be more important than trying to settle on a fixed doctrine about how to use them.

In the present discussion I will use motive primarily in the following way: motive has to do with *what impels one to act*. For example, jealousy is a motive, as are compassion, revenge, envy, and gratitude. My suggestion might seem stipulative, but it is meant to capture an especially important role for the concept of *motive*.[1] Motive can make an important difference to what one's act

[1] The complexity, and the multiple avenues of approach associated to this issue by numerous thinkers, are discussed in Leo Zaibert's contribution to this volume. He mentions some of the main views of this issue and suggests some of its persistent complexity.

is and what it counts for. If we do not know how you were motivated we do not know whether you participated in the conspiracy out of greed, ideological fervour, personal animosity toward the person conspired against, or because your brother was imprisoned by the regime. Motive can be partially constitutive of the act; it can help indicate what kind of act it is, what the behaviour *counts for*, so to speak. It tells us something about the character of the act if not the enduring character of the agent.

In contrast, one's intention generally concerns what one aims or means to do, where 'to do' is what one aims to bring about, accomplish, or realize. One intends (by participating in the conspiracy) to weaken the regime and perhaps to acquire a position in which to negotiate your brother's release from prison. If we say that one intends to avenge the horrible treatment your brother received at the hands of the regime that sounds like a *reason* for action that involves motive *and* intention. There is no bright line distinguishing them. However, motivation and intention here will be understood along the lines suggested.

With regard to the question of ethical motivation as a possible mitigating factor, consider the following cases, assuming them to be crimes (and in many jurisdictions they are crimes). We can suppose that the actor in each case regards him or herself as acting on an ethically sound motive.

a. In accord with a patient's wishes, a family member takes (active) steps to end suffering and life humanely, given that it is suffering that otherwise has no realistic prospect of being relieved, and active euthanasia is illegal in the jurisdiction.
b. To protest against hitherto unacknowledged military involvement that is costing lives and which has not been satisfactorily explained by the administration. We can imagine people blocking an important railway line that leads to a port where military equipment is loaded onto ships to be sent to the theatre of combat operations, or trying to get through an air base perimeter and sitting down on an active runway for military aircraft.
c. To intervene and use potentially lethal force in protecting persons from violent crime in a context in which it is evident that residents are underprotected by the police—either because of corruption, lack of manpower and resources, being intimidated by ruthless gangs, or for some other reason.
d. To publicly criticize and illegally obstruct access to an adoption agency that is suspected of offering for adoption at least some children who have been trafficked.

e. To protest against environmental degradation or against policies that endanger some already very vulnerable animal populations in the wild. Suppose protesters damage logging equipment and construction supplies at a construction site in an area impacted in the ways protesters oppose.

The criminal violation consists in the act, and it is not difficult to imagine different possible motives in each case. Also, in some cases it is evident that specific persons' welfare is at issue while in other cases there is not a clear, direct, or immediate connection with human welfare or with particular persons. There can be sharp disagreements over the *urgency* of an issue regarding its significance and its timeliness. The issue might be one that could be addressed in a patient, considered manner, though the protester is motivated by a sense of urgency about highlighting the issue and bringing it to the public's attention. I will suggest that subjective urgency, without a clear connection to the actual circumstances, is not a basis for mitigation. The protester might be prescient in the respect that the issue really will become pressing and important—later on—and drawing attention to that now will make a great difference. But it is doubtful that there are grounds for mitigation given the lack of urgency and because there is no special reason that this particular individual has for engaging in the offending act.

In case c. above it could be argued that the person who intervened actually had no business doing so, and is at fault for injuring the attacker. Some might praise or admire the intervener's motives and courage, but there is still the issue of whether the offender is taking the law into his own hands. Suppose police stood by, doing nothing to help; or if the persons most directly victimized really were quite helpless, that might make a difference to the evaluation of the action of the person who intervened. He might have been the only person in the immediate vicinity capable of effective defence of others. Granted, unclarity about the threat *to him* might complicate judgment about whether his action was justified. But there are scenarios in which only the helpful intervention keeps numerous people from being harmed, perhaps seriously. If those responsible for protecting persons are not there or fail to do their jobs then even someone otherwise not at risk in the situation might be justified in intervening to provide protection, especially if the person is motivated by concerns for persons being victimized and unable to protect themselves. In a case such as this, the urgency is manifest and that strengthens grounds for mitigating sentence. If after seeing off the attacker our hero then says, 'OK, time to pay up', meaning that he thinks each person owes him money for having helped them, that would be enough to disclose the motivation as having involved greed and thereby being undermined ethically.

In many cases there are alternative approaches available to the agent for pursuing their end or purpose and for realizing the value in question. One can participate in public hearings instead of damaging costly equipment and materials. One can write opinion pieces and letters to editors instead of actually interfering with the livelihood of others or doing damage to physical structures. Whatever one's sentiment toward the issue or the cause in question, when there is only subjective urgency on the part of the offender the case for mitigation is weakened considerably. If there are plausible non-criminal courses of action available, this weakens the case for mitigation on the basis of ethical motive. Granted, the non-criminal courses of action might work very slowly and uncertainly and might have dubious prospects for genuinely effective success. Still, mitigation of sentence should not become a way of showing endorsement of causes or offenders who are no more urgently situated in the circumstances than anyone else.

It is not possible to codify exhaustively what kinds of cases are suitable for considering mitigation of sentence, but there are some general considerations concerning urgency and the relation of the offender to the issue motivating their conduct that figure in whether there is a case for mitigation. Also, there is a difference between conduct that is meant to *make* a moral point and conduct that can be understood as *having* a moral point, though the agent in question was not acting primarily to make such a point. In case c. the person who intervened was not primarily making a moral point; the primary concern was to protect helpless people from assault. The act was not done to communicate a valuative stance (even if it had that as an effect). Part of what motivated the person to intervene is the nonfeasance of law enforcement or their absence and how that influenced the offender's decision to try to protect others. It would almost surely be a distortion to insist that such intervention is always *nothing but* self-important moral theatre. (Of course, someone *might* intervene in that way.)

The fact that conduct makes a moral point—whether or not that was the act's primary purpose—can cut both ways, we might say. On the one hand, it can be a basis for supporting a mitigated sentence for the offender. On the other hand, it can lead to a judgment that the offender was engaging in moral theatrics, especially if little or no risk is involved. Perhaps many people join protests for the excitement of engaging in political action, even if they are uninformed regarding the issues. In many contexts it is not very difficult to feign ethical motivation or to persuade oneself that just by virtue of being on a particular side in a dispute one is thereby motivated in an ethically admirable way. Mitigation of sentence is appropriate when there are good reasons to believe that the agent undertook the action as the most plausible (or in some case, only plausible) way to realize a defensible value that could not be effectively realized in some other way. Thus, mitigation needs to be recognizable as a just sentence even if—or because—the law does not provide for a just sentence given the agent's act.

3. Potentially Problematic Aspects of Mitigation

I will suggest some respects in which grounds for mitigation can be especially challenging and how it might be more uncertain than grounds for aggravation. That is not meant to undermine the case for mitigation, but certain types of care in judgment are required to support a case for mitigation. There is a long history of sentences being aggravated on the basis of numerous factors. That is not to say that of course such aggravation is justified. However, in numerous cases that does seem plausible and in any event, it will be helpful to consider whether mitigation is symmetrical with aggravation, and if not, why it is not.

In general, in a liberal political order maintaining a distinction between moral evaluation of agents and legal judgment of behaviour helps preserve liberal values. Nevertheless, as Jeffrie Murphy has noted, we (in liberal states) regard 'an abandoned and wicked heart', 'a depraved heart', 'a depraved mind', 'wickedness of disposition', and 'extreme indifference to the value of human life' as appropriate aggravating conditions to consider in sentencing (Murphy 1995: 79). 'The criminal may be punished primarily for breaking the rules, but we often feel free to give him some additional punishment if we think he broke the rules because of traits of character we find loathsome' (Murphy 1995: 80). Murphy notes that 'In many American states, for example, capital murder's *mens rea* requirement of "malice aforethought" may be implied from recklessness if a killer is said to have the mental state or character defect variously described in the terms above; ("an abandoned and wicked heart," "a depraved heart," "a depraved mind," "wickedness of disposition . . . ")' (Murphy 1995: 79). Many such expressions refer to how a person is motivated, with motivation as an aggravating factor beyond the harm caused by the behaviour in question. Granted, this may seem a holdover from earlier times during which moral considerations had a more direct and explicit role in criminal justice. But what is being retained is not simply arbitrary; it has continuing resonance for legal judgment, making it possible for sentencing to be an occasion for calibrating sentence on the basis of how the offender imparted features to the offence that are relevant to blameworthiness. This might be problematic to some extent for a liberal political order but it is in fact an enduring aspect of criminal justice.

It might seem that in the contexts of aggravation and mitigation reference to offenders' 'insides' shifts the focus of sentencing from what the person *did* and the harm caused to what is the offender *like*, and that (it can be argued) is not the law's business. I have suggested that motive can be significant to specifying what the conduct *counts for*, what kind of act it is. Motive informs and orients what the agent does and is integral to the reasons for that action for that person in those circumstances on that occasion. One potential difficulty is that *what one did* often depends on how things *turned out* (see Nagel 1979: 24–38). The relation between acts and their outcomes is clearly of considerable significance for the law. However, if motives are to be mitigating that should not be based on a consequentialist judgment. For example, the role of compassion or of malicious jealousy in one's conduct does not depend on outcome, though outcome might be evidence of motive, but even that can be ambiguous.[2] (It is especially ambiguous if the act is motivationally over-determined.)

Often, there can be uncertainty about whether a person is ethically motivated, while in many cases there is little doubt about there being aggravating conditions. Looking at the facts surrounding each case might make it fairly easy to hypothesize unflattering motives. Does terminating the agonizing life in the first case simplify the offender's life, relieving various burdens on that person? Can the person's behaviour in case d. be interpreted as possibly improving that person's chances in an upcoming political campaign? And so forth. Whether planned or more spontaneous, an offender's cruelty, degradation of the victim, and pleasure in causing suffering can be very difficult to conceal. Yet, morally admirable motives, in at least some kinds of cases, can be feigned or might be obscure.

Moreover, many of our actions might be motivationally overdetermined. We may be moved by numerous considerations and might not be able to disentangle them. (See Ryberg, this volume) That is not to say that we can never judge the genuineness and character of moral motives with confidence. It would be a kind of sceptical affectation to insist that our own motives or the motives of others are always hidden or are other than what we take them to be. All sorts of relationships, interactions, and practices would become impossibly

[2] If the result of intervening to bring suffering to an end increases suffering in a totally unanticipated way, that does not diminish the compassion of the motive.

tentative on that basis. But motives are not always evident to us and various factors can render them obscure or lead us to misrepresent them.

Suppose that after months of agonizing reflection a parent terminates life-support for their four-year-old blind, terminally ill child whose condition involves progressively worsening paralysis and unrelieved pain. Also, suppose the question of whether the parent is being financially ruined by the cost of continued life-support does not arise; the parent is wealthy, and in any case the cost of care is borne largely by insurance and the state. One could argue that, really, the parent is mainly concerned with their own suffering, rather than that of their child. But in the absence of evidence such an accusation might be just a gratuitous and callous slander, probably adding more suffering to the situation. Terminating the child's life so that pointless suffering ends, when it is done by a parent (without objection by the other parent or a guardian) can be understood in a way that is mitigating, as humane and respectful, and as not condemning the child to a kind of helpless, pain-dominated oblivion. It could be that in violating the law the parent is willing to face whatever consequences that might bring, and that could be evidence in favour of the ethical genuineness of the parent's motivation. Sentence mitigation can make the punishment proportional to the blameworthiness of the offender. Is that showing mercy? We can call it that, though the chief point in mitigation is being justly responsive to the facts of the situation.

Suppose an offender who was cruel in the commission of a crime and then unmoved in response to conviction, and who is then punished more severely than someone remorseful and plainly shocked by their own ability to cause harm. The sentencer need not claim that a cruel offender's crime is more *wrong* than that of a similar offence not involving cruelty. It may be more repellent without being more wrong. The aggravated sentence is a way of recognizing how the former offender's act is a more pronounced repudiation of fundamental values and it is not a groundless overreach on the part of the sentencer. (In this context the cruelty is relevant and significant rather than the lack of remorse later on.) This is a way of communicating that the offence was notorious for its disparaging unconcern with values the society regards as basic. That can be seen as an aspect of blameworthiness and thus, the judgment of culpability.

In mitigating sentence because of the offender's ethical motivation it is important to guard against doing so mainly out of sympathy with the offender's perspective or sensibility. It is not a matter of 'I'm with you.' Nor is it a matter of just admiring someone's integrity or courage. The offender's action needs to be recognizable as the just thing to do, because what the law specifies and requires is not adequate to supply the correct sentence in the case, where 'correct' has largely to do with proportionality and desert given the agency informing the act. The sentencer is considering together the act, the law, and the motive that makes for this act being meaningfully different from what we might suppose is the vast majority of violations of the law in question. This is not mercy, if mercy is *not punishing when one ought to punish* (i.e., because there are sufficient grounds to punish). Nor is it mercy if mercy is a kind of grace, an unmerited gift. The mitigation of sentence is—in the best of instances—motivated by concern for justice. It is not giving something else priority over justice. I mentioned the case of a parent terminating the life of their child, who has no prospect of recovery, is in considerable pain, and is not even able to be responsive to affection. That certainly seems a candidate case for mitigation and that is because law cannot be as fine-grained as the concreteness of actual moral life, and in a case such as this the desert of the parent is best understood in terms of the moral point of the motive. The parents, and the judge in the case, might regard the law that prohibits actively intervening to take a person's life as sound law. They could also see sentencing in need of a degree of specification that is at a level of resolution the law cannot reach. Mitigation of sentence provides that.

Many actions of the kind claimed to be morally motivated involve actors drawing attention to what they take to be urgent social, political, or economic matters, and the offenders often regard these matters as involving injustice that needs to be remedied. In such cases the state can be shown in an unflattering light, and might even be shown to lack, as Duff puts it, 'the authority and the standing to call this person to answer for his alleged crime' (Duff 2003: 185). Consider, for example, segregation in the United States in the early to mid-1960s. There was clear evidence that large numbers of people were victims of distributive injustice and blatant, often violent, bigotry. Duff says of the offender who is calling into question the standing of the state to punish, 'Suppose that he has been excluded—politically, materially, and normatively—from an adequate share in the community's goods: and that his exclusion has been recognized as a wrong done to him' (Duff 2003: 186). The injustice—though disputed—was only supportable on very dubious grounds and the harm caused was undeniable.

Many protesters opposed to segregation were persons directly and unfairly impacted by it. Their protest was often in the form of civil disobedience. In addition to those persons there were numerous other individuals who fought segregation in the United States. The morally objectionable character of laws regarded as unjust was highlighted by seeing people arrested for violating them, exposing to moral censure those enforcing and supporting the law, even if they themselves did not feel ashamed. This was a situation in which we might think there was little room for genuine moral debate about the injustice of the laws in question or the urgency of the issue though, for many generations large numbers of people did not agree; many people were firmly committed to segregation.

Many civil rights protesters were white and did not suffer the discrimination African-Americans were subject to, and that might seem to weaken the case for mitigating sentence for those not directly affected. However, they were protesting matters of fundamental civic importance that have an impact on the character of the rule of law, rights, and the standing of citizens, as well as on the civic culture of the society. That can be said to bring them 'closer' to the issue in a way that gives their protest direct genuineness and supplies a ground for mitigating sentence. This might be a way that their protests differ from some contemporary protests against environmental degradation or against corporate practices of laying off employees. There are many grounds for ethically motivated protest regarding a great many causes, practices, policies, and institutions. However, broadly treating ethical motivation as mitigating would risk conformity to law becoming discretionary; as though, if one has ethical objections, that is sufficient to ground sentence mitigation. That would stretch desert and blameworthiness in a far too discretionary manner. In addition, it would result in the law and in sentencing having uncertain or confusing communicative resonance. When a case involves obvious urgency and the direct involvement of the offender it is much clearer that there could be grounds for mitigating sentence than in other types of cases. Segregation, and agonizing ill-health and disability with no prospect of recovery, are issues of fundamental importance in a way that corporate layoffs or even clear-cut logging are not. Segregation concerns basic values and principles of the civic and juridical order in a way that most instances of protesting environmental policy do not.

Making a point, even when motivated by genuine moral earnestness, is not a sufficient basis for mitigation. There are good reasons to keep mitigation in a rather narrow channel as a way of preventing earnestness from being interpreted as genuine urgency.

4. Concerns About Character in Sentencing

The virtues and vices of citizens are not a direct concern of the liberal state. Moreover, a vast amount of moral life is not addressed by the state at all. That does not make the rule of law a morally neutral matter. That people have various freedoms and are protected from numerous kinds of harm is a fundamental aspect of the *moral content* of the rule of law of a liberal-democracy.[3] And there are moral reasons for limiting the involvement of the state in the moral lives of its citizens. (See Jacobs 2020, esp. chs 2 and 3.)

An individual is not assumed to have a certain kind of character because of their position in society, and the individual's agency is not confined by such a position. There is to be an equality of dignity of the members of a liberal state, whatever differences there might be on account of ability, wealth, character, and achievement. Yet, there are respects in which aspects of motivation reflected in one's criminal conduct can help in the specification of blameworthiness in a way that supplies a ground for mitigation of sentence.

Supposing that desert and proportionality are significant elements of sanction it might seem that the broadly liberal state should focus on what was done and whether it was voluntary and intentional rather than characteristics of the act reflecting the offender's moral sensibility and motivational orientation, as it were. However, the fact that an action is especially egregious and reprehensible on account of how it was motivated can be properly reflected in judgments of a person's blameworthiness and desert.[4] Desert is a basic ground for punishment even if other considerations are also included in the determination of sentence. Though law in the liberal state is not employed to evaluate the moral goodness or badness of persons, there are points in criminal proceedings where it is appropriate to recognize and respond to at least some moral features of the offender inasmuch as they informed the act in question.

In *In Search of Criminal Responsibility*, in the course of an extensive discussion of the role of character in the context of criminal justice Nicola Lacey writes: 'At a formal level, in significant developments in both the UK and the US, legislation and policy structuring sentencing has in recent years added impetus to character-based attributions; "three strikes" laws; other mandatory

[3] Some versions of the positivist notion of a clean break between law and morality are quite implausible. It is true that legality and morality are distinct and that the differences between them are significant. However, it is difficult to imagine a plausible conception of law—or at least the rule of law—devoid of moral considerations. Especially in a liberal democracy there are moral reasons to restrict the moral reach of the law, and the notion of the rule of law needs to be suitable to rational, voluntary agents. Legality has a distinct type of integrity but that, too, is connected in some ways with moral considerations. The moral presuppositions might be silent; but they are there.

[4] I am not claiming that desert alone is the justifying basis for criminal sanction. But in numerous works I have argued that desert is integrally important to criminal sanction that respects persons as agents though there are many ways in which the exercise of agency is influenced by factors individuals cannot control. But deterrence and reform, in particular, seem to me to be especially uncompelling as justifications of punishment. I address this issue in *The Liberal State and Criminal Sanction* (Jacobs 2020) and several articles, going back to 'Luck and Retribution' (Jacobs 1999).

sentences for certain kinds of offences; 'dangerous offender' policies of one kind or another all provide examples' (Lacey 2016: 64). She expresses concern about the ways in which 'responsibility will be decisively shaped by character-based judgments' (Lacey 2016: 64). There is concern that an enlarged role for character is antithetical to the liberal principle that sanction should concern what a person did and not what sort of person one is. Lacey points out that 'Part II of the Criminal Justice Act of 2003 fundamentally changes the rules on admissibility of evidence of bad character' (Lacey 2016: 154). Section 101(1) of the Act 'allows evidence of bad character, in the sense not only of previous convictions, but also of previous misconduct or reprehensible behaviour' (Lacey 2016: 154). Her overall discussion points out numerous respects in which considerations of character are finding their way into criminal proceedings and she highlights sources of serious concern raised by that trend. But mitigation on the basis of ethical motivation need not be part of a larger project of character-based judgment in criminal proceedings. If its application is measured and limited in some specific ways it can have a role that serves a commitment to proportionality.

The enlargement of a conception of legal responsibility to accommodate various features of character can be troubling, mainly because of the risk of criminal proceedings becoming a way of censuring and sanctioning offenders as 'bad people' instead of on account of their actions. Still, it does seem plausible to allow aspects of motivation—in a careful, measured manner—in sentencing. I say this because they tell us something about what sort of action the offender performed and they can indicate important features of how victims were impacted by this act, telling us something about blameworthiness for harm. The harm caused might be especially frightful and shocking, and that might be because of gratuitous cruelty, for example. Harm can be shocking even if it is entirely unintended and not a result of reckless or negligent behaviour. But such harm is sometimes explicable in terms of how the offender was motivated. Aspects of motivation might properly influence judgments of what punishment is deserved because of how those aspects were integral to the type of action performed, to *what one has done*. Still, it remains important to guard against using considerations about character extensively as basic elements of decisions about sanction because of how that can draw attention away from facts about the act for which the offender is being punished.

Fear of crime and fear of terrorism are among the social trends that have been especially pronounced recently and those have led to increases in criminalization, severity of sentences, and expanded powers of law enforcement.

They have also given impetus to character-based attributions. Referring to the last four decades of the twentieth century in the United States, William Stuntz wrote: 'Once liberal politicians like Johnson and Kennedy embraced punitive politics, the right's bluff had been called. Conservative politicians had two choices: they could back down, cede the crime issue to their liberal opponents, and admit that their tough rhetoric was cheap talk. Or they could follow suit and ramp up punishment' (Stuntz 2011: 239). This can easily involve an increasing concern that there are groups that reject some of the basic norms of society. And that can be reflected in enlarged inclusion of considerations about offenders' characters. Lacey argues that character-based attributions of responsibility have a growing role in US and UK criminal justice in ways that are troubling. She says that this happens 'when the sentiments underpinning norms toward equal liberties are fragile' perhaps on account of fears of crime and terrorism. What one *is like* can loom large along with what one *has done*.

Taking into account the moral qualities of motives need not be part of a general trend of drawing more and more about character into sentencing. The point is not to make a judgment that is illustrative of how a person's character and conduct overall are seen or how this offence is indicative of what must be deeply rooted aspects of the offender's character. There is a significant difference between a criminal justice system that punishes persons on the basis of their character (in addition to the harm they cause) and a system that acknowledges that actions that appear qualitatively similar can reflect very different exercises of agency, the differences largely attributable to motive. The point of the present discussion is not to make a case for character-based sentencing. Instead, ethical motivation can be crucial to the just sentencing of an agent independent of whether the motive is seen as a window into character. One's actual motive might be somewhat *out* of character. Typically, character and motive are closely related; character just is a set of enduring dispositions to choose, act, and respond in certain ways. But the main issue here is that there are instances in which the offender's motive is a ground for mitigating sentence without that being evidence of a durable set of dispositions characteristic of the offender. The issue is that in some cases not acknowledging the significance of motive can result in a misidentification of the significance of the offender's act and that could lead to questionable sentencing. In such cases sentence mitigation need not be a judgment of the offender's character in general. Nor need it be a kind of unmerited grace. It is a calibrating of sentence to the facts of the situation and the act. (See Zaibert this volume, for a discussion of mercy.)

5. Is Mitigated Sentencing Appropriate?

On the question of whether sentence mitigation is a matter of the sentence showing mercy, Leo Zaibert writes: 'If mercy has a place within the law, as both Nussbaum and I think, it is crucially within sentencing, where deontic strictures are considerably looser than in other areas. Deep sentencers can grant mercy in ways that legislators cannot—often it is good that they do' (Zaibert this volume). Mercy can be morally complicated and there are strikingly different contexts in which the question of mercy can arise. In one sense, mercy is *not punishing though doing so would be justified.* And even that can be motivated in a variety of ways. Showing mercy could be a gesture of grace on the part of one eager to demonstrate superior power and authority, or it could be humane concern for the person to whom mercy is shown. It could be a way of exhibiting concern for the fragility of another, realizing that punishment would be deeply wounding to the other person. It could be a way of acknowledging that the person being shown mercy already has a full understanding of their wrongdoing and whatever is to be communicated by punishment is already grasped.[5] Also, just as forgiveness, compassion, and even generosity can be morally misguided or misdirected so too, can mercy. There are situations in which being merciful would be unjust, and being merciful is not always doing more and better than doing justly.

Zaibert's discussion helpfully acknowledges that the most important features of mercy (in the context of criminal justice) are not mainly in contrast to the distorted conception of retributivism that Nussbaum employs as the main alternative.[6] And he notes: 'In sublimating mercy, Nussbaum appears to forget that mercy itself is but one important tool for dealing with ethically-motivated and other complicated offenders' (Zaibert this volume). Equity is another, and it perhaps more often has a key role to play in seeing that justice is done. The strongest case for mitigated sentencing is that it is the just thing in the situation. Rather than appealing to a value 'beyond' or 'above' justice, the mitigating sentence is striving to integrate a complex of factors so that they are brought together to arrive at a just result.

[5] Whether these examples of mercy have much to recommend them is another matter. I just want to illustrate different forms being merciful might take.

[6] Nussbaum (2016) and others (Thomas Scanlon 2013 for example) seem to believe that retributivism is a form of vengeance and that it aims to inflict pain. Neither of those is an element of most influential recent and contemporary conceptions of retributivism. Desert, proportionality, respect for rational agency, and in some influential theories, a communicative aspect concerning values rather than rage or retaliation are central to retributivism.

The discretion that is appropriate for sentencers is an opportunity for a calibrated judgment concerning the depth and character of the offender's blameworthiness involving a similarly calibrated judgment of proportionality. In that regard, mitigation is not a departure from desert though it is a judgment of desert that is not already addressed by the law. This differs from Walker's discussion of eclectic and hybrid sentences. (See Walker 1991: ch. 15). We have mentioned the complications that come with motivational overdetermination of an action and uncertainty about the efficacious motive. Even in the terminating life case, it could be that the parent finds the child's predicament and the emotional burden of it so unbearable that it cannot be borne any longer, although that is not how the person portrays their act to themselves or to the court. That it is unbearable is more or less a given; that does not mean that the parent's decision was not genuinely motivated by concern for the child's suffering, though that is bound up inseparably with the emotional factors. The concepts that structure and orient the elements of criminal justice are always realized in ways more or less thickly informed by concrete particulars and contextual factors and those can make for degrees of ambiguity and uncertainty. While law provides extensive guidance concerning sanction and it discriminates different kinds of cases that might otherwise be confusingly classified together it cannot anticipate every kind of case and every kind of actor. If there is a place for mitigated sentences on the basis of the moral quality of motivation it is for agents whose involvement in the situation is direct, urgent, and concerns value that cannot otherwise be realized in the concreteness of the situation.

6. Conclusion

The issue of the ethically motivated offender is one of the most difficult questions concerning the factors that constitute the culpability of an offender. The fact that 'person P did act A, which is a violation of law L' identifies the relevant agent to whom wrongfulness is to be attributed but in some cases what P was doing *in doing A* is not limited to the fact of violating a rule that defines an offence; what in addition is attributed to the agent enables us to ascertain more fully what the agent is answerable for in terms of their blameworthiness.

We might find that we regard certain motives as making an agent's conduct worse as culpable wrongdoing. Thus, sentences are sometimes aggravated. Likewise, being ethically motivated can moderate the blameworthiness of the agent. In such cases it is appropriate to register that through sentence mitigation. This is not a claim that if the moral character of the offender is generally admirable, that fact is a ground for mitigating sentence. That would raise questions about how faithfully a principle of equality before the law is being upheld in addition to representing a shift of attention to an agent's overall character, which would be a problematic reorientation of attention. Treating equals similarly does not mean exactly similar sentencing for every instance of a specific type of violation, and the differences that are properly recognized can include differences in motivation. Ethically honourable motives inform an act in a way that can merit recognition in assessments of desert. Once those are acknowledged it can seem artificial and perhaps even misleading to exclude them altogether or to insist that the act alone is what matters legally, not what the actor was doing in so acting.

As a final remark, I have argued that there is a case for sentence mitigation when the offender acts in a manner that involves urgency, direct engagement in the situation, and the agent's motive—to the extent it can be accurately ascertained—is morally intelligible but not in a way that is explicitly recognized by the law. It is not a sure thing that such cases point to how the law should be changed. It may not be possible to fully codify relevant types of behaviour and the form that ethically honourable motives can have. There is less of a case for mitigation when the agent is not directly engaged in the issue in question or when the offending act takes the form of protest and there are lawful alternative ways of expressing opposition.

References

Duff, R. Antony. *Punishment, Communication, and Community.* New York: Oxford University Press, 2003.

Jacobs, Jonathan. 'Luck and Retribution'. *Philosophy* no. 74 (1999): 73–93.

Jacobs, Jonathan. *The Liberal State and Criminal Sanction: Seeking Justice and Civility.* New York: Oxford University Press, 2020.

Lacey, Nicola. *In Search of Criminal Responsibility: Ideas, Interests, and Institutions.* Oxford: Oxford University Press, 2016.

Murphy, Jeffrie G. 'Legal Moralism and Liberalism'. *Arizona Law Review* 37, no. 73 (1995): 73–93.

Nagel, Thomas. 'Moral Luck'. In *Mortal Questions.* pp. 24–38. New York: Cambridge University Press, 1979.

Nussbaum, Martha. *Anger and Forgiveness: Resentment, Generosity,* Justice . Oxford: Oxford University Press, 2016.

Ryberg, Jesper. 'Sentencing Honourable Offenders: On the Complexities of Assessing Human Motives', Chapter 3 of this volume.

Scanlon, Thomas. 'Giving Desert its Due'. *Philosophical Explorations.* 16, no. 2 (2013): 101–116.

Stuntz, William. *The Collapse of American Criminal Law*. Cambridge, MA: Harvard University Press, 2011.
Walker, Nigel. *Why Punish? Theories of Punishment Reassessed*. Oxford: Oxford University Press, 1991.
Zaibert, Leo. 'How to Deal with Ethically-Defensible Criminality, or On Deep Sentencing', Chapter 2 of this volume.

PART II

SENTENCING ETHICAL OFFENDING IN PRACTICE: JURISDICTIONAL CASE HISTORIES

10

Sentencing Pro-Democracy Protesters in Hong Kong

Florence Lee

1. Introduction

This chapter examines how Hong Kong courts approach the sentencing of pro-democracy protesters within its evolving national security framework. Following a period of social unrest, sentencing decisions have assumed increased importance, reflecting a delicate balance between recognizing offenders' motives (their pursuit of democratic ideals) and upholding the government's priority of maintaining stability. These sentences have attracted significant international attention for their length and severity.[1] Government supporters claim that priority should be given to deterrence, while critics argue that penalties are excessive and silence dissent, emphasizing that those convicted were exercising fundamental rights to freedom of speech, assembly, and political participation.[2] Others objected to the broad application of national security legislation.[3] The sentencing of pro-democracy protesters in Hong Kong remains a source of tension in the struggle to uphold traditional common law values amidst a changing political landscape.

As the volume of cases of unlawful assembly, rioting, and national security offences has increased, a trend has emerged: deterrence-based sentences have become more severe. A number of questions lie at the heart of this chapter. How do judges sentence pro-democracy offenders who commit crimes with

[1] The sentencing of Hong Kong pro-democracy protesters has been covered by major global outlets and institutions across the world, including the US Department of State's Bureau of East Asian and Pacific Affairs, UK House of Lords and House of Commons, US Consulate General, BBC News, Human Rights Watch, Amnesty International, UN News, among others.

[2] For example, the UK's Minister for the Indo-Pacific, Catherine West, claimed that the sentencing of the Hong Kong 47 activists 'is a clear demonstration of the Hong Kong authorities' use of the NSL to criminalize political dissent'. For discussion, see Hawkins and Davidson (2024).

[3] For an overview of human rights concerns regarding Hong Kong's security trials, see Human Rights Watch (2024).

Florence Lee, *Sentencing Pro-Democracy Protesters in Hong Kong* In: *Sentencing the Ethically-Motivated Offender*.
Edited by: Julian V. Roberts, Leo Zaibert, and Jesper Ryberg, Oxford University Press. © Florence Lee 2026.
DOI: 10.1093/9780198993025.003.0012

honourable motives? Do the Hong Kong courts remain faithful to the principle of proportionality when sentencing in a politically shifting landscape? How do the courts assess the justifiability of mitigating sentences based on the perceived legitimacy of the cause? And finally, which honourable motives and circumstances have a mitigating effect on sentencing outcomes? The safeguarding of Hong Kong's stability is seen as a top political priority in Beijing. Courts have continued to apply sentencing principles such as fairness and proportionality (see e.g. Clayton 2018). However, the space in which judicial decision-making unfolds has been reshaped by the city's unique political landscape, including the passing of the National Security Law which is driven by a preventive and deterrent rationale.

2. Overview

Section 3 of this chapter outlines the changing landscape of national security laws in Hong Kong. The next two sections illuminate how courts grapple with the intricate balance between individual intent, honourable motives, and the added criminality of an agenda that seeks to undermine national security in cases through examining the sentencing outcomes of democrats who were charged with public order or national security offences between 2014 and 2021. It demonstrates that sentencing protesters in this context creates tensions that are not easily resolvable by the courts, as proportionality is often eclipsed by more dominant sentencing goals. On one hand, judges strive to uphold principles like proportionality which require a careful balance of assessing culpability and harm. On the other hand, courts are urged to prioritize purposes such as deterrence and legitimacy at sentencing, which reflects the prevailing political environment. The result is a complex sentencing landscape in which an offender's commitment to pro-democratic ideals is acknowledged but seen as a reason to impose tougher sentences to deter others. The final section reflects on the limits of honourable motives at sentencing in Hong Kong.

3. The Evolution of National Security Laws in Hong Kong

It is important to contextualize the security laws in Hong Kong before analysing the sentencing of pro-democracy protesters. The uniqueness of Hong Kong's constitution lies in the 'one country two systems' framework, which was designed by Deng Xiaoping to enable the unification of Hong Kong after being returned to China following British rule in 1997.[4] This framework enabled Hong Kong to retain its capitalist economy, common law system, independent judiciary, independent prosecution system, and fundamental rights after the handover until 2047 (Wesley-Smith 1996). The fundamental rights of each citizen in Hong Kong are enshrined in the constitution through the Basic Law, which guarantees, amongst others, the following civil rights: freedom of speech, freedom of the press, freedom of association, freedom of assembly, and freedom of demonstration.

The high degree of autonomy given to Hong Kong extended towards the enactment of national security laws. Typically, national security legislation in jurisdictions such as the United Kingdom or the United States is enacted by the central government, as opposed to regional authorities, who do not have the power to legislate on reserved matters. Unusually, the Basic Law contained several provisions delegating this power to the Hong Kong government. Article 23 of the Basic Law implements a constitutional duty on Hong Kong to 'enact laws on its own to prohibit any act of treason, secession, sedition, subversion against the Central People's Government, or theft of state secrets, to prohibit foreign political organisations or bodies from conducting political activities in the Region, and to prohibit political organisations or bodies of the Region from establishing ties with foreign political organisations or bodies'.[5] Grenville Cross described this as a 'remarkable concession and a great show of faith in the city', giving considerable autonomy towards the regional government to take national security into their own hands (2024: 3).

However, this distinctive constitutional framework inadvertently led to a legal lacuna in the area of national security legislation. In 2003, the Hong Kong government attempted to pass a National Security Bill which was met with resistance from citizens and institutions, who gathered to protest against the proposed bill.[6] Many of the bill's problems were attributed to the lack of defences to the proposed national security offences, as well as its limitations on the freedom of expression (see e.g. Fu et al. 2005). Despite making over 50 amendments to reflect the views of the protesters, the government ultimately withdrew the draft bill.[7] Arguably, the gap left by the failed attempt to enact national security legislation may explain why Hong Kong remained open to threats of national security.

[4] For a detailed overview of the 'One Country Two Systems' framework, see Yep (2009).
[5] Art. 23 of the Hong Kong Basic Law of the Hong Kong Special Administrative Region of the People's Republic of China.
[6] For a full history of the rise and fall of the National Security Bill in 2003, see Petersen (2005).
[7] For discussions of the draft bill, see e.g. Chen (2017).

3.1. Occupy Central

In 2014, Hong Kong experienced another social movement spurred by a decision by the National People's Congress to reform the electoral system by requiring candidates for the Chief Executive position to obtain a majority from a specified election committee. These developments resulted in the Occupy Central movement, a large pro-democracy protest that demanded, among others, true universal suffrage under the 'One Country Two Systems' model.[8] The *modus operandi* of the protest involved acts of civil disobedience through methods such as blocking major roads and setting up protest campsites in central locations of the city. Since the Occupy Central movement was largely peaceful, it did not trigger further national security legislation from Beijing. The aftermath saw leaders of the movement prosecuted for public order offences such as taking part in an unlawful assembly and conspiracy to cause public nuisance. These prosecutions signalled a growing intolerance of dissent.

3.2. Extradition Law Protests

The turning point in the evolution of Hong Kong's national security narrative came in 2019 and 2020, when Hong Kong experienced one of its largest protests which had a great impact on China's approach towards the imposition of national security laws (Lee et al. 2019). The protesters opposed the enactment of a bill to amend the Fugitive Offenders Ordinance, which enabled the extradition of offenders to countries including mainland China.[9] To quell social unrest, Beijing bypassed Hong Kong's legislature and imposed the Law of the People's Republic of China on Safeguarding National Security in the Hong Kong Special Administrative Region (NSL) in 2020, which created four new offences: secession, subversion, terrorism, and collusion with foreign forces.[10] This law contains mandatory minimum sentences for several offences, as well as elements of civil criminal law which leave little room for the consideration of mitigating factors at sentencing. This was followed by the enactment of the Safeguarding National Security Ordinance in 2024 which implements Article 23 by incorporating new national security offences into the regional

[8] For a fine overview, see Young (2015).

[9] The Fugitive Offenders and Mutual Legal Assistance in Criminal Matters Legislation (Amendment) Bill 2019 allowed mutual extradition arrangements to be made between Hong Kong and several other countries.

[10] Art. 1 of the NSL.

legislature.[11] The national security landscape has shifted from an uncertain sphere existing in a legal vacuum, which left room for the courts to grapple with honourable motives at sentencing as will be discussed later, to a far more centralized, security-focused framework based on risk prevention, aligned with China's governmental priorities.

4. Pre-NSL: a Recognition of Honourable Motives

In early post-2014 judgments, judges tended to sympathize with the democratic ideals of protesters even if they defied the criminal law. Honourable motives, such as a belief that Hong Kong should achieve universal suffrage, were once balanced against the need for public order and used to explain, but not excuse, conduct. Pro-democracy protesters were charged under public order offences and their inchoate counterparts such as unlawful assembly or unauthorized assembly. Judgments from this time reflected a more open judicial space for the discussion of ideals, values and pro-social motives in determining culpability and sentencing through contextualizing the harms of the unlawful conduct.

4.1. Grappling With Motives in *Wong Chi Fung*

The seminal case of *Wong Chi Fung* revealed differing judicial attitudes towards the treatment of honourable motives at sentencing public order offences.[12] The first defendant, Wong, was convicted of inciting others to take part in an unlawful assembly and of taking part in an unlawful assembly contrary to section 18 of the Public Order Ordinance before the Occupy Central protests.[13] The second and third defendants were convicted of the latter.[14] Wong, a leader of the student group 'Scholarism', opposed government proposals for national education. The unlawful assembly occurred at the closed forecourt of the Central Government Offices after a lawful protest expired at 10 pm, where Wong and others forced their way in around 10:20 pm. Several

[11] For example, s. 119 of the Safeguarding National Security Ordinance criminalizes the 'unlawful harassment of persons handling cases or work concerning national security', punishable by up to 10 years' imprisonment.
[12] *Secretary for Justice v Wong Chi Fung* [2018] HKCFA 4.
[13] ibid. [23].
[14] ibid. [23].

dozen protesters entered, resulting in injuries to security guards.[15] The court acknowledged that the political debate on the constitutional reforms had 'run high' but 'it is not the role or function of the courts . . . to enter into this or any other political debate'.[16]

At the Magistrates' Court, motives such as the offender's 'concern for societal problems', passion for politics, and a willingness 'to take action to realise their ideals', alongside the non-violent nature of the assembly, were powerful mitigating factors.[17] Community sentences were given to all three defendants (with a suspended sentence of three weeks' imprisonment for the third), showing that empathy towards honourable motives may lead to rehabilitative rather than purely punitive sentences.

The lenient sentences passed by the Magistrates' Court were later reviewed by the Court of Appeal, which placed a stronger emphasis on the need to enforce a deterrent-based sentencing framework. [18] The Court considered that a lack of genuine remorse, combined with the seriousness of the facts, required more emphasis on deterrence. This reduced the impact of honourable motives at sentencing.[19] Poon JA held that the magistrate had put 'disproportionate weight' on the defendants' circumstances and motives, noting that 'genuine' remorse does not come from a willingness to bear the legal consequences of criminal acts motivated by pro-democratic ideals.[20] Substitute sentences of six, eight, and seven months' imprisonment were imposed on the three defendants respectively.[21] This raises an issue about the court's attitudes towards conflating a defendant's refusal to show remorse with a lack of genuine contrition. In cases motivated by a political cause, defendants may accept the legal consequences while still standing by the *moral legitimacy* of their cause. Reluctance to show remorse is sometimes interpreted by the courts as a rejection of the need to protect public safety and stability, as will be evident in later cases.

The Court of Final Appeal had to determine the sentencing approach towards offenders who commit public order offences based on pro-social motives. An issue was: 'to what extent should a sentencing court take into account the motives of a defendant in committing the crime of which he or she has been convicted, particularly in cases where it is asserted that the crime was committed as an act of civil disobedience or in the exercise of a constitutional

[15] ibid. [15].
[16] ibid. [5].
[17] ibid. [35].
[18] ibid. [36].
[19] ibid. [39].
[20] ibid. [40].
[21] ibid. [41].

right'?[22] Although motive is a relevant factor affecting the appropriate sentence, the Court stated that for offences involving acts of civil disobedience in the exercise of constitutional rights, there is a 'bright line' between peaceful protested demonstrations and 'unlawful activity' which interferes with others' rights.[23] Protesters claiming to exercise constitutional rights will be 'unlikely to carry significant weight' in mitigation at sentencing, because by committing an unlawful act, they have already stepped outside those protected rights.[24] No guidance is provided on when such a 'line of acceptability' will be crossed.[25]

The Court gave another example of when offences are committed by way of an act of civil disobedience, which are motivated by genuine beliefs that laws are unjust, or done to protest against 'perceived injustice or in order to effect some change in either the law or society'.[26] The Court held that:

> Either type of behaviour may be actuated by the offender's conscientious objections and genuine beliefs and a sentencing court may properly take these into account as the motive for the offending, although the weight to be attached to that motive will necessarily vary depending on many other circumstances, including the facts of the offending and its consequences and the need for deterrence and punishment.[27]

There is a relationship between the cause the protesters wish to draw attention to—democratic or political change—and the consequences of the crime committed to draw attention to the problem. Citing John Rawls, the courts noted that the essence of civil disobedience is to challenge existing laws through non-violent, conscientious acts that are contrary to the law.[28] However, when protesters behave disproportionately, for instance, by causing excessive damage or disruption, they shift the nature of the act towards one where violence is a potential risk. In these cases, 'a plea for leniency at the stage of sentencing on the ground of civil disobedience will carry little (if any) weight since by definition that act is not one of civil disobedience'.[29] The third defendant argued that it should be a significant mitigating factor when '(a) the ideals behind a course of civil disobedience are consistent with the promotion

[22] ibid. [43].
[23] ibid. [68]–[69].
[24] ibid. [69].
[25] ibid.
[26] ibid. [71].
[27] ibid.
[28] ibid. [72].
[29] ibid. [74].

of a pluralistic, open and tolerant society or political order, and (b) the means undertaken by the offenders impose only minor injuries or damages to property'.[30] In rejecting this claim, the Court emphasized that they will not take sides in political debates, but focused on whether punishment would be necessary. The difficult task for the judges in this case is to take into account honourable motives at sentencing but at the same time adopt a pragmatic approach, giving greater weight to the need to enforce the law.[31]

Ultimately, the Court of Final Appeal reinstated the community sentences imposed by the Magistrates' Court, citing that it was within the discretion of the magistrate to emphasize positive factors, including the defendants' pro-social motives and 'idealism' for their offending.[32] The Court assigned honourable motives greater weight at sentencing, especially for 'minor' public order offences such as those in the present case. The Court upheld the sentencing guidelines crafted by the Court of Appeal, which created a structured approach towards when deterrence would be considered more or less relevant at mitigation. Factors that the court had to consider include: 1) the seriousness of the offence, 2) whether the offence is violent or non-violent, 3) the deterrent effect of sentences imposed, 4) proportionality, and 5) whether the offence is 'minor' or 'serious' in nature.[33] This shows that the constraint of proportionality is reimagined through a deterrent logic, creating a sentencing environment where proportionality is stretched to accommodate other factors at sentencing.

Interestingly, a *tiered* system for considering honourable motives was established. For 'minor' offences involving little violence and harm to property, the court may give proportionally more weight to motives, and less to the factor of deterrence; for 'serious' offences involving large-scale violence, the court would give deterrence and punishment greater weight with little or no weight for motives.[34] It is clear then that honourable motives can have more room to operate if the offence is minor, while a deterrent framework will be used in sentencing more serious cases. Deterrence is considered the most appropriate sentencing factor in large-scale unlawful assembly cases taking into account the circumstances of Hong Kong's past social unrest.[35]

[30] ibid. [75].
[31] ibid. [76].
[32] ibid. [105].
[33] ibid. [12].
[34] ibid. [123(4)].
[35] ibid. [120].

4.2. Sentencing after the Occupy Central movement—*Tai Yiu Ting and Others*

The cases after the Occupy Central movement introduced a more stringent proportionality analysis towards sentencing pro-democracy protesters. In *Tai Yiu Ting and Others*, nine defendants pleaded guilty to a mixture of offences including conspiracy to commit public nuisance, incitement to incite public nuisance, and incitement to commit public nuisance as a result of their actions prior to the movement.[36] The motivation for these offences included pressuring the government through acts of civil disobedience by blocking main roads in the city centre.[37] At trial, the judge challenged the reasonableness and 'unrealistic' expectations held by the defendants of how the protests would develop, stating that there are no grounds to think that, should citizens turn up to the protests, 'that mass expression of resolve was anticipated to have been sufficient to achieve the desired result and therefore removing any further need to cause further disruption in accordance with the proportionality principle'.[38]

At sentencing, the ninth defendant relied on *R. v Roberts (Richard)*[39] to argue that the honourable motives of the defendant should reduce culpability because the courts ought to 'balance' the right to freedom of expression and the 'conscientious motives' of protesters who act with a sense of proportion on the part of their offending to avoid 'excessive damage or inconvenience'.[40] Emphasizing the peaceful nature of the protests, counsel relied on *Roberts* to argue for the imposition of a community or suspended sentence, noting that proportionality should entail a fair weighing exercise to be conducted.[41] Many of the defence's claims were based on urging the court to exercise leniency and avoid custodial sentences.[42]

There will be leniency if a defendant expresses regret for the inconvenience that they caused to members of the public who has been affected.[43] However, none of the defendants expressed regret for what they had done. This raises the question of what form of regret matters for defendants who are driven by honourable motives. The Court clarified that the defendants do not need to 'give

[36] *HKSAR v Tai Yiu Ting and Others* [2021] HKCA 630 [2].
[37] *HKSAR v Tai Yiu Ting and Others: Reasons for Sentence* [2019] HKDC 450 [7].
[38] *Tai Yiu Ting* (n 36) [33].
[39] *R. v Roberts (Richard)* EWCA Crim 2379; [2019] Env LR 17.
[40] *HKSAR v Tai Yiu Ting and Others: Reasons for Sentence* [2019] HKDC 450 [47].
[41] ibid. [47].
[42] ibid.
[43] ibid. [58].

up' their political beliefs or political demands (which were not the concerns of the Court) but ought to apologize to the public for the harm they have caused. The Court concluded that proportionality requires a 'sense of proportion on the part of the offenders in avoiding excessive damage or inconvenience' which the defendants lacked.[44]

4.3. Proportionality: a Two-Way Street

The sentencing of pro-democracy protesters who engage in civil disobedience requires proportionality, both in terms of the protesters respecting the boundaries set by the law and consideration for their personal beliefs which drive their offending. The protesters' own sense of proportionality was assessed by the courts in determining their level of culpability. The Court held that while some restraint was exercised by the protesters in determining where to blockade, the incited protests caused widespread disturbances and harm to the public for almost three months.[45] Despite the defendant's steadfast beliefs in achieving universal suffrage for Hong Kong, they were deemed to fail a proportionality 'test':

> They failed to notice the ordinary folks who needed to use the carriageways in question to travel to work to make a living. The martyrdom the defendants exhibited was a contorted one in that the price that each of them was prepared to pay also had to be borne by the ordinary folks. Whilst the defendants were prepared to break the law and accept legal consequences to the extent the charges to be laid would meet their expectation, the excessive damage and inconvenience caused by the obstruction had to be borne by many others.[46]

Despite an acknowledgement of the defendants' underlying motivation of fighting for universal suffrage for committing the offences, the seriousness of the public nuisance caused by the protests meant that all the defendants except the sixth defendant (who was given a community sentence because of his young age) were sentenced to terms ranging from eight to 16 months' imprisonment.[47] The Court of Appeal dismissed the appeals against sentence. In cases like this, the courts made clear that honourable motives are subjected to

[44] ibid. [59].
[45] ibid. [66].
[46] ibid. [69].
[47] ibid. [83]–[146].

a narrower proportionality test at sentencing and may not be able to outweigh serious harm when public order is breached.

5. Post-NSL: the Diminishing Role of Honourable Motives at Sentencing

The NSL is what Pascoe labels a 'socialist legal transplant', which has implications for constraining the court's ability to consider honourable motives as mitigating factors in protest-related cases (2022: 25). Unlike common law, which recognizes that mitigation based on individual motives is important, the hybrid framework in the NSL is designed to prioritize state security through its codified and rule-based structure reminiscent of its civil law origins. Its structure leaves less room for moral nuance—honourable motives not only have less mitigating effect but are sometimes viewed as aggravating, signalling a lack of remorse as well as defiance.

This trend also rings true for the consideration of human rights by the courts. As Pascoe notes, 'although the courts will try to interpret NSL provisions in accordance with Hong Kong's prevailing human rights laws "as far as [is] possible", if a direct conflict were to arise, the NSL's stated crimes, penalties and extension of mainland jurisdiction are likely to hold sway over human rights standards' (2022: 20). The mandatory minimum punishments and a deterrence-heavy sentencing framework which features in the post-NSL legal landscape have significantly eroded the court's ability to treat political idealism as a ground for leniency, reshaping the sentencing of pro-democracy protesters into a more rigid process.

5.1. From Idealism to Aggravation

Recent judicial attitudes have shifted away from viewing pro-democratic motives as mitigating. Instead, such convictions are increasingly seen as signs of defiance, undermining remorse and justifying harsher punishment under a deterrent/preventive sentencing regime. In *Tong Ying Kit*, Tong drove a motorcycle that carried a banner with the anti-government slogan 'Liberate Hong Kong, revolution of our times' into three policemen during a protest in the city.[48] He was convicted of 'incitement of secession' under Article 21 and

[48] *HKSAR v Tong Ying Kit: Reasons for Sentence* [2021] HKCFI 2239 [2].

'terrorist activities' under Article 24 of the NSL.[49] This was the first case under the NSL in Hong Kong. On the first count, the Court of First Instance took into account the mandatory minimum sentences imposed by Article 21, which required the courts to impose a five to 10-year fixed-term imprisonment if the circumstances of the offence are 'of a serious nature'. If the circumstances of the offence are 'of a minor nature', then 'the person shall be sentenced to fixed-term imprisonment of not more than five years, short-term detention or restriction'.[50] In the present case, the political context in which Hong Kong faced a crisis of anti-China advocating for Hong Kong independence added to the 'serious nature' of the offence, justifying a starting point of six and a half years' imprisonment.[51]

On the second count, the NSL contains a somewhat vague mandatory minimum schema which states: 'A person who commits the offence causing serious bodily injury, death or significant loss of public or private property shall be sentenced to life imprisonment or fixed-term imprisonment of not less than ten years; in other circumstances, a person who commits the offence shall be sentenced to fixed-term imprisonment of not less than three years but not more than ten years'.[52] However, because the injuries caused to the policemen by the motorcycle were not serious, the court assessed that the 'in other circumstances' limb was applicable.[53] Tong later appeared on a television show stating that he displayed the slogan because of an urge to address Hong Kong's societal problems at the time, so he was driven by the compulsion to act due to an honourable political motive.[54] However, the court was unsympathetic to any political agenda, stating that the 'political agenda in count 2 was of a secessionist nature, which involves a contravention of fundamental provisions of the Basic Law'.[55] According to the court, there is an 'added criminality in that such an agenda is seeking to undermine national unification'.[56] No other mitigating factors were accepted. As a result, a starting point of eight years was given, with the final sentence being nine years' imprisonment (two and a half years from the second count running consecutively to that of the first count).[57] Since the 2019 political unrest in Hong Kong, this view has become

[49] ibid. [1].
[50] Art. 21 of the NSL.
[51] *Tong Ying Kit* (n 48) [23].
[52] Art. 24 of the NSL.
[53] *Tong Ying Kit* (n 48) [35].
[54] A television programme called 'National Security Law—the Cornerstone of Prosperity and Stability' contained 12 episodes and was produced by the Hong Kong police and Hong Kong's biggest television station TVB.
[55] *Tong Ying Kit* (n 48) [36].
[56] ibid. [37].
[57] ibid. [39], [43].

more prevalent within the courts of Hong Kong. Offenders like Tong who are motivated by pro-democratic or ideological values often do not plead guilty or show little remorse due to their strong beliefs. The result is that defendants protesting the erosion of democracy (or the like) can expect to serve longer sentences due to the lack of a discount from a guilty plea or a show of remorse, stemming from their strong belief in their pro-social values.

Under Articles 20 and 21 of the NSL, the offence of incitement to secession criminalizes the planning and participation of acts that undermine national unification, for example by advocating for independence.[58] In *Lui Sai Yu*, Lui pleaded guilty to this offence after posting about protest tactics on a Telegram channel named 'Channel of Anti-Communism and Hong Kong Independence'.[59] At sentencing, the court assessed not just the nature of the incitement itself, but also appeared to weigh the perceived political legitimacy of the underlying cause as well as the context of the social unrest seen in Hong Kong since 2019.[60] The court emphasized that messages posted by Lui advocating independence as the 'only way out' were seditious and, taking into context the protests in Hong Kong, constituted a serious nature.[61] A starting point of five years and six months' imprisonment was given, which was reduced by one-third for a guilty plea.[62] However, due to the mandatory minimum sentence of five years (and not up to 10) for an offence of a serious nature, a term of five years was imposed.[63] At sentencing, courts have predominantly focused on the political contexts of statements advocating independence, with little consideration for any honourable motives of defendants. The mandatory minimum sentences imposed by the NSL further create an undesirable effect where strong political agendas may act as an aggravating factor in determining the starting points or final sentences for particular offences.

5.2. Shifting Judicial Attitudes—'Hong Kong 47' Case

In the landmark 'Hong Kong 47' case, the courts once again demonstrated their sceptical attitude towards the consideration of honourable motives.[64] As the largest single prosecution under the NSL, 47 pro-democracy activists and

58 Arts 20 and 21 of the NSL.
59 *HKSAR v Lui Sai Yu: Reasons for Sentence* [2022] HKDC 384 [5].
60 ibid. [9].
61 ibid. [13].
62 ibid. [47].
63 ibid. [54].
64 *HKSAR v Ng Gordon Ching Hang and Others: Reasons for Verdict* [2024] HKCFI 1468.

politicians were charged with conspiracy to commit subversion under Article 22(3) of the NSL and sections 159A and 159C of the Crimes Ordinance.[65] In 2020 and 2021, the defendants took part in a scheme to gain a controlling majority in the Hong Kong Legislative Council, to veto budgets and expenditures intending to paralyse the operations of the government.[66] First, the court assessed whether the scheme was 'unlawful' within the definition of Article 22 and adopted a purposive but narrow mode of interpretation.[67] The agreed *modus operandi* of 'indiscriminate vetoing of budgets' was found to 'seriously interfere, disrupt or undermine' the performance or duties and functions of the government through creating a 'constitutional crisis' for the government.[68] Therefore, subversion did not necessarily involve the use or threat of force contrary to the *ejusdem generis* rule which limits the interpretation of general terms to only those of the same nature as the specific terms preceding them. In giving reasons for the verdict, the court rejected a defendant's defence which relied on motive—she argued that she would 'definitely veto' the budgets as she 'considered that the Government was "unjust" so that no budgets it proposed would truly benefit the people of Hong Kong'.[69] Determining her participation in the conspiracy, the court focused on her agreement to the scheme and did not consider her honourable motives at trial.

The defendants intended to pressure the Chief Executive to agree to the 'Five Demands', which were the objectives of the 2019 protests: 1) full withdrawal of the extradition bill, 2) amnesty for arrested protesters, 3) withdrawing the classification of pro-democracy protesters as 'rioters', 4) an independent inquiry into police brutality and misconduct, and 5) implementation of genuine universal suffrage for the Chief Executive and Legislative Council elections.[70] The Five Demands were driven by aspirations to achieve greater democratic freedoms for Hong Kong, arguably reflecting certain public concerns about the uncertainty of the values guaranteed by 'one country two systems' after the political turmoil. However, the court's interpretation of Article 22 NSL determined that the scheme created a constitutional weapon of 'mass destruction' intending to achieve the protesters' aims by paralysing government operations.[71]

[65] Charges include the offence of conspiracy under ss. 159A–C of the Crimes Ordinance and Art. 22(3) of the NSL.
[66] *Ng Gordon Ching Hang* (n 64) [2].
[67] ibid. [94]–[95].
[68] ibid. [100].
[69] ibid. [238].
[70] ibid. [179].
[71] ibid. [182].

One of the issues considered by the court was the 'convergence, compatibility and complementarity' between the penalty for the offence of conspiracy under section 159C of the Crimes Ordinance and Article 22 of the NSL.[72] Article 22 imposed a mandatory minimum sentencing requirement where offenders committing a 'grave' offence must be sentenced to 'life imprisonment or fixed-term imprisonment of not less than ten years; a person who actively participates in the offence shall be sentenced to fixed-term imprisonment of not less than three years but not more than ten years; and other participants shall be sentenced to fixed-term imprisonment of not more than three years'.[73] These mandatory minimum sentences reflect the overall direction that sentencing is heading towards—focusing on preventive rather than individualized justice, reflecting a sentencing system that reduces judicial discretion thereby preventing the implementation of proportional sentences. Emphasizing that the legislative intent behind the NSL is to be complementary with local laws, the court noted that common law principles of sentencing were applicable. Citing *Ma Chun Man*, the circumstances of a case were relevant to sentencing inchoate NSL offences.[74] Using incitement to secession as an example, the court detailed factors that were relevant at sentencing, including Hong Kong's 'risk' of endangerment to national security and the rule of law during the offence.[75] The result of a focus on the heightened political climate of Hong Kong and the mandatory minimum sentences imposed by the NSL is that honourable motives are not given much room to mitigate sentences since the overall judicial attitude seems to be reflecting an interest in preventing political stability and protecting state interest rather than focusing on individual motives.

Sentences for individual defendants are not mitigated because of their democratic or political motives. Instead, a 'holistic assessment' of the degree of planning, number of people involved and potential harms and outcomes of the plan to subvert was considered.[76] The mastermind of the plan and the first defendant, Tai Yiu-ting, was sentenced to 10 years' imprisonment (reduced from a starting point of 15 years). Despite being an eminent professor of constitutional law in Hong Kong and a firm supporter of the rule of law, the only mitigation in his case was an early guilty plea.[77] One may speculate about why defendants who clearly expressed a view towards the democratic movement in

[72] *HKSAR v Ng Gordon Ching Hang and Others: Reasons for Sentence* [2024] HKCFI 3298 [20].
[73] Art. 22 of the NSL.
[74] *Ng Gordon Ching Hang* (n 72) [23].
[75] ibid. [22].
[76] ibid. [36].
[77] ibid. [46].

Hong Kong chose not to plead their motive as a mitigating factor. Nonetheless, sentencing primarily focused on the degree of participation in the conspiracy (whether they were a 'principal offender or merely an 'active participant'), with the other defendants sentenced at the lowest end to four years and two months' imprisonment to seven years and nine months' imprisonment.[78]

Interestingly, a defendant who maintains a steadfast belief in his values may be treated more harshly than those who do not express a change of attitude or belief. The 28th defendant, Ng Kin-wai, relied on a letter explaining his reason for participating in the conspiracy, emphasizing that 'he took full responsibility for his actions and would not apologise for all the values he and his voters believed in and stood for'.[79] There were no other mitigating factors in his case. The court rejected mitigation for his firm beliefs in pro-democratic values. The court based his final sentence of 67 months' imprisonment on his active participation in the scheme. This sentence falls at the higher end of the range for other defendants.[80] In contrast, defendants who expressed a change of beliefs or took action to demonstrate genuine change are sentenced more leniently. The eleventh defendant, Pang Cheuk-kei, supported his plea in mitigation with a letter outlining his voluntary work in 'promoting' the Constitution of the PRC, the Basic Law, the NSL and the principle of "One Country Two System" to students in Hong Kong, which garnered a 3 months reduction resulting in a final sentence of 6 years and 6 months' imprisonment.[81] The fourteenth defendant, Ho Kai-ming Kalvin, told the courts he ceased any activities which may breach the NSL and 'was prepared to leave politics' in the future, a factor which the court considered in granting a reduced sentence of six years and seven months' imprisonment.[82] Expressing an attitude change, or renouncing prior political beliefs has in some instances led to sentence mitigation, suggesting that a retraction of those very beliefs may lead to leniency. This raises important concerns about whether the sentencing process is being used not just to punish, but to reshape political identity.

A reconsideration, or reflection, of one's honourable motive seems to play a role in reducing the sentences of pro-democratic protesters. The 25th defendant, Chu Hoi-dick Eddie was sentenced to a more lenient term of four years and five months' imprisonment in comparison with the other defendants, taking into account his confession that he had been 'overzealous,

[78] ibid.
[79] ibid. [229].
[80] ibid. [229]–[231].
[81] ibid. [104].
[82] ibid. [124].

irresponsible and too narrow-minded in fighting for universal suffrage'.[83] Chu admitted that 'he had failed to take into consideration of the political development and social stability in Hong Kong at the time . . . [and felt] sorry for his mistakes and was willing to take full responsibility'.[84] This type of mitigation is effectively considered by the courts as a demonstration of 'genuine' remorse, which had a greater mitigating effect than merely standing by one's values as the previous defendant did. Similarly, the twenty-sixth defendant, Cheung Ho-sum, showed remorse and 'reflected deeply upon the effect of his acts to the society', rendering his sentence to be reduced to four years and 11 months' imprisonment[85] due to his genuine remorse being a factor taken into account in determining the issue of remission. Remorse plays the most significant role in mitigation, particularly because the courts consider genuine remorse as a strong factor determining whether offenders are likely to reoffend. However, it may be argued that offenders who hold a steadfast or extremely firm belief in, for example, democratic values, may be less likely to show remorse and hence be sentenced to longer terms of imprisonment. This creates a paradoxical situation where the stronger the belief in their honourable (pro-democratic) motives, the more it may hurt defendants at mitigation, a trend which is evident in this case.

6. Conclusion: a Shrinking Space for Considering Pro-Democracy Motives

Three concluding observations can be made about the sentencing of pro-democracy protesters in Hong Kong. First, there is a clear shift in judicial sentiment over time in Hong Kong towards recognizing honourable motives when sentencing pro-democracy protesters. A more open judicial space existed before the enactment of the NSL, when the courts were more willing to entertain the idea that offenders commit offences such as civil disobedience motivated by certain political ideals and values. In certain cases, the court also acknowledged that deterrence is of little use in relation to defendants who adhere to their beliefs so strongly that no punishment would prevent reoffending.

The enactment of the NSL marked a shift in judicial attitudes, notably towards a more preventive and deterrent framework of sentencing where

[83] ibid. [210].
[84] ibid.
[85] ibid. [217].

honourable motives have less room to manoeuvre. In the post-NSL landscape, courts are more focused on the goal of preventing national security from collapsing (again) and avoiding a repeat of the violent social unrest of 2019. The overarching goal of preserving political stability in the aftermath of violent protests is a recurring theme in most judgments after 2019. This goal overshadows the consideration of political motives at sentencing and weighs heavily in the struggle to choose between proportionate versus deterrent sentences. This shift means that defendants who resile from their political beliefs and regret their offence obtain leniency at sentencing.

Second, a more theoretical point relates to how pro-democracy protesters conceive of their motivation versus how they are perceived by the courts. Defendants with pro-democratic motives, such as a belief in achieving universal suffrage and a greater rule of law for Hong Kong, often rely on their claim to enhance the moral legitimacy of their offence or to justify their actions. While the courts have been sympathetic to these motivations, they often see them as a reason to implement deterrent sentences to prevent re-offending. The court tends to contextualize these motives in relation to the disruptions and effects caused by the social unrest and apply a proportionality test to evaluate the seriousness of the conduct. Since the guidelines for sentencing protest-related cases in Hong Kong remain rooted in *Wong Chi Fung*, deterrence remains the main sentencing objective that guides outcomes of in these cases. The stronger the deterrence rationale, the weaker the effect of honourable motives at mitigation. Proportionality still influences judicial reasoning, but it operates in a framework that prioritizes prevention. The consequence is sentences of greater severity.

Finally, some cases reveal a link between strong pro-social motives and a lack of regret expressed by some defendants, which is sometimes seen as problematic for the courts. In other words, the more committed the defendants are, the more likely they are to remain active offenders. As a result, they often receive more severe sentences because of the more serious role they played, as well as their lack of genuine remorse or regret for their acts, especially if they stand by their cause. In these cases, a deterrence-based sentencing framework regards these offenders as more likely to reoffend, resulting in more serious sentences. This logic not only means that honourable motives play a negligible role in sentencing protest-related cases but may directly make their offending more serious in the eyes of the courts.

The NSL, as a Chinese legal transplant, has moved sentencing in Hong Kong away from common law traditions of recognizing defendants' moral agency as a key consideration at sentencing. While often expressing sympathy for ethical offenders, courts are bound within a legal space that leaves little room for mitigation based on honourable motive. The extent to which ethical motives will influence future sentencing decisions in Hong Kong remains uncertain.

References

Chen, Albert H.Y. 'The Hong Kong Basic Law and the Limits of Democratization Under "One Country Two Systems"'. *The International Lawyer* 50, no. 1 (2017): 69–86.

Clayton, Richard. 'Keeping a Sense of Proportion: Political Protest and the Hong Kong Courts'. *Public Law* (July 2018): 375–382.

Cross, Grenville. 'The Hong Kong Story: Evolution, Security and the Rule of Law'. *China Daily*, 2024. https://www.chinadailyhk.com/hk/article/585159. Accessed May 1, 2025.

Fu, Hualing, Carole J. Petersen, and Simon N.M. Young (eds). *National Security and Fundamental Freedoms: Hong Kong's Article 23 Under Scrutiny.* Hong Kong: Hong Kong University Press, 2005.

Hawkins, Amy, and Helen Davidson. 'International Outrage over Sentencing of 45 Pro-Democracy Activists in Hong Kong'. *The Guardian*, 19 November 2024. https://www.theguardian.com/world/2024/nov/19/international-outrage-sentencing-pro-democracy-activists-hong-kong.

Human Rights Watch. 'Hong Kong: 45 Democracy Advocates Harshly Sentenced'. 20 November 2024. https://www.hrw.org/news/2024/11/20/hong-kong-45-democracy-advocates-harshly-sentenced.

Lee, Francis L.F., Samson Yuen, Gary Tang, and Edmund W. Cheng. 'Hong Kong's Summer of Uprising: From Anti-Extradition to Anti-Authoritarian Protests'. *China Review* 19, no. 4 (2019): 1–32.

Pascoe, Daniel. 'Hong Kong's National Security Law: A Socialist Legal Transplant?' *The Chinese Journal of Comparative Law* 10, no. 1 (April 2022): 28–55.

Petersen, Carole J. 'Hong Kong's Spring of Discontent: The Rise and Fall of the National Security Bill in 2003'. In *National Security and Fundamental Freedoms: Hong Kong's Article 23 Under Scrutiny*, edited by Carole J. Petersen, Hualing Fu, and Simon N.M. Young, pp. 13–62. Hong Kong: Hong Kong University Press, 2005.

Wesley-Smith, Peter. 'Law in Hong Kong and China: The Meshing of Systems'. *The Annals of the American Academy of Political and Social Science* 547 (1996): 104–117.

Yep, Ray. '"One Country, Two Systems" and Special Administrative Regions: The Case of Hong Kong'. In *China's Local Administration: Traditions and Changes in Sub-National Hierarchy*, edited by Jae Ho Chung and Tao Chiu Lam, pp. 86–110. London: Routledge Curzon, 2009.

Young, Simon N.M. 'Hong Kong: Universal Suffrage, Constitutional Reform and the Occupy Central Protests'. *Public Law* (2015): 158–160.

List of Cases

HKSAR v Chan Ho Wun: Reasons for Sentence [2021] HKDC 1324
HKSAR v Lai Chee Ying and Others: Reasons for Sentence [2021] HKDC 457
HKSAR v Lee Cheuk-yan and Others: Reasons for Sentence [2021] HKDC 1572
HKSAR v Lui Sai Yu: Reasons for Sentence [2022] HKDC 384
HKSAR v Ng Gordon Ching Hang and Others: Reasons for Sentence [2024] HKCFI 3298

HKSAR v Ng Gordon Ching Hang and Others: Reasons for Verdict [2024] HKCFI 1468
HKSAR v Tong Ying Kit: Reasons for Sentence [2021] HKCFI 2239
HKSAR v Tai Yiu Ting and Others [2021] HKCA 630
HKSAR v Tai Yiu Ting and Others: Reasons for Sentence [2019] HKDC 450
R. v Roberts (Richard) EWCA Crim 2379; [2019] Env LR 17
Secretary for Justice v Wong Chi Fung [2018] HKCFA 4

List of Legislation

Article 1 of the Law of the People's Republic of China on Safeguarding National Security in the Hong Kong Special Administrative Region
Article 20 of the Law of the People's Republic of China on Safeguarding National Security in the Hong Kong Special Administrative Region
Article 21 of the Law of the People's Republic of China on Safeguarding National Security in the Hong Kong Special Administrative Region
Article 22 of the Law of the People's Republic of China on Safeguarding National Security in the Hong Kong Special Administrative Region
Article 23 of the Hong Kong Basic Law of the Hong Kong Special Administrative Region of the People's Republic of China
Article 24 of the Law of the People's Republic of China on Safeguarding National Security in the Hong Kong Special Administrative Region
Section 119 of the Safeguarding National Security Ordinance (Instrument A305)
Section 159A of the Crimes Ordinance (Cap. 200)
Section 159C of the Crimes Ordinance (Cap. 200)
The Fugitive Offenders and Mutual Legal Assistance in Criminal Matters Legislation (Amendment) Bill 2019

11
Sentencing Crimes of Civil Disobedience in Switzerland

Clémence Demay

1. Introduction

Civil disobedience assumes many different forms and often involves conduct which contravenes the law. As a result, courts grapple with complex issues when sentencing such conduct. Sentencing defendants for acts of civil disobedience engages both human rights law and the criminal law. These two bodies of law affect sentencing in different ways. Human rights law is engaged as the act committed falls within the scope of application of protected freedoms. With respect to the criminal law, civil disobedients invoke the so-called 'honourable nature' of their motive as a mitigation factor. This chapter explores the sentencing of what may be such 'honourably motivated' or 'human-rights-based' offences involving civil disobedience in Switzerland.

Between 2018 and 2022, Switzerland experienced a resurgence of civil disobedience campaigns (Demay 2022) alongside other forms of protest, particularly involving ecological protesters (Bluwstein et al. 2023). This trend parallels developments elsewhere in Europe, including France (Julliard 2024), Germany (Bhrem 2024; Bönnemann 2023), the UK (Hayes and MacGregor 2023; Cammiss et al. 2025), Belgium (Jadoul 2025) and Spain (Berglund 2023), as well as globally (Jones and Young 2024). The rising level of civil disobedience has also attracted increased attention from international institutions. Notably, the UN Special Rapporteur on the Aarhus Convention recently published a report on civil disobedience (Forst 2024) which included proposed guidelines for human rights-sensitive State responses to such protests (UNECE 2025; Forst 2025).

While these developments reflect renewed attention to civil disobedience, neither its practice nor theorizing about it is new (Delmas 2018; Cervera-Maral 2013). The practice goes back centuries and falls within what Tilly

Clémence Demay, *Sentencing Crimes of Civil Disobedience in Switzerland* In: *Sentencing the Ethically-Motivated Offender*. Edited by: Julian V. Roberts, Leo Zaibert, and Jesper Ryberg, Oxford University Press.
 DOI: 10.1093/9780198993025.003.0013

conceptualizes as 'Repertoires' used by social movements (2008). In recent years, it has given rise to considerable debate in criminal law and political philosophy.

No universally accepted definition of 'civil disobedience' exists (Celikates 2018; Forst 2024: 4), and the contours of its boundaries vary according to the epistemological frames of reference employed to analyse it (Demay and Loetscher 2022; Demay 2022). Still, international human rights law characterizes civil disobedience as a 'non-violent action that, while in violation of the law, is undertaken for the purpose of amplifying or otherwise assisting in the communication of a message' (OSCE/ODIHR 2020). Such acts may occur in public or private spaces (Human Rights Committee 2020: para. 6). Regarding private spaces, UN Rapporteur Clément Voule has emphasized that civil disobedience involving trespass requires careful scrutiny. Specifically, he notes that '[t]he use of trespassing offences for public assemblies carried out on the private property of individuals who object to those assemblies, or on critical infrastructure facilities, should be assessed strictly against principles of necessity and proportionality' (Voule 2021: para. 65). This position reinforces the idea that peaceful assemblies, even those that involve legal violations, must be evaluated with attention to international human rights principles, not solely through the lens of domestic criminal law.

The non-violent nature of civil disobedience invokes broader protections under international law, particularly the rights to freedom of peaceful association and assembly guaranteed by Article 11 of the European Convention on Human Rights (ECHR) and Article 21 of the International Covenant on Civil and Political Rights (ICCPR). As the Organization for Security and Co-operation in Europe (OSCE) notes:

> The term 'peaceful' should be interpreted to include conduct that may annoy or give offence to individuals or groups opposed to the ideas or claims that the assembly is seeking to promote.... An assembly can be 'peaceful' even if it is 'unlawful' under domestic law. In this regard, it is especially important to emphasise that the concept of 'peaceful' may include conduct that temporarily hinders, impedes or obstructs the activities of third parties, for example, by temporarily blocking traffic. (OSCE/ODIHR 2020: paras 47–48)

On the other hand, non-peaceful assemblies involving the use 'of physical force against others that is likely to result in injury or death, or serious damage to property' are not granted protection (Human Rights Committee 2020: para. 16).

In legal doctrine, civil disobedience falls within the traditional scope of freedom of expression and of association (Voule 2021: para. 60; Forst 2024 and 2025; OSCE/ODIHR 2020). This perspective aligns with political-theoretical accounts emphasizing its civic and democratic nature. Such acts are marked not merely by their non-violence, but by their orientation toward democratic engagement—even when they result in public disorder. These characteristics also distinguish civil disobedience from vandalism and other actions aiming to overthrow a political regime. Civil disobedience also differs from conscientious objection: the latter seeks exemption from the law rather than any general revision.

The democratic character of civil disobedience is nonetheless frequently criticized by those who seek to portray it as incompatible with the rule of law. This view regards acts of protest not as a legitimate, fundamentally protected political expression, but as crime. Cervera-Marzal (2013) and Delmas (2018) criticize this effort to delegitimize civil disobedience, arguing that it is based on four conservative assumptions,[1] each of which can be countered by a democratic theory of civil disobedience that affirms the legitimacy of civil disobedience within constitutional democracies.

Thus, the German philosopher Jürgen Habermas views civil disobedience as rooted in constitutional values (Habermas 1985: 101). Drawing on liberal democratic theory, John Rawls (1971) also conceives civil disobedience as a public, nonviolent and politically conscientious act, undertaken to changes laws or state policies (ibid. para. 55). It aims to call attention to severe injustice in a society that professes a commitment to equality and liberty (ibid. para. 11). Hannah Arendt (1972: 107–109), in contrast, embraces a more confrontational and dialogic vision, highlighting the political and dialogic nature of civil disobedience. For Arendt, such acts are not merely responses to legal or moral wrongs, but expressions of a collective desire to reform societal values.

In line with this theorization and the human rights-based approach to civil disobedience, the following definition is proposed: civil disobedience is an act pursued publicly, non-violently, and in the interest of a wider community (Demay 2022). It is not motivated by personal gain and simply challenges existing law. It is marked by civility and a constellation of features that underscore its democratic legitimacy. This civility is also necessary for the act to qualify as non-violent; the civil disobedience should not physically harm anyone. The

[1] These being: that civil disobedience is a challenge to majority rule; that it generates social disorder; that it is a challenge to the rule of law, and that it cannot be considered democratic if its perpetrators seek to avoid punishment for their act.

non-violence must be understood broadly: mere disruption caused by the offence or potential infringement in one's right cannot exclude an act from being classified as civil disobedience. The publicity dimension refers to two elements: both the fact that the reasons for committing the act of civil disobedience are communicated to the public and that the action is carried out by people who agree to identify themselves. When judges are faced with cases that meet these criteria for defining civil disobedience, political philosophers argue that they should mitigate sentence, as these acts respond to a particular democratic dynamic that justifies mitigation.

Civil disobedience challenges the existing legal order. When the law is violated, criminal courts must act. Citizens become civil disobedients to express their concerns about the need for new laws or political change. In response, criminal courts must determine whether these acts warrant punishment, and if so—what sentence is appropriate. In the present context, the specific questions addressed in this volume and this chapter are whether offenders convicted of crimes arising out of acts of civil disobedience deserve mitigation at sentencing, and which would legal arguments justify such treatment.

Judicial responses to crimes arising from civil disobedience vary widely, reflecting judicial discomfort with the political nature of these acts (Demay 2022; Demay and Krahenbühl 2023; Cammiss et al. 2025). Each judge's analysis is filtered through their interpretations of legal categories such as freedom of expression, freedom of assembly, or the 'necessity defence' and the 'honourable motive' in criminal law. Using their discretion, judges distinguish acts they perceive as justified from those they view as merely unlawful. Despite defendants' appeals to their fundamental rights, the prevailing trend in European courts is to convict activists (Bluwstein et al. 2023; Perrin 2024; Cammiss et al. 2025). The trend is the same when it comes to accepting the necessity defence (Mazzotti 2024).

In this context, in Switzerland, the moral and political motivations underlying civil disobedience are considered at sentencing when judges examine the 'honourable motive' argument advanced by activists. Activists often plead that the 'honourable motivations' behind their actions—seeking to denounce injustice, for example—should be considered at sentencing. Under the legal definition of this term, political motivations are not considered honourable; only moral or ethical motives are. 'Moral' and 'ethical' acts are interpreted as incorporating broadly shared societal values. As such, they are more worthy of sentence mitigation. By contrast, political claims are understood to serve narrower or more contested interests and should not affect judicial assessments of appropriate sentences. Yet the line between the two is both conceptually fragile and in practice difficult to draw.

2. Overview

This chapter examines how Swiss courts have employed the 'honourable motives' defence to justify mitigation at sentencing. It also critically assesses their reasoning in the light of the above human-rights principles and its implication for mitigation and conviction.

Analysis of judicial findings reveals inconsistency in the court's reference to 'honourable motive' to mitigate sanctions in cases of civil disobedience, leading to questions regarding the very applicability of the 'honourable motive' category to it. Courts are generally more inclined to find civil disobedient acts motivated by women's rights and environmental protection to be honourably rather than politically motivated. In contrast, those associated with animal rights or solidarity with migrants tend to be classified as political in nature rather than ethically-motivated. Civil disobedients claim to be acting in the name of justice, which can be interpreted as both moral or ethical and political. Courts disagree, but they rarely explain the reasons for this, instead adopting the questionable assumption that politics and morality can be clearly distinguished. Crucially, they do not explain the criteria they use to categorize some acts of civil disobedience as political and others as ethical and so mitigate or not the sanction.

In principle, more carefully justified rulings—explaining both when such motives are accepted and when they are denied—could allow the judiciary to refine its approach, generating a 'judicial dialogue' that incrementally clarifies the doctrine. In this way, courts could achieve some conceptual clarity. Meanwhile, a more principled approach already exists in European jurisprudence: the analytical framework provided by the theory of restriction to human rights, especially relating to freedom of peaceful assembly and the ECHR's argument regarding the 'general public interest debate' and its association with freedom of expression.

This chapter pursues both lines of argument. First, I demonstrate that the distinction between political and ethical is logically untenable as a justification for sentence mitigation. At the same time, I argue that the ECHR framework offers a stronger, rights-based method for assessing civil disobedience cases. Although courts rarely apply the ECHR to such cases, they could and should: the framework provides a principled, consistent, and rights-based method for determining when acts of civil disobedience cases warrant mitigation or outright dismissal. Moreover, it circumvents the conceptual and practical pitfalls of the 'honourable motive' doctrine, avoids engaging individual judges' political preferences, and is more likely to promote consistency and clarity in rulings. The chapter focuses on the 'honourable motive' strategy, not to test whether the category can validly encompass the political or moral nature of civil disobedience, but to show how any judicial attempt to do so to justify mitigation is inherently flawed. I will begin by outlining the legal origins, scope, and doctrinal treatment of 'honourable motive' in Swiss law, as a foundation for the critique that follows.

3. Sentence Reductions for Honourable Motives: The Legal Framework

Article 48 of the Swiss Criminal Code[2] states:

> The court shall reduce the sentence if: the offender acted for honourable motives; while in serious distress; under a serious threat; or at the behest of a person to whom he was duty-bound or on whom he was dependent.

In line with the broadly positivist orientation of Swiss criminal law (Viala 2011; Hurtado Pozo and Godel 2019), these circumstances are meant to be codified exceptions, with judges assessing them according to established statutory and doctrinal criteria rather than through moral or political reasoning.

4. Defining Honourable Motives

Case law defines an honourable motive as one 'to be assessed according to the ethical values recognised by the community',[3] values that must be considered 'superior' to political ones (Hurtado Pozo and Godel 2019; ATF 128 IV 53; ATF 101 IV 387), that is, 'deserving esteem, commanding consideration and

[2] Classified Compilation no. 311.00, Swiss Criminal Code of 21 December 1937 (Status as of 1 August 2025).
[3] ATF 101 IV 387. ATF stands for 'Arrêt du Tribunal fédéral' which designates the official decision of the higher Swiss federal court.

respect [and . . .] consistent with the ideas of honour and dignity'.[4] The rationale which distinguishes political and ethical values rests on concerns about arbitrariness regarding the censorship if courts engage in assessing the worth of activists' claims.

In practice, however, only vague guidelines assist judges as they assess the extent to which the motivation is political or ethical. Effectively, judges are encouraged to rely on their own intuitions when determining whether an honourable motive exists (Niggli and Wiprächtiger 2019; Dupuis et al. 2017). This is precisely where justice fails: as soon as individual judicial discretion is exercised, the judicial role shifts from applying codified criteria to personally evaluating a claim with moral criteria.

In activism cases, Swiss doctrine and case law insist that political motives and honourable motives do not overlap (Dupuis et al. 2017; ATF 101 IV 29; ATF 128 IV 53, c. 3). There is even an argument that the existence of one necessarily precludes the other (Donatsch 2018). Swiss jurisprudence has held that political motives range from altruistic idealism to self-interested opportunism. While risking personal safety to liberate others from oppression may seem admirable, courts note that not all political aims are meritorious. Hypotheticals in case law include violent acts committed to replace one oppressive regime with another, or to overthrow a democratically elected government simply because one disagrees with its policies. Accordingly, politically motivated acts cannot benefit from sentence mitigation under Article 48 of the Swiss Criminal Code.

This reasoning was articulated in a 1982 judgment that rejected sentence mitigation for activists who sabotaged an electricity line. In court, the defendants justified their action by referring to their opposition to repressive political regimes.[5] Since then, Swiss courts have consistently reaffirmed the principle that 'political' motives are distinct from 'honourable' motives in various cases ranging from pacifists[6] to animal rights defenders,[7] conscientious objectors, and anti-abortion activists.[8] By doing so, courts claim to draw a bright line: politically-motivated acts do not qualify as honourable and sanctions cannot be mitigated by invoking Article 48. Only ethically or morally motivated acts qualify as honourable. So in most cases where an activist asks for leniency because they acted to expose injustice or discrimination and wanted

[4] ATF 101 IV 387. All translations are by the author. The jurisprudence in Switzerland is published in German, Italian, or French. Official translations from one language to the other are sometimes available, but the original version always prevails.

[5] ATF 107 IV 29.

[6] ATF 112 IV 129.

[7] District Court La Côte 19 November 2020 PEl 7.024981.

[8] ATF 128 IV 53.

to raise public concern, courts have classified their motives as political rather than ethical. This logic was reaffirmed in Swiss decisions concerning civil disobedience linked to acts in solidarity with migrants,[9] workers,[10] or animals.[11] The civilly disobedient defendants were refused mitigation based on ethics or morals, yet judges often exercised discretion and found that sentences should be relatively light for other reasons (for example: young or advanced age, cooperation during the trial, clean criminal record).

5. Moral and Ethical or Merely Political? Climate and Feminist Activists Blur the Line

A detailed review of recent jurisprudence on civil disobedience cases reveals a surprising development: judges have sometimes mitigated punishment for environmental[12] and feminist defendants by framing their motives as ethical or moral—rather than political—despite acknowledging the political dimension of the conduct. This move departs from the traditional approach under Article 48 of the Swiss Criminal Code, which treats political motives as incompatible with honourable ones. It has allowed courts to treat these political activists differently from others whose motives have never been deemed to warrant mitigation for offences committed. The shift invites a critical assessment of the new prominence of 'ethical motivation' as a judicial criterion, promising deeper insights into its doctrinal and political implications.

Feminist activists were the first to benefit from this reasoning. In one case, female activists blocked a road with their bikes to protest against violence against women and gender minorities. The court mitigated sentence, finding that 'an honourable motive existed within the meaning of Article 48 . . . , i.e. women's rights'.[13] Disappointingly, the judgment offered no insight into why 'support of women's rights' qualified as an honourable motive, much less the standards by which the ethicality of this motive should be assessed. In so doing, it failed to provide the necessary clarification.

In another case, activists convicted of indecent exposure while protesting topless were praised by the judge for their peaceful conduct and for 'fighting

[9] Swiss Federal Tribunal 6B_1162/2019, 30 June 2020 and Swiss Federal Tribunal 6B_1368/2019, 13 August 2020.

[10] ATF 134 IV 216.

[11] Swiss Tribunal de police de La Côte, 20 December 2018, PE18.005962, p. 25: 'The decisive factor is the author's attitude towards the values protected by the law, to the exclusion of his political ideologies.'

[12] However, this trend varies across jurisdictions in the context of environmental activism.

[13] Vaud District Higher Court, CAPE, 14 January 2022, c. 9.5.

for the right of all' to build a 'fairer, more inclusive and more respectful' society.[14] Again, the judgment glossed over the protest's political objectives, simply asserting that the actions had an ethical or moral foundation that sustained the 'honourable motive' claim. This brief reasoning raises questions about whether judicial sympathy—or even gender stereotypes—played a role in the judgment, since such clemency has rarely been extended in similar contexts.[15] It certainly does not contribute to a systematic jurisprudence regarding honourable motives.

Environmental activism has followed a similar path. The Swiss Federal Court recognized in a road-blocking case that 'the harmful effects of climate change and the urgent need' to address them 'must be recognised as concerns of the highest respectability in today's democratic societies.'[16] In sentencing an activist who sprayed red paint on a bank's façade to denounce the financial sector's role in the climate crisis, the Court described environmental protection as 'an evolving ethical value'[17] that qualifies as 'honourable', despite its political nature, without further comment. However, mitigation was nonetheless denied in this case because the defendant refused to express remorse and indicated his intention to continue to damage property until governmental policies to tackle climate change were implemented:[18]

> That being said [. . . o]n the other hand, an honourable motive must in any case be denied when the violence of the activists' actions leads to damage or a risk of damage to the physical integrity of others. . . . It would therefore appear to be out of the question to recognise, in all circumstances, climate activists who have been convicted for their actions as having an honourable motive.[19]

This reasoning suggests an additional criterion: even where a cause is deemed honourable, mitigation may be denied if the offence involved 'violence' or even conduct which could possibly be construed as being violent. This judgment's expansive interpretation of violence, however, was not applied

[14] Lausanne District Court 7 July 2022, c. 10.

[15] See for example: ATF 129 IV 6; ATF 119 IV 301; TF, 6B_214/2011, 13 September 2011; La Côte District Court, 20 December 2018 PEl 7.024981; Neuchâtel District Court, 11 June 2021 POL.2020.689.

[16] Swiss Federal Court 6B_620/2022, 30 March 2023.

[17] Swiss Federal Court 6B_1061/2021, 9 May 2022; Swiss Federal Court TF 6S.337/1998. In this decision, the defendant (a Greenpeace activist), was recognized as having acted with an honourable motive (i.e. raising awareness on the environmental crisis) and his sentence was mitigated. The circumstances of the action were also key to the court's reasoning: the disobedience campaign in which he had participated was peaceful.

[18] UK judges seem to follow similar reasoning to exclude the relevance of activists' rationales for their actions. (See Cammiss et al. 2025 for a critique of this approach.)

[19] Swiss Federal Court 6B_620/2022, 30 March 2023.

in the feminist cases. As a result, judges end up distorting their reasoning in order to refuse mitigation, taking refuge behind an alleged distinction between violent and non-violent acts. Subsequent cases have applied this criterion, shifting the decisive factor from 'ethical/moral versus political motives' to 'non-violence versus violence'.[20] As an example of this shift, in the Federal Court judgment regarding a road blockage (discussed above), the judge held that, hypothetically, climate activists might receive mitigation if they acted to raise ecological awareness 'within a peaceful movement', but not where their actions caused or risked harm to others. The same reasoning emerged in another case where activists occupied a bridge to protest against climate inaction: alleged violence was cited to justify denying mitigation, even though the underlying motive was deemed ethical. In this case, merely causing a bus to be diverted was considered a form of violence that justifies dismissal of a claim to honourable motives. The Court found that:

> The harmful consequences of climate change and the need for action are neither disputed nor disputable. Nor can it be denied that [it is an] ethical cause . . . However, the means employed to express their concerns and claims significantly contravened legal provisions.[21]

In other words, the case law allows for a broad interpretation of 'violence' which extends to virtually all forms of public nuisance. In practice, this line of reasoning potentially denies mitigation to many acts of civil disobedience. It also disregards the human rights dimension of acts of civil disobedience. Furthermore, here too, there is no explanation of what distinguishes the case of the feminists where traffic disruptions were tolerated without discussion.

To summarize, unlike earlier jurisprudence involving migrant solidarity, workers' rights or animal rights activism, courts have treated feminist and environmental activism as morally or ethically (rather than politically) motivated, thereby permitting mitigation under Article 48. However, the judicial record is inconsistent, and the criteria for mitigation remain undefined. Outcomes depend less on coherent legal reasoning than whether a cause aligns with prevailing social values (at least insofar as the court understands them). This highlights the need for a clearer framework, either through a more reflective judicial dialogue about the criteria for mitigation, or through recourse to the rights-based approach of the ECHR. The latter would situate these cases

[20] ATF 149 IV 217; TF 6B_282/2022, 13 January 2023; 6B_145/2021; TF 6B_950/2024, 10 July 2025.
[21] Vaud District Higher Court, CAPE, 19 June 2024 Jug/2024/7 P 200.

within the broader framework of freedom of expression and peaceful assembly rather than leaving the assessment of whether the motive was honourable to individual judges to resolve.

6. Honourable Motives in Civil Disobedience Cases: a Critical Analysis

The criteria for deciding whether a perpetrator's culpability justifies mitigation remain unclear from the case law, reflecting a global trend at civil disobedience trials. The mismatch between the political motivations of acts of disobedience and the legal categories available to interpret them—such as 'honourable' versus 'political' motives—creates a fundamental tension. This tension gives the impression that judges choose outcomes without consistent safeguards, distinguishing 'honourable' acts from ordinary criminal offences and some politically motivated acts.[22] The resulting inequalities in the treatment of what is ascribed as ethical or honourable, versus political, are hard to justify doctrinally.

This practice also shows that courts bypass an important 'upstream' step: the constitutional theory of restriction of fundamental rights under Article 36 of the Swiss Constitution which directs courts to assess whether the protest was lawfully prohibited. To justify a restriction of a fundamental right, the state must demonstrate that this step is necessary in the interests of national security, public safety, or the economic well-being of the country, for the prevention of disorder or crime, for the protection of health or morals, or for the protection of the rights and freedoms of others and proportionate. In the ECHR system, these criteria are identical.

In cases of civil disobedience, the sanction imposed is considered a restriction on freedom of assembly or expression, and therefore these criteria must be met. It is particularly from the perspective of proportionality that the sanction and its severity are important in determining the admissibility of this restriction. To be proportionate, the restriction must (i) enable the public interest objective to be achieved (e.g. protecting public order), (ii) be necessary to achieve that objective, and (iii) be justified by a balancing of the public interests at stake. Such a proportionality analysis is more objective because it can be applied through relatively standardized criteria without requiring the judge to

[22] See also Cammiss et al. (2025) on the question of distinguishing protest trials from ordinary trials and on the contradiction of the separation between ethically and politically motivated offences.

evaluate the worth of political causes. Although prescribed by both the ECHR and the Swiss Constitution, this restriction test is often overlooked in civil disobedience cases, with cause-based assessments of extenuating circumstances instead imported into sentencing decisions—a practice I criticize above. If applied at the outset of the trial, these factors could provide principled reasons for declining to punish an act of civil disobedience altogether, or at least to mitigate the sanction.

These arrangements contribute to a dangerous precedent: consciously or unconsciously, judges encourage certain actions by mitigating sentences and discourage others by withholding mitigation, depending on their own political sensibilities. In practice, this undermines the prevailing doctrine that judges should refrain from evaluating the legitimacy of an offender's underlying political claims.

Indeed, freedom of expression should preclude judicial authorities from ruling on the admissibility of political claims. They should also avoid indirectly asserting the rightfulness or wrongfulness of those claims by qualifying them as 'honourable'. Simply evaluating the legitimacy of political claims, regardless of finding, opens the door to partiality and threatens the protection of minority views, a core element of freedom of expression.

Consider a controversial example. While assembling in solidarity with migrants may be considered honourable by some, marching to expel these same migrants may appear equally honourable to others. Courts justify differentiating between political and honourable motives on the basis that recognizing political motives as honourable would lead to arbitrary or inconsistent sentencing, depending on judges' political sympathies. Despite this rationale, allowing courts to separate moral or ethical (and therefore honourable) acts from political ones without articulating any clear rationale or criteria, inevitably leads to substantive assessments of the content of claims—precisely the kind of evaluation that courts seek to avoid.

Why, then, do authorities persist in applying this reasoning, especially in climate change and feminist cases? In continental legal systems—notably Switzerland, but also other states—the adage 'the law is the law'[23] applies to civil disobedience case and has a strong influence in criminal law. This adage

[23] This adage is representative of the dominant tradition of philosophy in continental legal systems, namely legal positivism. Legal positivists support the view that political motivation should not be taken into account, as law is not a political matter (Lenoble 2018; Coleman and Leiter 2010; Perrouty 2000; Troper 1994). The links between legal positivism and the legal rejection of the democratic origins of civil disobedience have been the subject of research (see Perrouty 2000; Turenne 2004; Demay 2022; Julliard 2024; Jadoul 2025).

is seen as important to translate a commitment not to question the law and respect the separation of powers. Following and strictly applying the law then becomes the evidence that judges are not questioning its political relevance and acting neutrally. Faced with civil disobedience cases, judge then encounter a paradox: while wishing to uphold the separation of law and politics, they also seek to apply the honourable motive and distinguish between 'moral' causes and 'political' causes. The 'trick' is to depoliticize certain causes by classifying them as ethical or moral rather than political, thereby fitting them into the positivist framework—at least superficially.

Such discretionary distinctions are open to criticism. By making these assessments, judges enter a field where they do not belong: evaluating the legitimacy or illegitimacy of a political cause. In doing so, they risk inserting politics into law, precisely the trap they seek to avoid. The separation mandated by the adage 'the law is the law'—excluding discussions on a law's purposes and origins—hampers nuanced reasoning and obscures the democratic significance of civil disobedience. If acts of civil disobedience were understood as addressing matters of public interest, they could be addressed as conflicts of rights rather than questions of moral worthiness. In such a framework, the balancing of competing rights and proportionality of state interference could justify leniency, without resorting to legalistic acrobatics about honourability.

We now turn to a more principled alternative: applying the theory of restriction of fundamental rights. This theory adopts an objective, principled framework that focuses on the justifiability of state restrictions or sanctions rather than the ethical or political motives of the defendant. It recognizes protected acts without engaging in discretionary moral or political evaluations at sentencing, while still leaving space for judicial consideration of these principles. Where restrictions on fundamental rights are disproportionate or unjustified, no punishment should be imposed, rendering debates over 'honourable' motives unnecessary.

7. A Human Rights-Based Approach

To avoid the pitfalls outlined above while recognizing the democratic nature of civil disobedience, an approach grounded in fundamental rights is required—one that rids itself of the problematic notion of 'honourable motives'. When citizens gather peacefully and engage in civil disobedience as an exercise of freedom of expression or assembly, their action should not be punished. Punishment is justified only when an act exceeds the permissible bounds of these freedoms, in light of permissible restrictions of fundamental rights (Mégret 2009; Demay 2022). In such cases, leniency through mitigation is the key to reconciling the protected nature of expression with the sanction imposed. This reasoning aligns with the approach developed by the European Court of Human Rights (ECtHR). Under Article 10 ECHR, the ECtHR evaluates whether acts of civil disobedience 'contribut[e] to a debate of public interest', particularly where freedom of expression must be balanced against other individual rights—and which may justify certain restrictions on freedom of expression (Roets 2019; Pin 2022). According to the ECtHR, an act of civil disobedience contributes if it raises issues of particular societal importance.[24] The justification is grounded in Article 10 of the European Convention on Human Rights (Besse 2018; Besse 2021).

Besse (2018; 2021) argues that offences relate to public-interest debates when they concern and contribute to matters such as public administration, policing, urban planning, the contestation or preservation of historical narratives, public health, or religion. The issues must be of interest to a broadly defined academic, regional, or national public, and media coverage is a useful indicator of public interest. Importantly, courts—not protesters—determine an act's contribution (Besse 2018; Besse 2021). When this criterion is met, freedom of expression may take precedence over competing rights, rendering otherwise unlawful acts permissible to the extent they serve an expressive purpose (Genton and Favrod-Coune 2022).

While the ECtHR initially reserved the application of the public-interest debate criterion in Article 10 ECHR to journalistic expression, its scope has recently been extended to other types of expression in the public interest, particularly relating to freedom of assembly and peaceful protests.[25] In these contexts, the peaceful character of a demonstration and the proportionality of the restrictions also play important roles when considering whether a punishment should be imposed. Thus, the acts are analysed through the prisms of both frameworks (Arts 10 and 11 ECHR).

Some recent ECtHR cases illustrate the application of the public interest debate criterion and the assessment of permissible restrictions on peaceful protest. They reveal how this criterion affects the sanction imposed. They also

[24] European Court of Human Rights 2022, para. 145. See especially: ECtHR, *Wingrove v United Kingdom* App. no. 19983/92, 24 February 1997, para. 58; ECtHR, *Satakunnan Markkinapörssi Oy et Satamedia Oy v Finland* App. no. 931/13, 27 June 2017, para. 165.

[25] ECtHR, *Baldassi v France* App. no. 15271/16, 11 June 2020; ECtHR, *Bumbes v Romania* App. no. 18079/15, 3 May 2022; ECtHR, *Nemytov and others v Russia* App. no. 1257/21 and 2 others, 27 May 2025; ECtHR, *Bogay and others v Ukraine* App. no. 38283/18, 3 April 2025; ECtHR, *Novaya Gazeta and others v Russia* App. no. 11884/22 and 161 others, 11 February 2025; ECtHR, *Mortensen v Denmark* App. no. 16756/24, 21 October 2025.

draw a line as to when a state must mitigate sentence to meet its obligation to safeguard freedom of expression. One notable series, collectively known as 'Macron's hangers-off', concerned French activists who had stolen official Presidential portraits from various town halls to draw attention to global warming and France's inadequate greenhouse gas reduction policies. The national courts have issued divergent rulings: some acquitted activists, recognizing their actions as 'political protest' covered by the freedoms of expression and assembly, while others found them guilty. Some of the activists who were found guilty appealed to Strasbourg.[26] The Court held in its ruling *Ludes and others v France* that these actions contributed to a debate of public interest[27] and confirmed that they fell within the scope of Articles 10 and 11 ECHR.[28] Importantly, while the Court affirmed the expressive dimensions of the acts,[29] it concluded that the punishment imposed by the national courts remained within the limits of the authorized restriction of their freedom, which involved suspended fines of between EUR 200 and EUR 500. The justification was that the activists had not returned the portraits; had they done so, the proportionality of the sanctions might have been called into question.[30]

A second illustrative set of cases concerns the expressive dimension of actions led by the 'Femen' movement in France. In one, a Femen activist at the Grévin Museum removed her shirt, revealing a political message denouncing authoritarianism on her torso and symbolically stabbed a wax statue of President Vladimir Putin. Prosecuted for exhibitionism and property damage, the French court held that it was not proportionate to punish such an expressive action contributing to a general interest debate and that imposing a penalty—even a lenient or administrative one—would constitute disproportionate interference with her right to freedom of expression, as the act contributed to a public interest debate.[31]

This reasoning was reinforced in the ECtHR decision in *Bouton v France*, which concerned another Femen activist who demonstrated in favour of

[26] ECtHR, *Ludes et autres v France* App. nos 40899/22, 41621/22, and 42956/22, 3 July 2025.

[27] ibid., para. 97. See also: ECtHR, *Verein KlimaSeniorinnen Schweiz et autres* App. no. 53600/20, 9 April 2024, para. 410: 'it's one "of the most pressing issue of the century"'.

[28] This approach is consistent with ECtHR, *Mamère v France* App. no. 12697/03, para 20; ECtHR, *Association Burestop 55 et autres v France* App. nos 56176/18 and 5 others, 1 July 2021, para. 87; ECtHR *Bumbes v Romania* App. no. 18079/15, 3 May 2022.

[29] ECtHR, *Ludes et autres v France* App. nos 40899/22, 41621/22, and 42956/22, 3 July 2025, para. 110.

[30] ibid., para. 113.

[31] Cour de cassation du 26 février 2020, n°19-81-827. The ECtHR ruling in *Mariya and others v Russia* App. no. 38004/12, 17 July 2017, shares thematic similarities, but provides a contrasting outcome. Although the ECtHR recognized the expressive nature of the act, it ultimately found that a fair balance had not been struck between the applicants' expressive rights and the rights of others. The French courts in *Bouton* drew on this jurisprudence while arriving at a different outcome.

abortion rights while topless in a church.[32] In both cases, courts found that the expressive dimension outweighed the potentially offensive or unlawful aspects of the acts, and no punishment was imposed. Crucially, both judgments emphasized the contribution of the protests to public debates on matters of general interest—women's rights—and recognized that expressive acts can justify leniency at sentencing without reference to the protestor's motive.

Finally, in *Bumbes v Romania*, the ECtHR considered an environmental activist who handcuffed himself to a barrier at a mining site. The Court held that the illegal nature of the demonstration did not justify punishing him for an essentially expressive and peaceful act, and underscored his protections under Articles 10 and 11 ECHR,[33] stressing that 'the imposition of a punishment, administrative or otherwise, however lenient, on the author of an expression that qualifies as political can have an undesirable chilling effect on public speech'.[34] By doing so, the judgment reaffirmed the importance of protecting peaceful political protest in a democracy, including acts of civil disobedience.

Taken together, these cases illustrate that acts of civil disobedience can be understood as expressive acts, protected by Articles 10 and 11 of the ECHR. Beyond that, when evaluated through the lens of general interest and proportionality, these freedoms may, in certain circumstances, exculpate or mitigate sentence for otherwise unlawful acts. By focusing on the stakes and context of expression, rather than on the honourable nature of motives, this approach reduces judicial discretion, ensures greater doctrinal consistency and fairness, and respects the inherently political nature of civil disobedience. If sanctions are applied, they should be proportionate, reflecting the balance between public interest and individual rights.

8. Summary and Conclusion

To sum up, the democratic nature of civil disobedience calls for mitigation at sentencing. Civil disobedience falls within the traditional scope of freedom of

[32] ECtHR, *Bouton v France* App. no. 22636/19, 13 October 2022, para. 48: 'the Court considers . . . that, having regard to its activist nature, the applicant's action, which sought to express her political convictions, in line with the positions defended by the Femen movement in the name of which she was acting, must be regarded as a "performance" falling within the scope of Article 10. The purpose of the applicant's topless *mise en scene*, was thus to convey, in a place of worship, a message relating to a public and societal debate on the Catholic Church's position on a sensitive and controversial issue, namely women's right to bodily autonomy, including the right to abortion.'

[33] ECtHR, *Bumbes v Romania* App. no. 18079/15, 3 May 2022.

[34] ibid., para. 101.

expression and of association which calls for either no sanction or a mitigated one to reflect its human rights-based nature. Thus, criminal courts should sentence civil disobedients with this in mind. In Switzerland, when mitigating sentence the courts employ the 'honourable motive' justification. The recognition of an 'honourable motive' implies drawing a line between ethically-motivated and politically-motivated acts. The case law regarding feminist activists and climate activists compared to the one regarding animal rights or workers or solidarity with migrants proves this line is blurred. The ECtHR approach to sentencing civil disobedience appears more principled. Looking at the ECtHR's case law, civil disobedience, when contributing to a public-interest debates, might be considered as the exercise of a protected freedom and therefore not punished, or at least with leniency. This approach reflects the democratic and civil nature of civil disobedience.

To conclude, when sentencing acts of civil disobedience, it is essential not to conflate distinct lines of reasoning. Reliance on the doctrine of honourable motives places the state in the position of deciding which causes are acceptable and which are not. This inevitably leads to unequal treatment between causes—and between courts—on the basis of opaque criteria and individual political preferences.

A more principled approach grounded in human rights recognizes the close link between civil disobedience and citizens' freedoms of peaceful assembly and expression. In some contexts, applying this framework may preclude any punishment. In others, a rights-based assessment—based on objective criteria like duration of the disturbance, recourse to violence, and so on—may lead to a sanction that is carefully calibrated to reflect the protected nature of the conduct. Ultimately, the 'honourable motive' doctrine is a flawed basis for sentence mitigation, and courts' reluctance to clarify its meaning or boundaries ensures that this flaw will persist. In contrast, a human rights approach offers a more coherent, democratic, and legally defensible foundation, reminding us that civil disobedience is vital to a healthy democratic society.

References

Arendt, Hannah. *Du mensonge à la violence: essais de politique contemporaine*. Paris: Calmann-Lévy, 1972.

Berglund, Oscar. 'Disruptive Protest, Civil Disobedience & Direct Action'. *Politics* 45, no. 2 (2023): 239–257.

Besse, Thomas. 'Le débat d'intérêt général: un fait justificatif conventionnel'. *Archives de politique criminelle*, no. 1 (2018): 87–97.

Besse, Thomas. 'Liberté d'expression et intérêt général: du droit spécial au droit commun'. *Droit pénal*, no. 1 (2021): 7–10.

Bluwstein, Jevgeniy, Demay, Clémence, and Benoit, Lucie. 'Ziviler Ungehorsam und Klimaprozesse in der Schweiz—worum wird an den schweizer Gerichten gekämpft? Désobéissance civile et procès climatiques en Suisse—quels combats se jouent dans les tribunaux suisses? Civil disobedience and climate trials in Switzerland—What are they fighting for in the Swiss courts?'. Report for the NGO Humanrights.ch, Bern 2023.

Bönnemann, Maxim. 'Civil Disobedience in the Climate Crisis.' *Verfassung Blog* (2023) https://verfassungsblog.de/editorial-english/.

Brehm, Johannes and Gruhl, Henri. 'Increase in Concerns About Climate Change Following Climate Strikes and Civil Disobedience in Germany'. *Nature Communications*, no. 15 (2024): 1–9.

Cammiss, Steven, Hayes, Graeme, and Doherty, Brian. 'Defending the Integrity Principle: Necessity, Remorse and Moral Consistency in the Protest Trial'. *Oxford Journal of Legal Studies* no. XX (2025): 1–29.

Celikates, Robin. 'Rethinking Civil Disobedience as a Practice of Contestation—Beyond the Liberal Paradigm'. *Constellation,* no. 23 (2018): 37–45.

Cervera-Marzal, Manuel. *Désobéir en démocratie: la pensée désobéissante de Thoreau à Martin Luther King.* Paris: les Forges de Vulcain, 2013.

Coleman, Jules L. and Leiter, Brian. 'Legal Positivism'. In *A Companion to Philosophy of Law and Legal Theory,* edited by Dennis M. Patterson, pp. 228–248. Malden: Blackwell Publishing, 2010.

Delmas, Candice. *A Duty to Resist: When Disobedience Should Be Uncivil.* Oxford: Oxford University Press, 2018.

Demay, Clémence. *Le droit face à la désobéissance civile. Quelle catégorisation pour un objet juridique non identifié?* Geneva/Bern: Schulthess, 2022.

Demay, Clémence and Krahenbühl, Mathilde. 'I don't want a child: an apolitical argument in climate change trials in Switzerland.' *Journal of Organisational Ethnography*, no. 3 (2023): 267–282.

Demay, Clémence and Loetscher, Audrey. 'Face à la crise de la non-durabilité, analyse de la réponse citoyenne au travers de la désobéissance civile.' In *Droit pénal de l'environnement,* edited by Anne-Christine Favre, Anne-Christine Fornage, and Loïc Parein, pp. 193–232. Bâle: Helbing, 2022.

Donatsch, Andreas, *Strafrecht III. Delikte gegen den Einzelnen*, 11th ed. Zurich:Schulthess, 2018.

Dupuis, Marc et al. *Petit commentaire Code Pénal.* Bâle: Helbing, 2017.

European Court of Human Rights. *Guide on Article 10 of the European Convention on Human Rights.* Strasbourg: Council of Europe, 2022.

Forst, Michel. 'State Repression of Environmental Protest and Civil Disobedience: a Major Threat to Human Rights and Democracy'. Paper by Michel Forst, UN Special Rapporteur on Environmental Defenders under the Aarhus Convention, UNECE, February 2024.

Forst, Michel. 'Guidelines on the Right to Peaceful Environmental Protest and Civil Disobedience.' Guidelines by Michel Forst, UN Special Rapporteur on Environmental Defenders under the Aarhus Convention, UNECE, October 2025.

Genton, Gaspard and Favrod-Coune, Pascal. 'Liberté d'expression et répression pénale. L'acte expressif répondant à une qualification pénale à l'aune de la jurisprudence de la Cour européenne des droits de l'homme'. *Semaine Judiciaire,* no. 8 (2022): 623–649.

Habermas, Jürgen. *Kleine politische Schriften/5, Die neue Unübersichtlichkeit.* Frankfurt-am-Main: Suhrkamp, 1985.

Hayes, Graeme and MacGregor, Sherilyn. 'Taking Political Time: Thinking Past the Emergency Timescapes of the New Climate Movements'. *South Atlantic Quarterly*, no. 122 (2023): 181–191.

Human Rights Committee. 'General comment No. 37 (2020) on the right of peaceful assembly (article 21)' UN Human Rights Committee, 2020.

Hurtado Pozo, José and Godel, Thierry. *Droit pénal général*. Zurich: Schulthess, 2019.

Jadoul, Marie. 'L'état de nécessité confronté aux actions des désobéissance civile écologiques'. *Revue de droit pénal et de criminologie*, no. 6 (2025): 363–395.

Jones, Erin and Youngs, Richard. *Civic Activists in an Intensifying Climate Crisis*. Washington DC: Carnegie Endowment for International Peace, 2024.

Juillard, Jean-Baptiste. 'Forme(s) de la contestation écologique: désobéissance civile, incivile ou violence légitime?'. *Cahiers Tocqueville des Jeunes Chercheurs*, no. 5 (2024): 30–58.

Lenoble, Jacques. 'Retour sur Droit, Mythe et Raison: comment penser l'obéissance à la loi? Sur les traces de Freud, Lefort et Castoriadis'. In *Le droit malgré tout. Hommage à François Ost*, edited by Yves Cartuyvels Yves et al., pp. 141–163. Bruxelles: Bruylant, 2018.

Mazzotti, Paolo. 'The Necessity Defence in (the Swiss) Climate Protest Cases: Democratic Contestation in the Age of Climate Activism'. European Law Journal, no. 29 (2024): 393–421.

Mégret, Frédéric. 'Civil Disobedience and International Law: Sketch for a Theoretical Argument'. *Canadian Yearbook of International Law/Annuaire canadien de droit international*, no. 46 (2009): 143–192.

Niggli, Marcel-Alexander and Wiprächtiger, Hans. *Strafrecht. Basler Kommentar*, 4th ed. Bâle: Helbing, 2019.

OSCE/ODIHR and the Venice Commission. 'Guidelines on Freedom of Peaceful Assembly'. Strasbourg/Warsaw, 2020.

Perrin, Bertrand. 'La conséquence sur la punissabilité d'une atteinte disproportionnée à un droit fondamental'. *Revue de droit suisse*, no. 143 (2024): 281–298.

Perrouty, Pierre-Arnaud. 'Légitimité du droit de désobéissance.' In *Obéir et désobéir: le citoyen face à la loi*, edited by Pierre-Arnaud Perrouty, pp. 59–75. Bruxelles: Éditions de l'Université libre de Bruxelles, 2000.

Pin, Xavier, 'Décrochage de portrait. L'état de nécessité c'est non! la démarche de protestation politique faut voir . . . '. *Revue de Science Criminelle et de Droit Pénal Comparé*, no. 4 (2022): 823–830.

Rawls, John. *A Theory of Justice*. Harvard: Harvard University Press, 1971.

Roets, Damien. 'Du vol d'un portait officiel du président de la République comme moyen de lutter contre le réchauffement climatique: « quelle justification »?'. *Recueil Dalloz*, no. 35 (2019): 1973–1978.

Tilly, Charles. *Contentious Performances*. Cambridge: Cambridge University Press, 2008.

Troper, Michel. *Pour une théorie juridique de l'État*. Paris: Presses Universitaires de France, 1994.

Turenne, Sophie. 'Judicial Responses to Civil Disobedience: A comparative Approach'. *Res Publica*, no. 10 (2004): 379–399.

UNECE. 'Guidelines on the Right to Peaceful Environmental Protest and Civil Disobedience by the UN Special Rapporteur on environmental defenders.' UNECE, October 2025.

Viala, Alexandre. Le positivisme juridique: Kelsen et l'héritage kantien, *Revue interdisciplinaire d'études juridiques*, no. 2 (2011): 95–117.

Voule, Clément. 'Exercise of the Rights to Freedom of Peaceful Assembly and of Association as Essential to Advancing Climate Justice'. Report of the Special Rapporteur on the rights to freedom of peaceful assembly and of association, United Nations, 2021.

12

Sentencing Climate Activists in Germany

A Critical Perspective

Katrin Höffler, Hauke Bock, and Tim Nicklas Wensien

1. Introduction

The increasing prevalence of civil disobedience in climate protests in Germany in recent years has sparked a debate about the appropriate criminal justice response. This chapter explores how courts have sentenced such acts in light of activists' motives and methods. We begin by situating climate protests within the broader framework of German criminal law and describing how existing offences have been applied to acts of civil disobedience. Building on this, we turn to the legal-philosophical debate on civil disobedience, tracing how scholarship has explored the tension between the rule of law and civil disobedience protests. Finally, we analyse how these theoretical and doctrinal tensions play out in practice by examining 19 recent sentencing judgments.

2. Criminal Law Assessment of Climate Protests

Any sentencing presupposes a prior judgment of criminal liability. The first step, then, is to ask how acts of civil disobedience (Chenoweth 2021) are classified under the criminal law (Bennett and Brownlee 2021; Coca-Vila 2023). The most common form of civil disobedience involves the obstruction of road traffic, often involving activists gluing themselves to the road. These disruptions constitute the offence of coercion (*Nötigung*) according to section 240 of the German Criminal Code (StGB). The statutory requirements are satisfied when a person 'by force or threat of serious harm' compels another person 'to do, acquiesce to or refrain from an act'. Criminal liability ultimately depends on whether the act is also deemed 'reprehensible' (*verwerflich*). Reprehensibility refers to the degree to which the conduct is worthy of condemnation. To assess

Katrin Höffler, Hauke Bock, and Tim Nicklas Wensien, *Sentencing Climate Activists in Germany* In: *Sentencing the Ethically-Motivated Offender*. Edited by: Julian V. Roberts, Leo Zaibert, and Jesper Ryberg, Oxford University Press.
 DOI: 10.1093/9780198993025.003.0014

this concept, it is essential to examine more closely the judicial interpretation of reprehensibility, which is closely tied to normative questions of civil disobedience and non-violent protest (Preuß 2024).

Reprehensibility is a vague legal concept which has attracted criticism for violating the legality principle, in particular the requirement of certainty (Werkmeister 2024; Kaspar 2024). The 'reprehensibility' in section 240 StGB also has roots in Nazi criminal law, where penal norms were often drafted with vague language that left wide scope for interpretation (Ambos 2019). The combination of an undefined concept of force (*Gewalt*) and the open-ended concept of reprehensibility leads to uncertainty (a violation of the German principle of legality, in particular a violation of the principle of specificity (*Bestimmtheitsgrundsatz*), Article 103 of the German constitution (*Grundgesetz*, abbreviated as GG below) regarding the risk of criminal prosecution for protesters). To safeguard the rule of law, section 240 StGB should therefore be reformed. As the following analysis will demonstrate, the current vagueness of the reprehensibility requirement can have both positive and negative consequences for climate activists.

The judicial evaluation proceeds through a tripartite framework: (1) the reprehensibility of the means of coercion, (2) the reprehensibility of the underlying motive, and (3) the proportionality between means and purpose (Homann 2023). Whether the means are blameworthy depends not only on objective criteria but also on the actor's subjective intent. The assessment of the reprehensibility of the means of coercion requires a fact-specific inquiry into the protest's circumstances: the duration and intensity of the disruption, its location and timing, the nature of the police response and public tolerance for temporary obstructions.

In assessing the reprehensibility of the coercive purpose, a central question is whether long-term political or moral objectives—such as demands for more effective climate policies—should factor into the analysis. The prevailing view in legal scholarship and jurisprudence rejects such considerations, as they would risk making criminal liability contingent on a judge's political views (BGHSt 35, 270 (276 ff.)). Following this traditional approach, only the immediate consequence—such as the deliberate disruption of traffic—can be considered.

Finally, courts must assess the proportionality between means and purpose. This requires a holistic evaluation of whether the offender's means are appropriate and not excessive in relation to the pursued aim. Although this balancing is primarily internal to the criminal law framework, it must also be interpreted in light of the broader constitutional context. This context includes the need to reconcile affected legal interests—such as the right to freedom of movement against the protesters' fundamental rights to expression and assembly under Articles 5 and 8 GG. If neither the means nor the purpose are inherently reprehensible, the analysis culminates in this holistic proportionality assessment. A particularly striking challenge within this framework concerns the potential for inconsistent outcomes: identical protests may be evaluated differently, depending on the normative orientation of the court—even though the exclusion of political motives should prevent this variability.

This issue was vividly illustrated by two divergent rulings rendered within the span of 24 hours. On 21 November 2022, a 31-year-old NGO employee was acquitted in a highly publicized decision (AG Freiburg (Breisgau), Beschl. v. 21.11.2022 – 24 Cs 450 Js 18098/22). In contrast, on the following day, a 29-year-old student teacher was convicted of coercion for the same conduct and sentenced to a fine of 40 day-fines of ten euros each (AG Freiburg (Breisgau), Urt. v. 22.11.2022 – 28 Cs 450 Js 23773/22). While the former court ruled that the conduct failed to attain the threshold of reprehensibility, the latter court reached the opposite conclusion. These contrasting outcomes underscore the discretion—and resulting legal uncertainty—arising from the application of the reprehensibility standard.

Although motives are irrelevant to the establishment of criminal liability, they are important at the sentencing stage (AG München BeckRS 2022, 43646; Kaspar 2024; Michael and Dersarkissian 2024). Under section 46 (2) StGB, courts must consider 'the motives and objectives of the offender' when determining sentence. Thus, even if climate protesters cannot evade criminal liability, their concern regarding the climate crisis should influence the nature and severity of sanction imposed. Whether such motives are regarded as legitimate political engagement or an undemocratic circumvention of democratic processes can therefore become a decisive factor at sentencing.

3. Habermas and the Legal-Philosophical Perspective on Civil Disobedience in Germany

The ambivalence of motives points beyond legal doctrine to questions about the moral legitimacy of civil disobedience and its role in democratic societies. In Germany, these questions have been most prominently explored by Jürgen Habermas, whose reflections provide a legal-philosophical perspective on civil disobedience (Habermas 1983). Habermas does not advocate legalizing such protests, warning that doing so could undermine its moral force by removing personal risk and diminishing its impact (Habermas 1983). Instead, he argues that civil disobedience must remain situated between illegality and legitimacy to retain its political and ethical impact.

For Habermas, the state's response to civil disobedience constitutes a 'test case for the rule of law' (Habermas 1883). Prosecuting such protests as ordinary crime risks what he calls 'authoritarian legalism'. Drawing on thinkers such as Rawls and Dworkin, Habermas (1983) identifies sentencing as the key to ensuring a proportionate state response. But how can legitimacy be recognized at sentencing without reducing judicial reasoning to a moral evaluation of political motives? The answer for Habermas lies within the constitutional order itself. The relevant distinction is not between ethically positive or negative motives, but between motives consistent with or opposed to constitutional values. Hence, rather than criminalizing motives, courts should distinguish between motives that align with the constitutional order and those that oppose it. Climate protection reflects a constitutionally endorsed value (Article 20a GG). While this does not legalize the act of protest, it lends legitimacy to the offender's motives which should be taken into account at sentencing. In this way, courts can avoid authoritarian legalism and move closer to passing the 'test case for the rule of law' (Habermas 1983).

4. Sentencing Protest-Related Offences

We now move to sentencing climate protesters. This section analyses 19 sentencing judgments to explore how courts have translated moral and constitutional arguments into sentencing decisions.

4.1. Criminal Law Theory and the Purposes of Punishment

A critical examination of how courts sentence climate activists requires consideration of the underlying purposes of punishment (Bennett and Brownlee 2021; Tudor and Rogers 2024). Traditionally, criminal law theory distinguishes between preventive and retributive aims: positive and negative forms of both general and special prevention on the one hand and retribution on the other (Kant 1798; Hegel 2017).

At the individual level, punishment seeks to rehabilitate. If rehabilitation is unnecessary, a custodial sentence is ruled out. In the case of climate activists, such 'resocialization' is of limited relevance. Climate activists are committed individuals who advocate for the benefit of society and the survival of humanity. Nevertheless, commentators and politicians have sought to frame these individuals as anti-social 'enemies of the state'. For example, one conservative politician described them as the 'climate Red Army Faction', referring to the political terrorists active in Germany until the late 1990s (Höffler 2022). Yet an examination of groups such as 'Last Generation' reveals that their appeals are directed at the state, urging legislators to strengthen climate protection. Thus, the state is not seen as an adversary but as a means of improving society. However, this perception may shift if the same state responds to peaceful activism with excessive punishment.

Applying Merton's theory of anomie (Merton 1938) reveals the risks of a punitive approach. A growing discrepancy between the desired goals (focusing democratic discourse on effective climate action) and the actual consequences (stigmatization and punishment) can lead to a state of anomie. This dynamic is particularly acute given that many activists have previously engaged in lawful means of protests that were politically ignored. This disregard itself risked producing a state of anomie. In this framework, frustration, caused by a perception of excessive punitiveness when sentencing coercion may transform into radicalization (Höffler 2022). Thus, a harsh judicial response at sentencing risks undermining the democratic commitment of individuals who are currently engaged in protests that urge politicians to implement more effective climate policies, a goal recognized by the German Constitutional Court (Bundesverfassungsgericht; see Höffler 2022).

Individual deterrence likewise offers little justification for punitive sentencing. Climate protesters act out of conscience, convinced of the legitimacy of their actions. From their perspective, their goal is to prevent the greatest catastrophe in human history. The threat of imprisonment or fines carries little weight compared to the existential threat of the climate crisis. While some believe this problem has been exaggerated, it is supported by scientific research (Forster et al. 2024; Lynas et al. 2021). There is also no evidence for a general deterrent effect (as suggested by the German Chancellor, Friedrich Merz) since the majority of the population already rejects the methods used by groups such as 'Last Generation'. The public does not need to be deterred from such conduct.

A more persuasive rationale for sentencing climate activists lies in the goal of strengthening public trust in the rule of law (Kaspar 2014). Even those sympathetic to the protesters' aims must acknowledge that a democratic state provides alternative means to influence the government. In a democracy, those seeking change should campaign in elections, participate in referenda, and build consensus through political engagement. These are the established rules. Those who do not adhere to them are subject to the same laws as anyone else who breaks the law. Maintaining public confidence in the rule of law must be preserved. At the same time, inadequate climate control policies have the potential to erode trust in the state and the legal order—particularly if excessive responses to climate protests divert attention from governmental inaction (Höffler 2023). The rule of law must therefore respond proportionately to unlawful protest, rather than making examples of individuals to demonstrate resolve (König 2023). Sentencing plays a crucial role in striking this balance. This issue will be examined in greater detail in the following sections.

4.2. Sentencing in Germany

The sentencing ranges for the criminal offences typically committed during climate protests permit the imposition of fines or custodial sentences. Imprisonment is a possible legal consequence of climate protests, provided that the relevant criminal provisions are fulfilled. The determination of the sentence depends on the objectives pursued at sentencing. As in all western jurisdictions, the imposition of the most severe sanction (imprisonment) requires particularly compelling justification. The issue of the controversial consideration of constitutionally compliant motives (*verfassungskonsensuale Fernziele*, discussed above), also applies at sentencing.

The legal basis for sentencing in Germany is set out in section 46 StGB. According to section 46(1) StGB, the culpability of the offender constitutes both the foundation—pursuant to the 'scope of discretion' or *Schuldrahmentheorie* of the Federal Court of Justice (Bundesgerichtshof, abbreviated as BGH below) and the limits of sentencing (BGHSt 28, 318, 319; BGH StV 1983, 18, 19; BGH, wistra 1984, 177, 178). Section 46(2) StGB enumerates both aggravating and mitigating considerations. Once the statutory penalty range of the relevant offence is established, the court must determine sentence within this range (BGHSt 7, 28, 32). At this stage, the relationship between the theories of sentencing and their objectives must be clarified and the different weightings and interdependencies taken into account.

Imprisonment of one to six months is permitted only where necessary for preventive purposes (section 47(1) German Criminal Code (StGB)), and preventive justifications for incarceration are particularly difficult to establish (for example BGH, NStZ 2024, 476 Rn. 4). This creates tension between the relatively minor nature of many climate protest offences—committed by otherwise law-abiding individuals—and the imposition of imprisonment. Even in the range of six months to one year, it is possible for a court to substitute a fine of 180 to 360 day-fines. In this range, however, fines are less likely. Here the imposition of a custodial sentence no longer requires an explicit preventive justification. However, this penalty still risks being disproportionate in light of the typically low seriousness of these offences and the adverse effects of incarceration on the prisoner.

For sentences ranging from one to two years, substitution by fine is only permissible in cases of aggregated sentencing, rendering fines generally unavailable. Beyond this point, custodial sentences are the only legally permissible sanction. To conclude, the imprisonment of climate activists requires either the questionable pursuit of preventive aims (in the lower sentencing range) or the attribution of significantly elevated culpability (in the mid-to-upper sentencing ranges).

5. Analysis of Sentencing Judgments

When sentencing climate activists, courts confront a tension between the constitutionally protected aim of climate protection and the necessity of upholding the rule of law. Sentencing decisions are based on sections 46 et seq. StGB which require consideration of both offender-related and offence-related factors. Within this framework, courts assess arguments in mitigation and aggravation of sentence. In order to shed light on the sentencing in cases of climate protests, we analysed a small number of judgments (regarding the 'Last Generation'). Few judgments involving prison sentences have been published. We therefore analysed unpublished judgments in which custodial sentences were imposed. We collected all relevant unpublished judgments to which we were able to gain access.

In total, 19 judgments were analysed, containing information on the convictions of 30 individuals (in some cases, the information relating to the individuals was redacted, meaning only limited analysis was possible). Of these, 18 were issued by courts of first instance (Amtsgerichte), and one by a district court (Landgericht). Consequently, some of the judgments may not yet be final as appeals may still be pending. However, this does not undermine the analysis of sentencing considerations. The offences were committed between January 2022 and May 2024, and the convictions recorded between April 2023 and April 2025.

For the purpose of this chapter, we focused on the reasons for sentencing relating to each offender. Aggravating and mitigating factors were assigned to four categories: (1) personal circumstances, (2) motivation and objectives, (3) the context of the offence, and (4) the criminal act. Within these categories, factors mitigate or aggravate. The arguments advanced in the judgments were then assigned to the respective categories. This does not constitute a quantitative analysis: each aggravating or mitigating factor was only recorded once in the relevant category. This resulted in a comprehensive overview of the sentencing considerations as articulated in the judgments.

Considering the dataset comprised only cases in which custodial sentences were imposed, it is no surprise that aggravating factors predominate. The focus of the analysis is therefore on identifying the reasons that led to the imposition of custodial sentences for relatively minor offences arising from climate protests. The youngest individual sentenced to a custodial term was 22 years old, the oldest 68. Accordingly, their personal circumstances varied significantly: some were students, others employed, unemployed, or retired. The shortest unsuspended custodial sentence was two months, the longest 22 months (this case involved 40 offences). The majority of custodial sentences were seven months or less. Suspended custodial sentences were evenly distributed from three to eight months.

5.1. Legal Principles: Sentencing for Climate Protesters

As noted, the BGH adheres to the *Schuldrahmentheorie* whereby the degree of culpability establishes both the upper limit and—at least indirectly—the appropriate form of punishment. Where criminal liability has only marginally been established, this strongly suggests a low level of culpability. This determination does not rest on complex doctrinal questions but rather the fundamental issue of whether the conduct falls within the protective scope of the relevant criminal provisions. From a strictly retributive standpoint, the imposition of imprisonment under such conditions appears untenable.

One must also bear in mind that the protesters—in addition to addressing and protecting the climate, a constitutionally accepted goal of action—also invoke the freedom of assembly and freedom of expression (Articles 5(1) and 8(1) GG), albeit in the form of civil disobedience (Weinstock 2016; Welchman 2022) which is precisely what makes this a special area of legal tension. This characteristic should, in any case, be regarded as a mitigating—rather than aggravating—factor in sentencing (Michael and Dersarkissian 2024; Tudor and Rogers 2024; Rönnau 2023). Nevertheless, should the culpability framework in principle permit imprisonment, such a sentence must also be evaluated in light of its preventive utility. As discussed, the necessity of preventive incarceration in this context is, at best, highly questionable. It remains unclear why a monetary fine would not suffice under these circumstances.

A transition from fine to custodial sentence at the lower end of the sentencing scale can only be justified if it is evident that a fine would fail to deter or rehabilitate. However, given that offences associated with climate protests typically entail relatively low culpability, only short-term imprisonment could be considered proportionate. Moreover, the more intrusive nature of imprisonment demands a corresponding reduction in sentence severity when compared to fines, due to the increased burden placed on the individual.

Custodial sentences are particularly defensible in cases where the offender acknowledges—or where it is otherwise evident—that a fine would be ineffective. Escalating to imprisonment solely on the basis of a prior conviction or a general risk of reoffending is, by contrast, premature if a larger fine would deter (Bruns and Güntge 2019). It would be more appropriate to think about other reactions outside the StGB: One could say that if the state were to pursue a good climate protection policy, this would also be the best 'criminal policy' for preventing climate protests involving mostly minor crimes (Höffler 2023). To integrate protesters into its efforts to protect the climate, the state needs to engage with these people. The state should ask them how they can work collaboratively to address global warming. In this way, the anomic state in which the activists find themselves would recede. After all, the climate movement has employed legal forms of protest for many years and only recently switched to 'peaceful resistance' in recognition that there is now less time to act. Accordingly, the only justification for imposing imprisonment in the context of climate protest is when a fine is insufficient. This highlights the limitations of a binary sanctioning system and the need for more flexible penalty structures that go beyond the dichotomy of fines and imprisonment (Wensien, forthcoming).

5.2. Use of Imprisonment in Cases of Unlawful Climate Protests

Repeated offending combined with a lack of remorse on the part of the perpetrator can lead to the imposition of short prison sentences for protest-related offences. In the judgments, all cases resulted in imprisonment. In our view, the distinction between constitutionally-aligned and non-aligned motives was assigned insufficient weight. Had it been weighted appropriately, a fine rather than imprisonment may have been imposed. The following section analyses the mitigating and aggravating factors that nevertheless resulted in a term of custody.

a) Mitigating factors

(1) Absence of prior convictions and confession (as part of Vorleben, *§ 46 Abs. 2 Part 5 StGB)*

The absence of relevant prior convictions is normally regarded as a mitigating factor. This also applies in cases where multiple offences are adjudicated in a single proceeding, but there has been no previous conviction. Legislators and courts consider prior law-abiding behaviour indicative of a positive prognosis. Where this is accompanied by a full acceptance of guilt by the defendant, this should mitigate sentence. A confession may reduce the need for extensive evidentiary proceedings and is interpreted as a sign of remorse and acceptance of responsibility.[1] Both positively influence the sentencing decision, including the question of whether to suspend a custodial sentence under section 56 StGB.

(2) Altruistically motivated offences

Where an offence is not committed out of self-interest or for material gain but instead arises from deeply held convictions, this mitigates—especially when it relates to ethically significant objectives (see the intention of § 46 Abs. 2 Part 2 StGB). Actions motivated by a genuine commitment to the common good—such as the protection of the climate—may be classified as altruistic rather than egoistic. Although the conduct remains unlawful, the ethical intent serves to mitigate, particularly where it relates to constitutionally-enshrined values such as those set out in Article 20a GG.

(3) Contextual consideration: environmental and climate protection

The societal relevance of the offender's motive may also mitigate sentence. This aspect addresses the societal legitimacy of the offender's perceived moral or altruistic objective. Judicial reasoning increasingly acknowledges that the climate crisis constitutes a global challenge (e.g., 'It is beyond dispute that the global warming caused by resource consumption and emissions represents an existential threat to humanity', AG Erding 07.04.2025). Where the protest remains

[1] Although German law does not recognize a guilty plea, defendants may acknowledge responsibility through a confession. This step abridges the criminal proceedings and generally results in a more lenient sentence.

non-violent, causes no lasting damage, and is conducted in co-operation with authorities (e.g. by vacating sites upon police instruction), this may reduce the harmful consequences of the act. The peaceful nature of civil disobedience and its intention to raise awareness of a real threat may be treated as a mitigating factor.

This approach stands in marked contrast to the negatively assessed factor of 'disregard for the legal order', which is discussed subsequently. Protests involving criminal acts but lacking socially recognized legitimacy (e.g. the blockade of a refugee shelter, for racist reasons) are addressed in § 46 Abs. 2 group 1 StGB and punished more severely despite the similarity of method and consequences. However, in cases where many aggravating factors are present, the offender's motive plays a diminished role. In these cases, even a motive explicitly regarded as morally commendable by the judge appears insufficient to prevent the imposition of a severe sentence.

(4) Capacity for insight and social prognosis

If the accused demonstrates insight into the wrongdoing of their conduct and credibly commits to comply with the law in future, this can significantly mitigate sentence (it addresses special prevention aspects, § 46 (1) 2 StGB). This circumstance may justify the imposition of a fine rather than a custodial sentence or permit a suspended sentence where the offence would otherwise warrant imprisonment.

The analysis suggests that individuals strongly committed to their cause, and who persist, are less likely to commit to refraining from further unlawful protests. As all cases analysed involved custodial sentences, this mitigating factor was seldom applied and mainly in relation to co-defendants sentenced to fines or where a suspended sentence was imposed despite additional aggravating elements. One judgment explicitly states: 'The court does not regard the accused as unteachable in the sense of abandoning climate activism. On the contrary: engaging in climate protection is a constitutionally recognised concern (Article 20a GG), and a strong commitment to this cause is undoubtedly lawful—arguably even imperative in light of the threats posed by climate change. Rather, the accused's incorrigibility lies in his unwillingness to pursue future activism within the bounds of the law.' (AG Heidelberg 19.10.2023).

b) Aggravating factors

(1) Substantial damage and multiple affected legal interests

Causing considerable financial harm is a significant aggravating factor. (For example, when the protests trigger increased operational costs, clean-up efforts, traffic disruption, or property damage.) Aggravation is further compounded when multiple legal interests are infringed, e.g. when a road blockade not only obstructs public traffic but also impedes emergency services or endangers third parties. Harm to the public—especially where health is concerned, such as medical emergencies—is given particular weight. This factor is most prevalent when multiple criminal provisions are breached during the same protest.

(2) Reoffending and speed of recidivism (as part of Vorleben, *§ 46 (2) Part 5 StGB)*

The courts frequently refer to the rapid recurrence of offences as an aggravating element—termed 'accelerated recidivism' (AG Heilbronn 14.04.2023). Where further protest-related offences are committed despite pending proceedings, previous fines, or even suspended sentences, this is viewed as clear evidence of recalcitrance on the part of the offender. In such circumstances, it is assumed that more lenient sanctions have proven ineffective: 'Given the high rate of recidivism and the demonstrated disregard for the legal order, a fine is no longer adequate to influence the accused' (AG Passau, 10.12.2024). A refusal to respond to previous sanctions and an explicit ejection of the legal consequences can result in custodial sentences without suspension—even for crimes of moderate seriousness.

(3) Lack of remorse and declaration of future offences

Where defendants openly declare their intention to continue offending regardless of criminal liability, this is ascribed to their antisocial character: 'The defendants, by their own stated motives and goals . . . consciously choose to break the law and infringe upon others' rights to draw attention and pursue political objectives. While their concern for the climate crisis is commendable, this cannot justify a self-authorised breach of the law.' (AG Erding, 07.04.2025.) Unlike general recidivism, here the court does not wait for another offence to be committed but treats the declaration alone as evidence of a continued and culpable disregard for the law. Courts see this as not only a refusal to reintegrate but also as a potential threat to the community. In some cases, problematic justifications are made based on the offender's beliefs: 'This ideological motivation necessitates, for reasons of special prevention, the imposition of even a short custodial sentence.' (AG Erding, 07.04.2025).

(4) Degree of organization and strategic planning

Offences that are strategically coordinated and designed for maximum public impact arc deemed more serious. Where symbolic sites such as the

Brandenburg Gate, major airports, or critical infrastructure are deliberately targeted, courts recognize a highly-planned approach. If the legal process is then used as a platform for activism, courts see that the legal system is being instrumentalized and impose harsher sentences.

(5) Disregard for the rule of law

Where offences are committed repeatedly, courts often cite a disregard for constitutional principles. A democratic society offers many legitimate means of protest, including demonstrations, petitions, letters to politicians and so forth. Declining these avenues and choosing to break the law is seen as challenging the state's monopoly on the use of force. As one of the courts puts it: 'Vigilantism is impermissible in a state governed by the rule of law. The law must not be dictated by the strongest, loudest, or most radical.' (AG Tiergarten, 17.07.2024.) This attitude results in harsher sentencing. Since civil disobedience inherently involves legal violations, this factor tends to be automatically aggravating—mitigated only partly by the underlying moral motive.

(6) General deterrence

Several judgments explicitly refer to general deterrence: 'Given the brazen violations of legal norms and others' rights by members of "Last Generation", a strong general preventive response is required to uphold the legal order and deter further offences.' (AG Tiergarten, 26.05.2023). This is particularly emphasized in politically-motivated actions by organized groups seeking public attention. Sentencing aims to send a clear signal to discourage imitation: 'There is a heightened need for general deterrence to prevent members, sympathisers, and imitators of "Last Generation" from engaging in similar conduct.' (AG Neubrandenburg, 20.09.2024.)

(7) Predictions of future behaviour

Following the imposition of a custodial sentence, courts often consider whether suspension with probation may be possible. In cases where only short custodial terms are imposed (e.g. three or four months) and no favourable prognosis can be established (§ 47 (1) StGB)—owing to the offender's stated intention to reoffend or indifference to sanctions—courts reject suspension. This demonstrates that conditional leniency is unavailable to those without remorse or who openly reject judicial authority: As one judgment noted, citing a defendant: 'No sentence will stop me from continuing these offences; fines are meaningless to me – they just join a pile of unpaid bills.' (AG Heilbronn, 14.04.2023.)

6. Discussion

These sentencing decisions require closer examination. With regard to mitigating circumstances, it is unclear whether the absence of prior convictions was adequately taken into account. As noted, the lack of prior crimes should mitigate even in cases of multiple offending. However, it appears that if a single judgment combines the sentencing decisions for multiple offences, this overrides the defendant's previously clean record—contrary to the requirements of the law. The aggravating sentencing factors identified in these cases also require critical reflection. Can they justify the imposition of custodial sentences? This use is questionable in light of prohibitions against double counting of factors (*Doppelverwertungsverbot*) and where the special additional requirements for imposing short-term prison sentences under section 47 StGB are not fulfilled.

The prohibition on double counting stipulates that circumstances constituting elements of the offence may not additionally be taken into account as aggravating factors at sentencing. However, the analysis of the judgments reveals that courts often refer to the choice of road blockades as a means of advancing one's own political views in order to establish the reprehensibility (*Verwerflichkeit*) element of the offence. This choice of protest is framed as violating the norms of democratic discourse and as an attempt to impose views on society. Yet if this reasoning already serves to establish the offence itself, it must not also be invoked to justify a harsher sentence (Höffler et al. 2025). An element of the offence cannot simultaneously serve as an aggravating factor; it is effectively 'baked into' the offence definition, yet this happens in many cases.

With regard to the harms caused and the protected legal interests, it must also be taken into account that demonstrations—as a form of collective expression—inevitably result in certain public costs such as those for emergency services, clean-up efforts, or traffic disruptions. These costs are, by legislative design, to be tolerated in the interest of preserving a democratic discourse. There is no evidence that the acts of civil disobedience which were the subject of these judgments generated costs exceeding those typically associated with lawful expressions of protest—raising significant doubts as to whether they may justifiably be treated as aggravating factors.

The claim that emergency services could be impeded is unconvincing. The tactics deployed by these groups typically stipulate that at least one protester remains able to facilitate passage of emergency vehicles. This was true in all the cases reviewed. It is also questionable why detailed planning of these protests serves as an aggravating factor. In many of the cases, the planning was aimed precisely at preventing harm to third parties and minimizing collateral damage. It is unclear why a carefully planned, well-defined act should result in harsher punishment than a spontaneous protest.

From the perspective of respect for the rule of law, it is troubling that courts have invoked the idea that 'the strongest must not dictate the law' as an aggravating factor in protest cases. Regardless of one's stance on the protesters' motives, it can hardly be argued that the climate movement acts from a position of strength in Germany, given prevailing public opinion and political majorities. On the contrary, the ineffectiveness of strategies such as road blocks appears to have contributed to the fact that, for instance, the 'Last Generation' has now largely abandoned such forms of protest.

Two points must be noted with regard to general deterrence as an aggravating factor. First, if criminal laws are violated (which, as shown above, is at least debatable in these cases), they must be applied equally to preserve public trust in the legal order. However, this alone does not explain why such trust can only be preserved through the imposition of custodial sentences. A confident rule-of-law state can—and arguably should—demonstrate its legitimacy by acknowledging a violation of the law while imposing only mild and proportionate sanctions. Second, this is especially true given that harsh punishments are unlikely to deter other climate activists. The very nature of committed protest actors (*Überzeugungstäter*) like climate activists is that they perceive their actions as necessary. Thus, attempts to set an example by punishing individuals harshly are unlikely to succeed. Custodial sentences, therefore, cannot be justified on grounds of general deterrence.

The sentencing in the cases reviewed reveals the inadequacy of the criminal law in addressing the underlying issue. Prison sentences are unlikely to resolve the anomic condition that motivates the acts in question, and this leaves the repressive response of the courts open to serious normative challenge. After all, the state has the alternative of fulfilling its constitutional duty under Article 20a GG as mandated by the Federal Constitutional Court (BVerfGE 157, 30), by adhering to its own climate goals. Doing so would resolve the anomic situation animating the protest without the need for repressive measures. This path is preferable not least because the exercise of state power through punishment itself requires justification (Benjamin 1965). This justification is absent when a less invasive, equally effective and constitutionally acceptable alternative is available.

7. Conclusion

This chapter has analysed a small subset of cases relating to climate protests, those resulting in a sentence of imprisonment. The vast majority of judgments involving climate activists resulted in the imposition of fines rather than imprisonment. In the cases analysed, the mitigating factors were primarily first-time offending, confessions, and demonstrable remorse. Conversely, where numerous aggravating aspects dominated—particularly repeat offending, lack of remorse and declarations of continued lawbreaking—short custodial sentences were imposed.

General deterrence emerged as a recurring preoccupation: sentences seeking not merely to sanction the individual but to deter other, potential protesters. Courts have drawn a sharp distinction between the commendable aim of climate protection and unlawful disruptions. Particularly in cases of persistent offending, courts have felt compelled to mark the boundaries of lawful protest through the imposition of custodial sanctions.

The individualized approach remains evident in the cases analysed which constitute only a small subset of the judgments rendered against climate protesters: co-defendants with differing degrees of remorse or co-operation correspondingly received very discrepant sentences. But even while acknowledging the moral or constitutional legitimacy of environmental objectives, courts consistently reaffirm the principle that neither noble intent nor ideological conviction can exculpate the defendants. This tension—between the ethical imperative to act and the legal imperative to comply with the law—provides a lens through which to view the limits of civil disobedience under the rule of law in the context of sentencing climate activists.

References

Ambos, Kai. *Nationalsozialistisches Strafrecht*. Baden-Baden: Nomos, 2019.

Benjamin, Walter. 'Zur Kritik der Gewalt'. In *Zur Kritik der Gewalt und andere Aufsätze*. Berlin: Suhrkamp, 1965.

Bennett, Christopher and Kimberley Brownlee. 'Punishment and Civil Disobedience'. In *The Cambridge Companion to Civil Disobedience*, edited by William E. Scheuerman, pp. 280–310. Cambridge: Cambridge University Press, 2021.

Bruns, Hans-Jürgen and Georg-Friedrich Güntge. *Handbuch Strafzumessung* (3rd edn). Hürth: Carl Heymanns Verlag, 2019.

Chenoweth, Erica. *Civil Resistance: What Everyone Needs to Know*. Oxford: Oxford University Press, 2021.

Coca-Vila, Ivó. 'Punishing the Last Citizens? On the Climate Necessity Defence.' *Res Publica*, (https://link.springer.com/article/10.1007/s11158-023 09642-y), 2023.

Forster, Piers M. et al. 'Indicators of Global Climate Change 2023'. In *Earth System Science Data* 16, no. 6 (2024): 2625–2658.

Habermas, Jürgen. 'Ziviler Ungehorsam—Testfall für den demokratischen Rechtsstaat' (1983). In *Ziviler Ungehorsam im Rechtsstaat* (3rd edn), edited by Peter Glotz, pp. 29–53. Berlin: Suhrkamp, 2015.

Hegel, Georg Wilhelm Friedrich. 'Grundlinien der Philosophie des Rechts'. In *Gesammelte Werke*, Band 14, edited by Klaus Grotsch, pp. 5–280. Hamburg: Meiner Verlag, 2017.

Höffler, Katrin. '"Klima-RAF" herbeireden: Radikalisierung durch Labeling und Druck'. *Verfassungsblog*, 17.11.2022.

Höffler, Katrin. 'Ziviler Ungehorsam—Testfall für den demokratischen Rechtsstaat.' *Verfassungsblog*, 25.05.2023.

Höffler, Katrin. 'Braucht es eine "Kritik der Gewalt"?' *Neue Strafrechtswissenschaft* 1, no. 4 (2024): 355–372.

Höffler, Katrin, Johannes Kaspar, Tobias Reinbacher, and Andreas Werkmeister. 'Die "Letzte Generation" als kriminelle Vereinigung?'. *Neue Kriminalpolitik* 37, no. 2 (2025): 175–193.

Homann, Vanessa. 'Heiligt der Zweck alle Mittel? – Die Strafbarkeit der "Letzten Generation" im Rahmen ihrer Klimaproteste Teil I: Einzelne Straftatbeständ'. *Juristische Arbeitsblätter* 55, no. 7 (2023): 554–558.

Kant, Immanuel. *Die Metaphysik der Sitten, Erster Teil: Metaphysische Anfangsgründe der Rechtslehre,* Allg. Anm. E zu den §§ 43–49, Akademie-Ausgabe, Band VI. Berlin, 1798.

Kaspar, Johannes. *Verhältnismäßigkeit und Grundrechtsschutz im Präventionsstrafrecht.* Baden-Baden: Nomos, 2014.

Kaspar, Johannes. 'Volle Härte oder volles Verständnis?' In: *Klimakrisenrecht*, edited by Phillip Hellwege and Daniel Wolff, pp. 165–191. Tübingen: Mohr Siebeck, 2024.

König, Stefan. 'Kurzer Prozess für Klimaaktivist:innen – Warum Strafverfahren light der falsche Weg sind'. In *Kleben und Haften – Ziviler Ungehorsam in der Klimakrise*, edited by Maxim Bönnemann, pp. 95–106. Berlin: Verfassungsbooks, 2023.

Lynas, Mark, Benjamin Z. Houlton and Simon Perry. 'Greater than 99% Consensus on Human Caused Climate Change in the Peer-Reviewed Scientific Literature'. *Environmental Research Letters* 16, no. 11 (2021): 114005.

Merton, Robert K. 'Social Structure and Anomie'. *American Sociological Review* 3, no. 5 (1938): 672–682.

Michael, Lothar and Sarah Dersarkissian. 'Verfassungsrechtliche Grenzen der Strafzumessung bei Klimaaktionismus'. *Neue Juristische Wochenschrift* 77, no. 4 (2024): 194–200.

Preuß, Tamina. 'Widerstand gegen den Rechtsstaat?' *Neue Zeitschrift für Verkehrsrecht* 37, no. 2 (2024): 61–71.

Rönnau, Thomas. 'Grundwissen – Strafrecht: Klimaaktivismus und ziviler Ungehorsam'. *Juristische Schulung* 63, no. 2 (2023): 112–115.

Tudor, Steven and Nicole Rogers. 'Climate Change and Criminal Law.' In *Becoming a Climate Conscious Lawyer*, edited by Julia Dehm, Nicole Graham, and Zoe Nay, pp. 100–131. Melbourne: La Trobe, 2024.

Weinstock, Daniel. 'How Democratic is Civil Disobedience?' *Criminal Law and Philosophy* 10, no. 4 (2016): 707–720.

Welchman, Jennifer. 'Environmental Civil Disobedience'. In *The Routledge Companion to Environmental Ethics*, edited by Benjamin Hale, Andrew Light, and Lydia Lawhon, pp. 783–793. London: Routledge, 2022.

Wensien, Tim Nicklas. *Das strafrechtliche Fahrverbot bei verkehrsunabhängigen Anlassdelikten* (forthcoming).

Werkmeister, Andreas. 'Politische Fernziele im Zusammenhang von Nötigung und Mord – zugleich zum Umgang mit Strafgesetzen nationalsozialistischer Provenienz'. In *Jahrbuch für Recht und Ethik*, p. 32. 2024 (in press).

13

Sentencing Ethical Offending in Italy

Gianmarco Bondi

1. Introduction

Countries answer the question of whether courts should mitigate sentences in cases of 'ethically motivated' offenders in different ways.[1] Italy is a jurisdiction in which the criminal law explicitly acknowledges the potential relevance of pro-social motives at sentencing. In addition to general mitigating factors, the Code includes a specific factor relating to ethical offending—described as motives of 'particular moral or social value'. In this chapter, I examine the mitigating circumstance of 'having acted for motives of particular moral or social value' under Article 62 para. 1 no. 1 of the Italian Criminal Code. I explain how the Italian model operates and how it may contribute to the broader discussion around sentence mitigation for ethically motivated offending.

2. Overview

The chapter is structured as follows. Section 3 introduces the matter. Section 4 categorizes the domains and issues in which this mitigating factor has been invoked. Sections 4.1 and 4.2 explore the relevant case law relating to this circumstance, highlighting the shortcomings in the current interpretation of this mitigating factor—principally the lack of consistency and restrictive interpretation of the provision. Section 5 advances a number of reform proposals.

[1] This chapter draws on research conducted within the framework of the Research Project 'Origins and development of the general part of criminal law in the common law systems'—PRIN 2022—CUP: F53D23003630006. Translations from Italian to English are by the author.

Gianmarco Bondi, *Sentencing Ethical Offending in Italy* In: *Sentencing the Ethically-Motivated Offender*.
Edited by: Julian V. Roberts, Leo Zaibert, and Jesper Ryberg, Oxford University Press. © Gianmarco Bondi 2026.
DOI: 10.1093/9780198993025.003.0015

3. The Mitigating Factor of 'Having Acted for Motives of Particular Moral or Social Value'

The mitigating factor of 'having acted for motives of particular moral or social value' is specified in Article 62 para. 1 no. 1 of the Italian Criminal Code. It applies to any criminal offence and permits up to a one-third reduction of the sentence. This mitigating circumstance has two parts: an objective element—the nature of the motive—and a subjective or individualized one, namely whether the crime was actually motivated by that reason (see Romano 2004: 672). The first element is more controversial than the second, as reaching consensus on which motives justify a reduced sentence is challenging (see Zaza 2002: 280).[2] Courts can consider this mitigating factor for any offence, regardless of its level of seriousness. For instance, the mitigating circumstance of ethically motivated offending is even claimed, albeit almost always unsuccessfully, in cases of terrorism and murder. However, in light of its potential breadth of application, the provision lends itself to inconsistent sentencing outcomes (see Preziosi 2013: 870).

A motive is the cause of the conduct—an impulse, instinct, or feeling that drives the individual to act (see Malinverni 1977: 287). Purpose, on the other hand, is the objective that the individual wishes to achieve (see Veneziani 2000: 6, 263). Motive can either be conscious or unconscious, whereas purpose is necessarily conscious since the act of setting goals requires deliberate reflection by the individual. Under the specific mitigating factor, positive motivation must be 'particular', or 'exceptional'. Motives are expected to go beyond merely average valuable behaviour. Scholars such as Miletti have noted that the Criminal Code's 'general mitigating factors' include those sufficient to reduce the seriousness and political significance of the crime even when they do not possess 'exceptional' moral or social value (see Miletti 2016: 200–201).[3] Furthermore, the defendant must believe that the motivation does in fact contribute to the common good (see Malinverni 1960: 87).

There are two principal forms of motives identified in the law: *moral* and *social* values. Legal scholars regard the former as ethical when they accord with the individual's principles (such as maternal love or non-violent political activism), and the latter as laudable because they are viewed favourably by the

[2] Reconciling 'objective' moral truths with 'subjective' decision-making is notoriously complex, including at the sentencing stage. For a defence of moral realism, see Moore (2010).

[3] Miletti lists the following examples of grounds for general mitigation: an injustice suffered not personally but by a friend; anger, pity, fear; political, religious, or erotic passion; the lesser gravity of the act resulting from the means used; and the abuse of rights.

community (examples include patriotism and protecting the environment; see Mantovani and Flora 2023: 426). Despite this distinction, case law suggests that in practice the two categories overlap, as both are unclear and subjective (see further below).

In an effort to distinguish between the two categories, Malinverni (1960: 87) and Nuvolone (1982: 436) suggest that 'moral' values are traditional and relatively stable. In contrast, 'social' motives are more fluid and contested, and therefore vary over time. However, this distinction appears to have lost currency. Scholars now generally consider both types of motives to be dependent upon, and informed by, the context in which the judicial decision is made (see Zaza 2002: 283). Considerations of moral or social beliefs are influenced by historical contingencies: they are evaluated according to the shared understandings of ethics and society at any given moment in time. As a consequence, both personal ethics and societal ideals evolve constantly (see Iadecola 2000: 724).[4] One example is nationalism, which no longer attracts the level of social support it had at the time of the Criminal Code's adoption in 1930 (under the Fascist regime).

Generally, a degree of congruence between the offence and the underlying motives is required for mitigation to be awarded. The conduct must not only reflect the defendant's personal reasons but must be appropriate to those motives. For instance, a 'mercy killing' executed in a manner that inflicts extreme and prolonged suffering upon the victim would not satisfy this requirement (see Pulitanò 1984: 231). The offender's motivations are also expected to be unselfish: the offender must not be a beneficiary of the crime. Regarding the subjective element, it is not enough for the individual to believe that they are pursuing a moral goal. An altruistic reason is frequently deemed necessary so that the offence is not regarded as self-serving (see Nuvolone 1982: 437). According to Mantovani and Flora (2023: 426), a community-oriented or civic-minded component is needed as well. On the other hand, Manzini (1981: 244) recognizes that egotistic reasons may still warrant mitigation if they originate from a noble and honourable impulse that is not wholly selfish. Drawing a clear line between altruism and egotism is difficult: while acting altruistically may indicate the presence of moral or social values, it cannot, on its own, be the decisive element (see Zaza 2002: 286). Certain categories of human feelings fall outside this domain; for instance, jealousy is not accepted, given its negative moral character.

[4] On the surface, this perspective might appear to contrast with the view that values in the Constitution should be considered when applying this mitigating factor.

In Supreme Court case law, the term 'particular' implies that the motives should be 'exceptional' and exceed ordinary ethical behaviour. A balancing act must be performed between the two competing interests: those underlying the motives for the crime and those harmed by it. In addition, the Court requires ethically defensible reasons to be the *sole* cause of the crime. An ethically laudable motive cannot justify mitigation if it coexists with other, undeserving motives. This combination frequently occurs in practice. (The problem of mixed or ambiguous reasons is discussed by Ryberg 2026.) Nor is it enough that the crime takes place within a broader activity loosely associated with a social benefit, such as journalism (see Zaza 2002: 287).

The Supreme Court further requires that moral motives be accepted across the entire social spectrum. Motives of social value must likewise align with the objectives of society at a given historical moment. Forms of protest involving violence are excluded (see Marinucci, Dolcini, and Gatta 2024: 703). Broadly, the key feature in the existing jurisprudence is the requirement of near-universal social approval of the reasons (see Zaza 2002: 286).

To determine whether the mitigating factor of 'motives of particular moral or social value' applies, it is necessary to distinguish between two legal concepts: the intrinsic unlawfulness of the criminal conduct and the nature of the motives that led the offender to commit the crime. Without this distinction, the two concepts collapse into one another, as the adverse impact of the crime eclipses the positive character of the motivation, precluding any reduction in sentence. This conflation also creates a logical fallacy, since it denies any differentiation between the 'wrong' in the criminal act and the 'right' in the reasons for it. Ultimately, this deprives the mitigation of both meaning and relevance, since the commission of the crime would bar any leniency relating to the offender's motives. Nevertheless, the Supreme Court's case law focuses on the illegality rather than the reasons (see Fiandaca and Musco 2024: 459–460).[5] The rationale is that any criminal conduct, being criminal, is never worthy of moral or social approval per se. Ultimately, this approach severely limits the application of this mitigating circumstance (see Marinucci, Dolcini, and Gatta 2024: 703; Mantovani and Flora 2023: 426).

The ethically motivated mitigating factor mirrors the aggravating factor of 'having acted for abject or futile motives' under Article 61 para. 1 no. 1 of the same Code, as inferred from its wording (see Pulitanò 2023: 320).[6] An 'abject'

[5] The authors note the exclusion for those who for motives of social justice employ violence. In fact, this is acknowledged in recent Supreme Court rulings, see Cass. pen. 23.4.2024, No. 16945.

[6] The mitigating circumstance is defined negatively in relation to the aggravating one. According to Manzini (1981: 244): 'It must involve motives that are not only neither abject nor futile, but inherently

motive requires reasons that are reprehensible and capable of provoking widespread public outrage (e.g., the killing of a minor solely because they refused to engage in begging). A motive is rejected as a source of mitigation when there is a clear lack of proportionality between the reason for the crime and the gravity of the offence (e.g., intentionally causing a collision that injures another driver merely because one was overtaken by them on the highway) (see Padovani 1988: 216).

4. The Principal Domains and Core Areas

The mitigating factor of 'motives of particular moral or social value' arises in many types of crime. The focus is on what motivated the person to act contrary to the criminal law, not on the nature or gravity of the crime (such as the protected legal interest or level of harm). This dynamic suggests that nearly all criminal offences may potentially be supported by individually or collectively virtuous reasons, implying a broad scope of potential application. It is therefore worth analysing the decisions (and the legal reasoning) of the courts concerning this mitigating circumstance and grouping them into general categories to draw conclusions regarding its viability in practice.

Two principal domains and four core areas emerge. The domains are the public and the private. The 'public sphere' encompasses conduct affecting fellow citizens and includes the areas of 'politics' and 'justice'. The 'politics' subset comprises acts of terrorism or subversive activity; violent or unlawful protests; hate speech (particularly fascist salutes); and conscientious objection to compulsory military service. The 'justice' subset features acts of summary justice; crimes by police officers during the course of their duties; crimes by security guards outside the bounds of legitimate self-defence; and the use of defensive devices to prevent crime, resulting in death or bodily harm.

Conversely, the 'private sphere' encompasses acts affecting familial or social relationships and includes the 'family' and 'work' areas. The 'family' subset comprises assisting the illegal immigration of a family member; false declarations regarding the civil status of a child; unlawful acquisition or retention of housing; 'culturally motivated criminal law', such as 'honour killing' or 'honour violence'; religiously motivated crime; 'mercy killing'; crimes committed (often against property or for profit) to support relatives; and violations

noble, or that otherwise evoke leniency, which make an exception, that is, to those motives that usually determine the crime in question.' For a contrasting view see Zaza (2002: 280).

of drug laws to aid family or friends. The 'work' subset features tax or environmental crimes committed to avoid bankruptcy, pay suppliers, or preserve jobs at a struggling company; and illicit medical treatments by doctors with the honourable intention of assisting patients.

4.1. The Public Domain: Politics and Justice

In recent years, many defendants have invoked the mitigating factor of 'motives of particular moral or social value' for political crimes. The Supreme Court has consistently rejected such appeals, holding that, by definition, political motives are divisive (see Trapasso 2009: 4248; Cass. pen. 24.10.2007, No. 46306). Allowing political reasons to justify mitigation would risk legitimizing any political movement in Italy, including those contrary to the Constitution (see Cass. pen. 5.2.2019, No. 27985). Furthermore, according to the Court, there is no moral or social value in using violence to pursue political aims.

In the case of the so-called 'Red Brigades' (Marxist-Leninist terrorists convicted of murder and attempted murder), the Supreme Court stated that the mitigating factor has no effect when defendants use violence (see Cass. pen. 14.5.1980, *Picchiura*).[7] The Court stressed that criminal acts, even if politically or socially motivated, cannot attract mitigation when they involve violence. Personal beliefs are insufficient proof of moral worth; in such cases the goals must correspond to values recognized by the community. In this case, the terrorists' 'ethical' motives were deemed irrelevant, since violence, according to the Court, is condemned by Italian society (see Cass. pen. 13.3.1984, *Bartoloni*). A socio-moral standard based on collective consensus is thus established, and it is clearly incompatible with terrorism (see Cass. pen. 30.1.1992, *Arbore*; Cass. pen. 16.4.2008, No. 25275).[8]

Protesters have frequently requested mitigation, including defendants in cases involving violent actions against public infrastructure (e.g., railways) or unlawful entry into buildings (e.g., to advocate for the right to housing). The Supreme Court rejected mitigation for individuals who blocked a railway

[7] See also Cass. pen. 5.10.1984, *Monaco* and Cass. pen. 7.10.1986, *Alunni*. Particularly with reference to the motive of participating in a subversive organization, see Cass. pen. 22.1.1991, *Seghetti*. On political motivation as non-universal, see Cass. pen. 1.5.1993, No. 11344.

[8] For a case concerning an international terrorist attack at an airport, see Cass. pen. 5.5.1989, *Khalil*. On the nature of such attacks—deprived of rational justification, brutal, and objectively inconsistent with the purported goals—and on their opposition to the ethical conscience of the broader community, see Cass. pen. 28.4.1988, *Othmann*.

to protest against the cost of travel (see Cass. pen. 15.12.2004, No. 2205).[9] Similarly, in a demonstration aimed at preventing the transport of military equipment from a US base in Vicenza to Pisa, the Court denied mitigation. It noted that the military base was authorized by the Italian state and supported (or at least not opposed) by the majority of the local population, given the common values and historical friendship between Italy and the United States (see Cass. pen. 29.4.2010, No. 20312).[10] Finally, in a case involving violent resistance to the eviction from a building used as a social centre, the Supreme Court again denied mitigation, observing that such acts do not enjoy societal support while the concept of private property does attract consensus (see Cass. pen. 27.11.2019, No. 15387).[11]

The Supreme Court has similarly denied mitigation in hate-speech cases, including fascist salutes and events honouring fascists (see Galluccio 2020). The Court held that sentiments of particular moral or social value cannot be confused with ideological expressions, which reflect the temporary orientation of particular groups and diverge from social consensus. The Court rejected the mitigating factor in such cases because this conduct conflicts with the constitutional principle opposing fascist ideology (see Cass. pen. 17.2.2023, No. 12049).[12]

When Italy had compulsory military service, courts addressed the mitigating factor of 'motives of particular moral or social value' in the case of conscientious objectors (see Palazzo 1979: 539; Lariccia and Tardiola 1999: 815). The Supreme Court denied mitigation in an instance where the defendant refused both military service and the civilian alternative. The defendant was deemed to be disregarding constitutionally-enshrined civic duties (including conscription; see Cass. pen. 22.3.1991, *Poli*; Cass. pen. 17.2.2005, No. 14628).

Turning to the 'justice' domain, numerous cases involve vigilantes acting out of their own view of justice rather than seeking state protection. These pleas

[9] For the 'No-TAV' movement's actions carried out against the building of a high-speed train network in the Val di Susa area (Piedmont), see Cass. pen. 27.4.2018, No. 54424 and Cass. pen. 11.12.2019, No. 19764. For an instance in which the mitigating factor was awarded—for three environmental activists sentenced for the crimes of violence and disruption of public service, together with 'generic mitigating factors', see Trib. Bologna 12.1.2024, No. 191.

[10] For an opposing view when the mitigating circumstance was applied where the defendants aimed at preventing, or at least delaying, the construction of military installations meant to host nuclear missiles and at soliciting support for the pacifist movement, see Trib. Ragusa 14.4.1984, *Barker*.

[11] For a case where resistance by violent means to avoid eviction from a social centre was deemed worthy of this mitigating factor, see Trib. Milano, 27.6.1990.

[12] On pacifist actions, see Cass. pen. 7.12.2016, No. 197. The Court denied mitigation for participants in an illegal counter-protest against a neofascist demonstration, noting the defendants' involvement in violent crimes including arson and vandalism. It emphasized that invoking values of the Italian Resistance, anti-fascism and the Constitution is irrelevant if the actions are also driven by illegitimate motives, see Cass. pen. 27.11.2008, No. 11236.

generally concern forms of extrajudicial justice. In one such case, a mother seriously injured a man and killed his wife after discovering that the man, aged 80, had committed sexual acts against her young son, with the wife failing to intervene. The Supreme Court held that this extreme reaction, although understandable, did not meet the threshold to justify the mitigation for acts of particular moral or social value. The Court acknowledged the existence of law enforcement and judicial authorities capable of promptly and legitimately punishing such crimes. Reliance on the appropriate public institutions defines a civil society (see Cass. pen. 14.7.2010, No. 29939).

The Supreme Court generally rejects requests for the mitigating factor where police officers broke the law in the course of investigations.[13] In one case, police officers themselves supplied heroin in an effort to combat drug trafficking. The Court ruled that police abuse of power or criminal conduct carries no moral or social value, even if they assist in fighting crime. Violations of the law by law enforcement are not regarded positively by the public, particularly when legal alternatives exist. However, the Court granted 'generic mitigating factors' and imposed a minimum sentence (see Cass. pen. 28.4.2004, No. 31339).

The Supreme Court has also tried cases involving private security guards acting outside the scope of their legal powers. In one case, a guard attempted to stop fleeing suspects by blocking the street and firing three shots, killing one person. Prior to the shooting, the guard had intercepted police radio communications. The Supreme Court rejected the request for mitigation. The Court stressed that the state police, and not private security personnel, were responsible for protecting the public (see Cass. pen. 1.6.2023, No. 46809).

Finally, the courts have been asked to assess the use of residential protection technologies which resulted in injury or death. In one case, a farmer had set up a system in which a rifle would automatically fire at anyone entering his sheep barn. There had been frequent thefts in the area. During an attempted burglary, the weapon killed a thief. The Latina Court of Assizes applied the mitigating factor, in view of the repeated thefts suffered by the farmer and others. The Court held that the farmer's actions were motivated primarily by a desire to protect the local community from crime, even though the conduct was violent. The evaluation was based on the conscience of the local community (see Court of Assizes of Latina 16.12.1986, *Cimini*).

[13] In an isolated example to the contrary—which evokes the so-called 'ticking-bomb scenario' (see Fornasari 2020)—police officers tortured suspects to learn where a NATO general was being held during his kidnapping by members of the Red Brigades. The Tribunal of Padua ruled in favour of mitigation for this crime (see Trib. Padova 15.7.1983, *Amore*; Pulitanò 1984: 231).

4.2. The Private Domain: Family Life and Employment Settings

The ethical offending mitigating factor frequently arises in contexts involving close personal ties. Familial, social, and professional relationships often generate emotions that can trigger criminal conduct. Committing a crime to assist a relative aligns with general perceptions of ethical conduct and therefore frequently leads to pleas for mitigation. The family is also the locus of cultural and religious identities, giving rise to requests for reduced punishment rooted in those elements.[14] In one case, the Court of Appeal of Trieste granted the mitigating circumstance for aiding the illegal immigration of a family member. The defendant met his non-EU-citizen brother at the border and drove him into Italy. The Court deemed this act worthy of some mitigation (see Court of Appeal of Trieste 20.5.2008, No. 194).

The Supreme Court has also ruled on false declarations regarding parenthood. In one case, two defendants were convicted of providing false personal details for their biological child so that he would be registered as born to an Italian citizen, thereby acquiring citizenship. The appellant argued that part of Italian society supported citizenship for children born in the country. The Supreme Court denied the mitigating factor in this case, stating that general consensus must involve the entirety—or near-entirety—of society, not just a significant minority. The Court further held that the pursuit of better living conditions is a personal aim, not a shared ethical or social value, and therefore the motive did not reflect collective opinion (see Cass. pen. 31.5.2018, No. 27746). In a different case, the Court of Appeal of Turin, in a decision upheld by the Supreme Court, granted the mitigating circumstance where a person falsely claimed paternity of a minor. The desire to provide a father to a child without one, the value placed on the social function of fatherhood, and maternal consent were found sufficiently compelling to justify mitigation (see Court of Appeal of Turin 23.5.2019, No. 3761).

Crimes relating to housing have triggered appeals under the ethical offending provision. In one case, the Supreme Court denied mitigation to a person who built a dwelling in violation of urban planning laws. The residence was solely for the benefit of the defendant's family. The Court stated that ethical conscience does not allow unlawful construction for such reasons as it harms the overriding public interest in urban planning (see Cass. pen. 28.9.1983, *Salvatore*). Violently resisting eviction has likewise failed to attract

[14] On 'culturally-motivated crimes', see Bernardi (2006). In the domestic setting in particular, see Grandi (2022).

mitigation. The Supreme Court held that such conduct cannot be accepted by reference to shared values even when the evicted person is vulnerable. The defendants' personal beliefs were insufficient, given that their unlawful conduct significantly interfered with the rights of the property owner (who had incurred considerable financial burdens, see Cass. pen. 14.7.2021, No. 299; Cass. pen. 16.12.2021, No. 2104).

Claims for mitigation for 'motives of particular moral or social value' have also emerged in cases of 'culturally motivated crimes'. Pleas relating to 'honour killings' or 'honour violence' belong to this category. Such appeals were more common in the past but have recently declined in frequency, in part because they have almost always been rejected. For example, the Supreme Court declined mitigation when the conduct, although altruistic, involved the killing of a child and the subsequent concealment of the body, driven by a desire to preserve honour and avoid public scandal. In this case, the Court refused to accept that this motive held exceptional moral or social value (see Cass. pen. 14.12.1970, *Ramazzotti*).[15] In a contrasting example, the Trapani Court of Assizes ruled that mitigation was applicable in the case of manslaughter committed by a young man who, having assumed the de facto role of 'head of his family', beat and abused his younger sister, resulting in her death. The Court of Assizes stressed that the defendant's intention was to suppress behaviour deemed immoral (see Court of Assizes of Trapani 21.10.1987, *Eliseo*).

Cultural motives also relate to religious beliefs. The Court of Assizes of Cagliari was asked to adjudicate the case of a minor who died after her parents, Jehovah's Witnesses, denied her a blood transfusion. The Court of Assizes refused mitigation in this case, deeming the religious motive irrelevant. It held that by denying the medical treatment, the parents accepted the risk of their child's death (see Court of Assizes of Cagliari 10.3.1982, *Oneda*).

Courts have examined claims for the mitigating factor in several cases of 'mercy killing' (see Girani 2024). These usually involve spouses or parents of a terminally ill person. The Supreme Court routinely opposes mitigation on this ground. In one case, a man sought a reduced sentence for killing his bedridden wife who had advanced dementia. He claimed to have acted out of despair over her condition and attempted suicide afterwards. The Supreme Court found that mitigation requires that the crime be committed in pursuit of a noble end,

[15] For the murder of a wife for not being a virgin, see Cass. pen. 27.1.1981, *Nappo* (see Volta 1989: 958), and, with reference to a 'rival', see Cass. pen. 8.2.1988, No. 12863. For the killing of a wife's lover, see Cass. pen. 30.1.1985, *Fiumaro*. For the murder of a sister's boyfriend out of opposition to the relationship between the two, where 'generic mitigating factors' were granted, see Cass. pen. 12.10.1995, No. 11043, and, for that of causing bodily harm, see Court of Appeal of Lecce 10.9.2019, No. 1101.

in accordance with the prevailing values of a specific time and place. It insisted on two points: the choice of means, especially when it involves taking a life; and the possible existence of a selfish motive. In the case at hand, the act resulted in the loss of life in order to terminate suffering, both for the victim and the defendant. It follows that, even without the aim being purely selfish, the motives for the killing clearly included an element of self-interest (see Cass. pen. 11.12.2007, No. 47039).[16]

In a case involving a woman who killed her terminally ill daughter and then attempted suicide, the Supreme Court again rejected the mitigating factor. The daughter suffered from a severe autoimmune disease that had reached its terminal stage; in a few months, it would have led to her death, accompanied by unbearable suffering. The mother had been her primary caregiver for years, but medical treatment had recently failed to alleviate the daughter's agony. The Tribunal of Pesaro initially found mitigation to be applicable (see Trib. of Pesaro 1.6.2009, No. 69),[17] but the Supreme Court overturned this decision. In view of the mother's attempt to take her own life and die alongside her daughter, the Court agreed that the defendant had not acted out of selfish motives. Nonetheless, it observed that the manner of the killing—together with the daughter's final plea—trumped the compassion evoked by other aspects of the case. It ruled that such conduct does not attract sufficient societal support (see Cass. pen. 17.11.2010, No. 43954).

So-called 'Robin Hood' crimes also trigger claims for the mitigating factor of 'motives of particular moral or social value'. These crimes are marked by a desire to help others, irrespective of any personal benefit. In a case where the defendant escaped custody to assist a sick relative, the Supreme Court ruled that the mitigating circumstance applies only where the degree of altruism and self-sacrifice exceeds that of the average person. The Court emphasized the importance of the 'exceptionality' test, stating that mitigation for moral or social value is not justified for 'unexceptional' selflessness, even when an act is motivated by a desire to provide care for an ill family member. However, the more

[16] Similarly, the Court refused to award mitigation for a husband who strangled his 88-year-old wife while she slept, despite his claim of financial hardship and lack of family support for caregiving. The Court acknowledged the burdens of caregiving but ruled that these do not constitute morally or socially valuable motives for murder and concluded that prevailing social and ethical views did not support the husband's actions. See Cass. pen. 6.7.2017, No. 7390. See also Cass. pen. 7.11.2018, No. 50378 and Cass. pen. 9.1.2019, No. 747.

[17] Another lower court decision awarded mitigation for a husband who killed his terminally ill wife by suffocating her with a pillow while she slept. She had been suffering from advanced lung cancer with brain metastases, leading to severe cognitive decline, and he had devotedly cared for her at home, honouring her wish to avoid institutionalization. His act was driven by a sense of compassionate love and a belief that ending her suffering was justified by their deep emotional bond and her deteriorating condition. See Court of Assizes of Modena 9.11.2023, *Cioni*.

general 'generic mitigating factors' were recognized, warranting some mitigation (see Cass. pen. 5.10.2005, No. 39856).[18]

The mitigating factor based on ethical conduct has also been claimed by family members or friends supporting those facing drug addiction. The Court of Appeal of Milan denied pro-social mitigation for an individual's physical attack on their addicted brother, even if the intention was to prevent him from consuming drugs. In this case, the Court found that using violence and wounding with a knife were not ethically acceptable means of resolving family or personal problems. The defendant's goals were deemed neither noble nor altruistic and not supported by the community (see Court of Appeal of Milan 23.5.2006, No. 2004). In a contrasting example, the Tribunal of Como applied this mitigating circumstance to parents who abducted their addicted daughter to prevent her from leaving home and buying drugs (see Trib. of Como 19.9.1988, *Volpe*).[19]

Shifting to the 'work subset', the following scenarios are relevant: committing tax crimes or crimes against the environment with the aim of saving a business, and illegal treatments administered by doctors for their patient's benefit. The Supreme Court intervened in the case of a company's legal representative who failed to pay the tax due for two consecutive years in an attempt to avoid bankruptcy, pay suppliers, and preserve jobs. Here, the Court affirmed that not paying taxation debts conflicts with a fundamental duty that enables the State to protect and promote fundamental rights, such as those in Article 32 (health) and Article 34 (education) of the Italian Constitution (see Cass. pen. 24.3.2023, No. 30952; Cass. pen. 22.3.2024, No. 14725).[20] Finally, the Supreme Court found that the pro-social mitigating factor was relevant for a medical doctor who prescribed drugs containing narcotics to a user, as an 'improper' maintenance therapy. The Court stressed that despite their illegal nature, the

[18] See also Court of Appeal of Lecce 27.1.2025, No. 113. For passing of counterfeit banknotes to render assistance to a sick father, see Cass. pen. 21.10.2009, No. 49674. For refusal to perform official acts, embezzlement, and falsification of a public document, committed in the exercise of her duties as court-appointed guardian of an incapacitated person in a situation of economic hardships, see Cass. pen. 11.11.2014, No. 49785. For theft by snatching to provide for a seven-year-old son, see Court of Appeal of Palermo 23.9.2015, No. 3209 and Cass. pen. 13.7.2015, No. 3967. For robbery to buy medicines for a son, see Cass. pen. 24.3.2021, No. 15595. For minor drug dealing to support the family, found to be relevant to the amount of the penalty but not for the application of this mitigation, see Court of Appeal of Naples 20.3.2023, No. 3065.

[19] In another case, the Supreme Court ruled that providing drugs to another addict, even without payment and out of altruistic motives, does not diminish the social harm of drug distribution and is therefore undeserving of mitigation. See Cass. pen. 22.3.1990, *Lucarini*.

[20] The Supreme Court reached similar conclusions with regards to pollution because of the needs of production and with the end of protecting jobs, where it concluded that the imperatives to safeguard water and the environment are themselves ingrained in primary social and moral values in modern society (see Cass. pen. 10.11.1993, No. 439).

doctor's actions had temporarily removed the patient from the trafficking network (see Cass. pen. 28.4.2004, No. 31339; Amato 2005: 2101).

4.3. Summary

This survey of recent accumulated case law has demonstrated the variability in judicial responses to claims for mitigation under the ethical offending provision. In addition, the provision has been narrowly interpreted, and as a result many offenders with a plausible claim for mitigation have been denied any such reduction in the sentence.

5. Reforming the 'Ethical Offending' provision

Considering the doctrinal and case law analysis presented, the mitigating factor of 'having acted for motives of particular moral or social value' seems unsatisfactory due to its strict requirements, which result in it being seldom awarded. In lieu of mitigation for an ethical motive, courts seem to prefer two other options: granting 'generic mitigating factors' and/or imposing the minimum punishment in the statutory range. This approach might be attributable to the difficulty in distinguishing the elements deemed necessary by the Supreme Court's decisions—namely, identifying important reasons of moral or social value that are shared by virtually every member of society, and that also constitute the sole motive, excluding any personal or self-interested considerations for the offender's actions. How might the provision be reformed to ensure more coherent application? Defining what constitutes moral or social value is inherently problematic.

First, the application of the mitigating factor should involve a balancing test. Under this approach, the pro-social motive could be recognized with a lower threshold—namely, even if it is not universally shared, provided that it is accepted by at least the majority of a specific target group. For example, a court following this rule might apply mitigation for protests organized by members of an ethnic minority seeking independence for a region of the country. Viewed through this lens, the moral or social value of the motive would be assessed not on the basis of the general population of the state but instead on that of the affected subgroup or region. Unlawful actions by an independence movement may be seen as ethically significant within the minority group, even if not wholly accepted by the broader nation, and their actions might be viewed more sympathetically based on the group's ideals of home rule.

Additionally, the mitigating factor could be justified if the pro-social motive coexists with other, less noble motives, as long as the former is found to prevail over the latter. This could be the case for 'mercy killing'. While there may be a selfish motive influencing the decision to end someone's life, judges would ascertain whether the *primary* motivation behind the act is to alleviate the victim's suffering, thereby confirming that the homicide derives mainly from compassionate reasons. For instance, a wife might end her terminally ill husband's life to stop his suffering and possibly in part because of the burden of being a caregiver. Although the act may have been partially influenced by the caregiver's personal burden, it still stems from a genuine ethical concern for the welfare of the victim.

The degree of mitigation granted should reflect the extent to which the motive of moral or social value is shared across society and its role in the offence, in a directly proportional manner. That is, the greater the alignment with community views, and the more significant the motive's influence on the actions, the greater the mitigation awarded.

Second, guidance for the interpretation of this mitigating factor should first and foremost be found in the rights and freedoms that are protected in the Constitution or constitutional acts, as well as in international human rights conventions and charters (see Marinucci, Dolcini, and Gatta 2024: 704; Padovani 2023: 318). Any motive is potentially relevant if it is compatible with the principles and values enshrined in these foundational documents. This framework would also make it possible for an individual's personal ethics to be understood as a basis for leniency, even if they are not broadly accepted within a particular segment of the community.

Reference could be made to the Italian Constitution, as well as the European Convention on Human Rights and the Charter of Fundamental Rights of the European Union. For an example of such a 'constitutional orientation', one might consider striking workers who use violent picketing to prevent access to a factory where the lack of safety measures had previously caused workplace deaths. Despite committing a crime, their motive aligns with Article 41 of the Italian Constitution which establishes respect for human safety as one of the limits to the freedom of private economic initiative (see Marinucci, Dolcini, and Gatta 2024: 704). For the "international charters' orientation', one might consider activists who disrupt operations on an industrial site to protest against environmental harm. Even though their actions are criminal in nature, they are motivated by a commitment to safeguard the environment (see Demay 2026). Environmental protection was explicitly recognized by Article 37 of the Charter of Fundamental Rights of the European Union (see Marinucci, Dolcini, and Gatta 2024: 705). Recently, the Supreme Court has adopted a similar interpretation of the mitigating circumstance, making clear that the motives must be assessed in light of the principles and social values enshrined in the Constitution, as they provide a unifying standard of judgment for the entire community (see Cass. pen. 7.3.2024, No. 26254).

6. Conclusion

The mitigating factor of 'having acted for motives of particular moral or social value' is designed to recognize ethical reasons for criminal behaviour at the sentencing stage. However, the provision is vague, and has been interpreted in an overly restrictive way, to the detriment of meritorious defendants.

The mitigating factor consists of two elements: an objective one (identification of motives of particular value, either morally or socially) and a subjective one (the actual influence of those motives in determining the criminal conduct). The former is the more ambiguous, as it requires the judge to clarify ethical standards that shift across space and time. This survey of case law confirms that courts often award mitigation only to recognize motives which attract near-unanimous consensus in Italian society. This restrictive approach risks denying mitigation for certain causes that are worthy of some reduction in the sentence.

This chapter has categorized Italian case law, organizing judgments according to their impact in the public and private spheres, and in the respective subfields of politics and justice, and family and work. This taxonomy illustrates the heterogeneous domains in which claims for mitigation arise. This wide spectrum, ranging from terrorism and conscientious objection to mercy killing and corporate criminal law, highlights both the breadth of the pro-social mitigating circumstance and the variability of judicial responses. Rather than invoking this form of mitigation in earnest, courts generally follow the safer paths of granting 'generic mitigating factors' or imposing a sentence near the statutory minimum.

Against this backdrop, several reforms would introduce greater coherence in the application of ethical offending mitigation. First, courts ought to adopt a more generous test, awarding mitigation even when the ethical motive does not enjoy universal approval or when it co-occurs with less commendable motives. Greater flexibility avoids the unfairness of applying a simple dichotomy. Second, this chapter has suggested founding the pro-social mitigating circumstance in states' constitutions and international human rights charters. This would strengthen judicial objectivity and social legitimacy while simultaneously promoting consistency of application.

Ultimately, Article 62 para. 1 no. 1 of the Italian Criminal Code demonstrates that engaging with the moral dimension of offending at sentencing is both possible and appropriate. Challenging the overly rigid ways in which the Italian Supreme Court has interpreted this form of mitigation would not only enhance its application in Italian sentencing practice but also contribute to the comparative scholarship on sentencing ethically motivated crime.

References

Amato, Giuseppe. 'Ancora sulla somministrazione di sostanze stupefacenti da parte del medico.' *Cassazione penale*, no. 6 (2005): 2101.

Bernardi, Alessandro. *Modelli penali e società multiculturale*. Torino: Giappichelli, 2006.

Demay, Clémence. 'Sentencing Crimes of Civil Disobedience in Switzerland', Chapter 11 of this volume. Oxford: Oxford University Press, 2026.

Fiandaca, Giovanni and Musco, Enzo. *Diritto penale. Parte generale*, pp. 459–460. Bologna: Zanichelli, 2024.

Fornasari, Gabriele. *Dilemma etico del male minore e ticking bomb scenario. Riflessioni penalistiche (e non) sulle strategie di legittimazione della tortura*. Napoli: Edizioni Scientifiche Italiane, 2020.

Galluccio, Alessandra. *Punire la parola pericolosa? Pubblica istigazione, discorso d'odio e libertà di espressione nell'era di internet*. Milano: Giuffrè, 2020.

Girani, Rebecca. 'Questioni di fine vita: l'omicidio pietatis causa e la circostanza attenuante dell'«aver agito per motivi di particolare valore morale o sociale».' *Archivio penale*, no. 3 (2024): 1.

Grandi, Ciro. 'I reati contro la famiglia e contro la persona culturalmente motivati: teoria ed evoluzione della prassi.' *Archivio penale*, no. 3 (2022): 1.

Iadecola, Gianfranco. 'Circostanze attenuanti comuni.' In *Codice penale. Rassegna di giurisprudenza e di dottrina*, edited by Lattanzi, Giorgio and Lupo, Ernesto, p. 724. Milano: Giuffrè, 2000.

Lariccia, Sergio and Tardiola, Andrea. 'Obiezione di coscienza.' *Enciclopedia del diritto* III (1999): 815.

Malinverni, Alessandro. 'Circostanze del reato.' *Enciclopedia del diritto* VII (1960): 87.

Malinverni, Alessandro. 'Motivi (dir. pen.).' *Enciclopedia del diritto* XXIV (1977): 287.

Mantovani, Ferrando and Flora, Giovanni. *Diritto penale*, p. 426. Padova: CEDAM, 2023.

Manzini, Vincenzo. *Trattato di diritto penale italiano*, p. 244. Torino: UTET, 1981.

Marinucci, Giorgio, Dolcini, Emilio, and Gatta, Gian Luigi. *Manuale di Diritto Penale. Parte Generale*, p. 703. Milano: Giuffrè, 2024.

Miletti, Marco Nicola. 'Elemosina giudiziaria o trionfo dell'equità? Il ripristino delle attenuanti generiche nella penalistica italiana del secondo dopoguerra.' In *Attualità e storia delle circostanze del reato. Un istituto al bivio tra legalità e discrezionalità*, edited by Bartoli, Roberto and Pifferi, Michele, pp. 200–201. Milano: Giuffrè, 2016.

Moore, Michael S. *Placing Blame. A Theory of the Criminal Law*. Oxford: Oxford University Press, 2010.

Nuvolone, Pietro. *Sistema del diritto penale*, p. 436. Padova: CEDAM, 1982.
Padovani, Tullio. 'Circostanze del reato.' *Il Digesto penale* II (1988): 216.
Padovani, Tullio. *Diritto penale*, p. 318. Milano: Giuffrè, 2023.
Palazzo, Francesco. 'Obiezione di coscienza.' *Enciclopedia del diritto* XXIX (1979): 539.
Preziosi, Stefano. 'Le circostanze del reato.' In *Trattato di diritto penale - Parte generale Vol. II: Il reato*, edited by Cadoppi, Alberto, Canestrari, Stefano, Manna, Adelmo, and **Papa, Michele**, p. 870. Torino: UTET, 2013.
Pulitanò, Domenico. 'L'inquisizione non soave, fra pretese «necessità» e motivi apprezzabili.' *Foro italiano*, no. 2 (1984): 231.
Pulitanò, Domenico. *Diritto penale*, p. 320. Torino: Giappichelli, 2023.
Romano, Mario. *Commentario sistematico del Codice penale*, p. 672. Milano: Giuffrè, 2004.
Ryberg, Jesper. 'Sentencing Honourable Offenders: On the Complexities of Assessing Human Motives', Chapter 3 of this volume. Oxford: Oxford University Press, 2026.
Trapasso, Maria Teresa. 'Riflessioni in tema di rilevanza attenuante dei "motivi politici" e di autonomia interpretativa in materia di "provocazione".' *Cassazione penale*, no. 11 (2009): 4248.
Veneziani, Paolo. *Motivi e colpevolezza*, pp. 6 and 263. Torino: Giappichelli, 2000.
Volta, Raffaella. 'Applicabilità dell'attenuante di cui all'art. 62 n. 1 del codice penale ai cosiddetti "delitti d'onore".' *Rivista penale*, no. 10 (1989): 958.
Zaza, Carlo. *Le circostanze del reato*: 280. Padova: CEDAM, 2002.

14

Sentencing Political Protesters and White-Collar Offenders in Chile

Javier Wilenmann and Carla Sepúlveda

1. Introduction

The current volume addresses the role of motives, particularly positive motives, at sentencing. The nature of the offender's motive may influence a court's sentence. The nature of the crime may also play a role. If ethical offending affects sentencing, should legislators and courts treat benign motives differently depending on the type of offence being sentenced?

In recent years, sentencing in Chile has been significantly shaped by the introduction of special rules applicable to particular categories of offences. This stands in contrast to the traditional sentencing framework, which relied on a single sentencing regime across all crimes. Sentencing has thus become increasingly fragmented. While these special rules often aim merely to exclude certain punishments or to limit judicial discretion, they have also addressed specific aggravating and mitigating circumstances. The treatment of motives—and the relative weight of contextual factors—has been markedly inconsistent across offence types. Particularly striking is the legislature's inconsistent approach to taking benevolent motives into account at sentencing. In this chapter, we examine sentencing in two such contexts: political protesters and white-collar offenders.

Over the past decade, Chile has experienced both peaceful and violent demonstrations connected to widespread socio-economic inequality. In responding to mass unrest, Chilean legislation has treated protest-related conduct as aggravating the seriousness of the base offence, particularly with respect to property crimes. Security concerns predominate in this area of law. In this chapter we discuss sentence mitigation in cases of activism or organized protest (such as those explored in other chapters of this volume), and ask

Javier Wilenmann and Carla Sepúlveda, *Sentencing Political Protesters and White-Collar Offenders in Chile*
In: *Sentencing the Ethically-Motivated Offender*. Edited by: Julian V. Roberts, Leo Zaibert, and Jesper Ryberg,
Oxford University Press. © Javier Wilenmann and Carla Sepúlveda 2026. DOI: 10.1093/9780198993025.003.0016

whether such considerations should extend to large-scale, relatively violent, and uncoordinated protest. Following widespread demonstrations sparked by perceptions of economic inequality and dissatisfaction with rising living costs in 2019, the legislature's response appears to be negative: at least for property offences, harsher sentences are deemed necessary. Accordingly, a mandatory aggravating factor was introduced for offences committed at the time of public disorder (art. 449 ter of the Penal Code). The factor now states:

> Art. 449 ter. When the offences punished under Paragraphs 3 and 4 of this Title [burglary and theft] are committed on the occasion of a public calamity or a disturbance of public order, whether the perpetrator acts as part of a group or individually but under its cover, the corresponding custodial sentence shall be increased by one degree.
>
> In the case of the conduct penalised under the first paragraph of Article 436 [simple robbery], and when the circumstances described in the preceding paragraph are present, the corresponding custodial sentence shall be imposed, excluding its minimum degree.[1]

As a result, individual motives are excluded from consideration, while protest serves as an aggravating circumstance. At the same time, the Chilean government undertook a comprehensive reform of sentencing in relation to corruption and white-collar crime. Emerging from the same social climate of unrest and demands for greater equality, this reform sought to counteract perceptions of impunity by introducing a sentencing framework specifically applicable to white-collar offences. Its stated objective is to make sentencing proportional to culpability and the harm associated with white-collar offences, making harsh punishment more likely for offences with high culpability or harm. Within this framework, motivational factors assume a prominent role, functioning as both aggravating and mitigating circumstances. Mitigation applies, for instance, where an offender 'acted without seeking personal benefit' (art. 13.1.a, Act 21.595) or 'in the interest of persons in need or out of necessity' (art. 14.1.a). In stark contrast to the protest context, then, motives are explicitly recognized as relevant considerations in sentencing white-collar crime.

[1] Statutory custodial sentences in Chile are divided into 'degrees' (grados), each corresponding to a sub-range of the overall penalty. The first paragraph of this provision aggravates the penalty by shifting the minimum and maximum penalty by one degree. The second paragraph raises the minimum sentence while leaving the maximum unchanged.This effect is more intense than adding a general aggravating factor, since the latter could be counteracted by grounds for mitigation, while the former cannot.

2. Overview

This chapter explores this 'twin-track' sentencing regime which recognizes claims for mitigation for one profile of offender but not for another. We start by considering the case for mitigation or aggravation related to motives in each context that we explore, namely sentencing in protest-related and white-collar cases. The following section contextualizes the protests in Chile, the offences involved in the 2019 riots, and analyses whether such offences should be treated more harshly or leniently than non-protest-related cases. The chapter then explores the evolution of white-collar sentencing in Chile and the recognition of altruistic-motivation circumstances. Finally, the chapter explores both the causes and normative justifications for treating offences differently.

On a descriptive level, we explain the legislative intervention on sentencing factors related to motivation, leading to diverging outcomes by reference to context-specific causes as well as the broader trend towards sentencing fragmentation in Chilean criminal law. While our chapter discusses only a single legal system, there are implications for other regimes. On a normative level, we argue that while the recognition of benign motives for specific crimes might help courts craft proportional sentences, it creates a need to justify this approach. As a result, we argue that legislatures should consider whether these sentencing regulations are normatively justifiable. Justifying differences between offences represents a significant challenge in a fragmented sentencing field.

3. Mitigation for Property Offences in the Context of Political Upheaval?

How should courts sentence offences committed during political and other forms of protests? Should these offenders be accorded leniency or punished more harshly? Or should courts disregard the offender's motive? We do not address here the broader question of whether protest-related offences ought to be punished at all. That issue has been debated by Latin American scholars who stress the democratic value of protest and highlight its recognition as a fundamental right in a functioning democracy (Gargarella 2008, 2012). Our concern is narrower: how should courts sentence offences committed as part of a political protest?

As other contributions to this volume illustrate, this is a controversial issue from a normative perspective, dependent on several variables: (i) the extent to which a given protest-related crime threatens the rights of others; (ii) the type and seriousness of offences, including violent offences harming property or public order; and (iii) the motives of those sentenced, whether their conduct was intended to draw attention to a social issues or simply reflected personal goals. We focus on property-related offences (such as damage, theft, or burglary) committed during protests that may have included violence. In the 2019 Chilean riots, acts of arson, damage to public and private property (cars and sometimes commercial businesses), and looting occurred. We do not analyse cases where no individual rights are threatened under variable (i) or where offences are considered not very serious under variable (ii). We analyse only more serious acts.

In recent decades, many communities—from Hong Kong and Paris, to Minneapolis, Santiago, and Bogotá—have experienced large-scale and occasionally violent protests. Courts have thus faced the challenge of how to sentence offences committed during such events. Our concern here is not with small-scale disruptions by committed activists pursuing a specific cause, such as climate change interruption of traffic, but with mass, often volatile protests. Such large and loosely organized events can give rise to what has been termed a 'mob criminality'—large groups, bound by weak and short-lived cohesion, which act collectively, out of emotion rather than reason (Sánchez 2025). Motives may range from altruistic to vengeful and are rarely shared uniformly by all rioters. Anger against governing institutions tends to emerge during such protests.

This form of protest has occurred across Chile's political history. Political protests were pivotal in the early 1970s, when frequent clashes involving supporters and opponents of President Salvador Allende were used by the military to justify the US-backed coup of September 1973. They again proved decisive in the late 1980s and early 1990s, when mass demonstrations contributed to Chile's peaceful transition to democracy. With economic growth in the 1990s and early 2000s, protests waned, only to re-emerge through youth movements highlighting persistent economic inequality (Donoso 2013; Somma 2016). This movement culminated in October 2019, when millions took to the streets for over three months in what became known as the *estallido social*, or social eruption (Somma et al. 2020; Wilenmann and Feddersen 2022).

The protests and riots of 2019 were unprecedented in their scale and impact. They were sparked by widespread frustration arising from inequality and rising living costs (Araujo 2019, 2022). Over time, the discourse shifted towards other issues such as police brutality (Wilenmann and Feddersen 2022). While largely peaceful, some incidents involved arson, looting, and violent clashes with police, leading to thousands of arrests and prosecutions. Statistically, the offences committed by protesters fall into in four categories, where property crimes account for the largest share (11,156 cases, almost half the total), followed by public order offences (7,965 cases), assaults against police officers (3,293 offences), and arson (732) (*Informe Estadístico Estallido Social* 2025). Criminal justice institutions thus played a central role in a state apparatus overwhelmed by disorder. The most common charge was commercial, particularly involving looting. This accounted for 18 per cent of all crimes prosecuted in connection with the *estallido* and 58 per cent of all property offences (Farías et al. 2023; *Informe Estadístico Estallido Social* 2025). In total, 2,940 cases of property crime resulted in convictions.

Mitigation was not considered by the courts in these cases. Rather, courts raised the question whether existing aggravating factors should be applied to justify harsher penalties. Article 12, number 10 of the Penal Code establishes a general aggravating circumstance for offences committed 'at the time of public disturbance'. Courts had applied this factor both before and during the 2019 *estallido social* to aggravate sentences for property and other offences.

In January 2020, Congress sought to strengthen the judicial emphasis on aggravation in such cases. A reform introduced a specific aggravating circumstance for property offences committed 'in times of calamity or disruption of public order'.[2] Although similar to Article 12, number 10, the new provision was expressly directed at property offences, signalling a legislative intention to punish protest-related offences with individual victims more harshly. As the new provision was intended to specifically address protest-related looting/burglary, it was originally drafted only in connection with non-domestic burglary. At this stage, the seriousness of the offence, rather than the offender's motive, was placed at the centre of sentencing decisions. Some centre-left politicians objected, arguing that the diversity of protesters' motives during the *estallido* warranted an individualized approach to sentencing in such cases. In the event, their objections were disregarded.

The bill initially targeted specific forms of public disorder but later evolved into a general aggravation for looting. Late in the legislative process, its scope was expanded to encompass property crimes committed 'at a time of public calamity or disturbance of public order', alongside the creation of a new looting offence defined by the destruction or appropriation of goods during such

[2] It is worth noting that in England and Wales, the definitive sentencing guidelines include 'offence committed in the context of public disorder' as an aggravating factor. Courts must follow these guidelines unless it would be contrary to the interests of justice to do so. This aggravating factor was added to the guidelines following nationwide social unrest occurring in 2011. See: https://sentencingcouncil.org.uk/guidelines/non-domestic-burglary/?source=7511.

events. The legislative focus thus shifted from conduct and motivation to the context of the offence. Sentencing moved away from an individualized model where culpability and motive determine the outcome, towards a categorical approach.

As the provision was enacted after the main events of the *estallido*, its impact on sentencing practice is difficult to evaluate. Nonetheless, courts have since applied it to property offences committed in protest contexts, reasoning that a protest, by definition, involves some disturbance of public order.[3] If this reflects general judicial practice, the legislative aim of increasing the severity of punishments for protest-related property offences has been achieved.

Is this approach defensible? Could offending while participating in massive, disorganized protests ever be morally justified? Protests are sometimes described as forms of uncivil disobedience because they may involve violence. Yet one might argue that the concept of violence is being applied too broadly. Property harm that does not entail physical or psychological harm to individuals might be excluded from the category of relevant violence (Scheuerman 2021). If so, property damage could be regarded as more acceptable in protest contexts than in other circumstances, rather than as justifying aggravation. This requires a typology of property damage.

Scheuerman (2021) distinguishes between three types of protest. **Symbolic property damage** targets objects of expressive or symbolic value and is not generally considered violent. **Disruptive property damage** aims to obstruct or sabotage practices perceived as unjust; this includes arson and sabotage and carries greater risks of personal harm. **Seizing property**, such as looting, is a third category. While sometimes defended as a form of political protest, Scheuerman contends that such actions are only justifiable as a last resort, where proportionate, focused, and with minimal risk to human life. He highlights the devastating impact looting can have on small businesses and restricts this justification to cases of extreme need (such as stealing food to prevent loss of life, ibid.: 100). On this view, protest-related looting rarely provides grounds for mitigation.

A more convincing justification for mitigation in cases of property damage would cite the democratic necessity of political protests. Rioting in these circumstances can be understood as an extreme means of expressing legitimate grievances when lawful avenues for protest or change are closed (Flanigan

[3] See, for example, a judgment by the Santiago Court of Appeal on 6 December 2023, Rol N° 5857-2023. The case involved two women accused of stealing items such as hand sanitizer, baby cologne, hair dye, toothbrushes, and medications from a closed pharmacy. A similar reasoning was applied by the San Miguel Court of Appeals on a judgment in September 2022, Rol N° 2287-2022.

2025). The harm it causes cannot be separated from its expressive function: '(at least some of) the harmful and destructive acts characteristic of the practice are themselves expressions of dissent' (Flanigan 2025: 281). Under this view, rioting may thus be morally evaluated not only in relation to the aims and means of the group but also with reference to each participant's role and responsibility with respect to the offence.

From this perspective, proportionality is not assessed solely by reference to the harm caused or the success of specific demands, but by the proportionality of the violence in relation to the injustice which triggered the protest. Both collective rioting and individual acts must be proportionate to the wrongs they seek to denounce. As Flanigan argues, breaking a shop window may be proportionate in response to systemic injustice, even if its adverse impact on shopkeepers is significant (Flanigan 2025: 286–288). The adequacy of such targets should be judged in light of citizens' complicity or responsibility for the injustice, or alternatively as a demand of solidarity requiring some personal cost.

On this account, certain criminal acts committed during riots could merit mitigation, provided they are proportionate and appropriately targeted. This would not entail categorical mitigation but rather an individualized, case-by-case consideration. The Chilean legislature, however, has not engaged with these arguments. It has simply elected to emphasize aggravation alone.

This position could be justified in three ways. First, from a contextual rationale: large-scale protests threaten public order and the state's capacity to maintain control. The traditional concern for public order reflects this view, suggesting that heightened deterrence is required. Secondly, from a culpability perspective: offenders who opportunistically take advantage of disorder to offend are deemed more blameworthy. Thirdly, in the Chilean case, looting, damage, and arson occurred on a widespread scale—they were not targeted crimes. The proportionality test for mitigation in case of violent protests thus appears absent. This suggests that, at the very least, a general rationale for mitigation cannot be found. Of course, this does not imply outright that general aggravation is a desirable outcome. A more desirable legislative outcome would allow judges the discretion to weigh sentencing factors in an individualized manner.

4. Mitigation for Altruistic Offending in White-Collar Crime?

The last decade not only brought reforms aimed at increasing the severity of sentencing for property offences but also transformed Chile's regulation of white-collar crime (Wilenmann and Bascuñán 2023a). For decades, Chilean commentators described the field in 'Sutherlandian' terms (Sutherland 1940, 1945). This approach conceives of conduct largely resistant to criminalization, where elite actors successfully shield corporate misconduct from criminal law and, in the rare cases prosecuted, face derisory penalties (Winter 2013; Correa and Winter 2014). This landscape shifted dramatically during the 2010s, following two waves of corporate scandals that prompted legislators to widen corporate criminal liability and increase penalties for corruption offences (Wilenmann and Bascuñán 2023a).

The most significant reform was also triggered by the political upheaval of the 2019 *estallido social*. The lenient punishments associated with major scandals of the 2010s became a focal point of public anger. In response, legislators sought to address corporate abuse by enacting a sweeping reform of white-collar and corporate criminal law. This culminated in Act 21.595 of 2023, commonly referred to as the Economic Offences Act. For present purposes, its most notable feature is the central role it assigns to motivational factors in sentencing.

The Act is more ambitious than earlier reforms that introduced special sentencing regimes. It amended numerous provisions across different categories of white-collar crime and broadened corporate criminal liability (Wilenmann 2023b; Wilenmann and Bascuñán 2023b). Like its predecessors, the Act aimed to increase the severity of expected penalties. Sections of the business community criticized it for being too punitive. However, unlike earlier reforms that increased severity by limiting mitigating factors or excluding the use of probation as a sanction, the Economic Offences Act established a far more comprehensive sentencing framework (Wilenmann 2023b). Its purpose was to align punishments with the distinctive characteristics of white-collar criminality, ensuring that judges were more attentive to factors that made offences either more or less serious. The principle of proportionality (to the seriousness of the offence) was identified as the central aim of the reform, and as the means of correcting the leniency previously perceived in white-collar cases.

To this end, legislators introduced a sentencing grid requiring courts to evaluate cases along two axes: harm and culpability (Wilenmann 2023b). While harm had long been a relevant criterion under Article 69 of the Penal Code, the innovation lay in the explicit requirement to assess the offender's level of culpability (Rodríguez Collao and Pinto Bustos 2025). Culpability engages the offender's motives for the crime (van Weezel 1997). The incorporation of motivation into a mandatory sentencing framework constitutes a novel development in Chilean criminal law.

The Economic Offences Act links culpability to two principal factors: (i) the abuse of power or leadership positions by the offender; and (ii) the offender's motives. Accordingly, motives are formally recognized in white-collar sentencing through two mitigating provisions. One reflects diminished culpability (a general mitigating circumstance) and a second exceptionally low culpability (a special mitigating circumstance). Since self-interested profit is presumed to be the default motive in white-collar crime, its absence allows for a finding of lower culpability. Where the absence of personal gain reflects an altruistic motivation (Wilenmann 2023a and 2023b) this is viewed positively, emphasizing the offender's moral character and disposition (Rodríguez Collao and Pinto Bustos 2025: 154).

Such an approach is normatively defensible. Although white-collar crime is often perceived as being driven predominantly by financial gain (Gottschalk 2020), concerns for social justice or altruism related to individual third parties can also motivate individuals to offend (Agnew 2014). As Gottschalk observes, '[a]n entrepreneur can commit financial crime to ensure that all employees have a job they can return to. A trusted employee can pay bribes to make sure that the company will have new orders to survive in the future. An executive may commit embezzlement to be able to help his adult children to recover after personal bankruptcy' (2020: 8). From a deterrence perspective, if financial gain motivates white-collar crimes, an offender without such a motivation is unlikely to reoffend. From a retributive point of view, although the argument is less straightforward, it may be also argued that the consideration of the interest of others make the case less blameworthy (Haugh 2014). For our purposes, such motivations may be relevant for assessing culpability in a white-collar case.

In the Chilean case, this logic is most clearly embodied in what might be termed a 'Robin Hood clause' which provides mitigation where the offender acted to assist others in need. In such cases, culpability is classified as very low, thereby reducing the likelihood of imprisonment. In theory, based on the mechanics behind the new white-collar sentencing framework, the fact that a special mitigating circumstance applies when white-collar crime is perpetrated for altruistic motives would only make imprisonment possible if the statutory penalty associated with the crime was exceptionally severe. Although case law has yet to emerge regarding this provision, possible scenarios include employees stealing to fund urgent medical treatment for a relative or even helping a business to remain trading (Haugh 2014). In such cases, a full defence of necessity may not apply, as alternative behaviour might have been available. Nevertheless, the legislature has deemed such defendants less blameworthy than those offenders without such an altruistic motive.

This framework raises an important question: why should ethical-motive mitigation be restricted to white-collar offences? If proportionality is the guiding principle of sentencing policy, and if motives are central to assessing proportionality, there seems little justification for restricting such considerations to a single category of crime. And why this category of offending in particular?

One explanation of why motivational mitigation has been restricted to economic crime lies in the policy environment of white-collar law. Unlike other areas of criminal law, it is relatively insulated from two dominant policy concerns: prison population management and incapacitation. The criminal law often functions as a tool to manage offender populations, with sentencing policy shaped by assessments of dangerousness and recidivism risk. In practice, resource constraints and the volume of cases explain measures such as presumptive imprisonment for certain offences. By contrast, white-collar offenders are less likely to reoffend, more capable of reformation, and more costly to detect, prosecute, and convict.

This context helps explain why white-collar sentencing has evolved towards a framework centred on culpability and harm—including the offender's motive—while other areas of sentencing remain dominated by more pragmatic considerations. The result, however, is that white-collar crime is the only domain where proportionate punishment is pursued with rigour, while other areas of law remain driven by more instrumental goals.

5. Inconsistent Responses to Offending in a Fragmented Sentencing Regime

As the preceding analysis demonstrates, the evolution of Chile's sentencing regime from a generalized framework to a fragmented field has generated paradoxical outcomes concerning altruistic motivations. In the case of property (and other) offences, no statutory provisions exist to mitigate sentence to reflect altruistic motives. Since judges typically assign sentences at the lower end of the statutory scale (Wilenmann et al. 2019; Morales Peillard and Salinero Echeverría 2020), motivations play no further role in ordinary cases. By contrast, when property offences occur during protests, the motivational context has been construed as an *aggravating* circumstance. The heightened perception of risk and the association of protest with violence, crystallized during the 2019 *estallido social*, have reinforced this approach. Ethical arguments concerning the legitimacy or necessity of protest and riot have found little resonance among legislators or judges.

The opposite trend prevails with respect to white-collar crime. Motives—altruistic ones in particular—play a decisive role within the new sentencing framework. The statute directs judges to assess motivations when evaluating culpability. This permits findings of low or very low culpability, resulting in mitigated sentences. Sentencing outcomes may change significantly, rendering otherwise ineligible offenders eligible for probation or authorizing less intrusive forms of supervision.

It would be overly simplistic to attribute this duality to factors relating to social class, suggesting that crimes associated with the poor are punished harshly while leniency is extended to the powerful. Both reforms were, in fact, enacted with the expressed aim of increasing severity. Both emerged during a period of widespread protest and civil unrest, reflecting legislators' responsiveness to public demands for action. However, this punitive response to white-collar crime was sought within a framework emphasizing desert and proportionality; in the case of protests and property crime, no such considerations exist. Public security concerns predominate in the latter cases.

These divergent approaches reflect the increasing fragmentation of sentencing in Chile. Because reforms are pursued piecemeal rather than through a general framework, legislators enjoy considerable latitude to introduce disparate rationales across different areas of criminal law. On one view, this enhances the legislature's capacity to respond rapidly to the distinctive characteristics of different offences. Considerations relevant to one form of offending may not apply to another. Under Chile's traditional sentencing framework, the whole system of aggravation and mitigation is structured according to criteria designed for dealing with violent crime. As a result, other categories of offending remained largely insensitive to relevant contextual or motivational factors. This reality triggered a backlash by the legislature, rooted in a desire for harsher penalties, and also related to the perceived inability of courts to achieve proportional sentencing outcomes (Wilenmann and Gambardella 2023). Fragmentation may thus add depth to an otherwise undifferentiated sentencing framework.

Yet fragmentation also creates space for divergences that extend beyond the consideration of relevant factors for specific categories of crime. The present case illustrates this dynamic starkly. In reforming sentencing for property offences, legislators approached these crimes as threats to the state's ability to respond to mass disorders. The central rationale was to preserve public order during the *estallido social*. Participation in looting or similar crimes was therefore treated as aggravating, in order to distinguish protest-related offending from non-political property crime. This approach is hard to justify. As noted earlier, we do not see a strong case for general mitigation for offences associated with looting and arson in a context of widespread, non-targeted protests. At the same time, there also seems no justification for widespread aggravation in these cases.

In contrast, a distinctly different approach was adopted with regard to sentencing white-collar crimes. Although the reform sought harsher penalties for serious economic crime, its rationale was clearly founded in desert principles. Motivations were treated as intrinsic to culpability and explicitly recognized as potentially mitigating. The contextual logic that justified aggravation in the protest setting was deemed irrelevant. Again, this appears plausible in isolation.

We believe, however, that in a fragmented sentencing field, normative justification for sentencing rationale should not only refer discretely to each sentencing framework, but differences in treatment ought also to be justified. The fact that motivation is considered by judges only in white-collar cases requires justification. One may argue that white-collar crime should be assessed predominantly from a retributive, desert-oriented perspective, whereas common and violent crime ought to remain more sensitive to order-maintenance and other policy considerations. A fragmented sentencing framework makes such differentiation possible. But if proportionality is predominant across crime categories and motivation is deemed relevant for assessing culpability, there is no justification for restricting altruistic motives to white-collar crime. Proportionality is a fundamental sentencing principle and is not one that is restricted to certain forms of offending. Our chapter reveals the normative incoherence of Chilean sentencing: the stark divergence in the importance accorded to benevolent motives across offence types reflects fundamental inconsistencies in the underlying orientation of criminal law that are unjustifiable.

6. Conclusion

There is no principled impediment to extending the white-collar reasoning to all forms of offending. This would have to apply to property offences unless expressly excluded. In a context where, even after the reform of white-collar crime, social injustice is seen as expressed in the existence of a different set of rules applicable to the crimes of the powerful, such a reform would be desirable. Yet protest-related mitigation has gained little support. Unconvinced of the normative arguments justifying or excusing looting and more violent forms of protest, legal scholars have yet to advance an argument in its favour. The legislature and the public are even more opposed to such a possibility. From the perspective of principled and consistent sentencing, they are both in error.

References

Agnew, Robert. 'Social Concern and Crime: Moving beyond the Assumption of Simple Self-Interest'. *Criminology* 52, no. 1 (2014): 1–32. https://doi.org/10.1111/1745-9125.12031.

Araujo, Kathya. 'Desmesuras, Desencantos, Irritaciones y Desapegos'. In *Hilos Tensados: Para Leer El Octubre Chileno*, edited by Kathya Araujo. Santiago: USACH, 2019.

Araujo, Kathya. *The Circuit of Detachment in Chile: Understanding the Fate of a Neoliberal Experiment*. Cambridge: Cambridge University Press, 2022.

Correa, Carlos, and Jaime Winter. 'Prisión Preventiva y Delincuencia Empresarial En Chile'. *Perspectiva Penal Actual* 3 (2014): 209–234.

Donoso, Sofía. 'Dynamics of Change in Chile: Explaining the Emergence of the 2006 "Pingüino" Movement'. *Journal of Latin American Studies* 45, no. 1 (2013): 1–29. https://doi.org/10.1017/S0022216X12001228.

Farías, Javiera, José Manuel Fernández, Tomás Pascual, and Hugo Rojas. 'Los delitos del estallido social y el rol de la Defensoría Penal Pública en Chile en 2019'. *Derecho PUCP*, no. 90 (May 2023): 79–114. https://doi.org/10.18800/derechopucp.202301.003.

Flanigan, Edmund Tweedy. 'Why Riot? An Expressive Theory of the Justification of Rioting'. *Free & Equal: A Journal of Ethics and Public Affairs* 1, no. 1 (2025). https://doi.org/10.16995/fe.17733.

Gargarella, Roberto. 'Un Diálogo Sobre La Ley y La Protesta Social'. *Derecho PUCP*, no. 61 (December 2008): 19–50. https://doi.org/10.18800/derechopucp.200801.001.

Gargarella, Roberto. 'Law and Social Protests'. *Criminal Law and Philosophy* 6, no. 2 (2012): 131–48. https://doi.org/10.1007/s11572-012-9140-6.

Gottschalk, Petter. *Corporate White-Collar Crime Scandals: Detection, Investigation, Reconstruction*. Cheltenham: Edward Elgar Publishing, 2020. https://doi.org/10.4337/9781839105999.

Haugh, Todd. 'Sentencing the Why of White Collar Crime'. *Fordham Law Review* 82, no. 6 (2014): 3143–3188.

Informe Estadístico Estallido Social. Ministerio Público, 2025. https://www.fiscaliadechile.cl/node/44805.

Morales Peillard, Ana María, and Sebastián Salinero Echeverría. '¿Cómo Fallan y Controlan La Ejecución de Las Penas Sustitutivas Los Jueces?' *Revista de Derecho (Valdivia)* 33, no. 1 (2020): 319–341. https://doi.org/10.4067/S0718-09502020000100319.

Rodríguez Collao, Luis, and Andrea Pinto Bustos. 'Graduación de la culpabilidad en la determinación de la pena del delito económico'. *Pro Jure Revista de Derecho - Pontificia Universidad Católica de Valparaíso* 63 (January 2025). https://doi.org/10.4151/S0718-68512024063-1483.

Sánchez, Rocío. 'Delitos Cometidos En Escenarios de Catástrofe o Calamidad. Antecedentes Criminológicos Para Interpretar Las Circunstancias Agravantes de Responsabilidad En El Derecho Penal Chileno'. *Política Criminal* 20, no. 39 (2025): 187–219.

Scheuerman, William E. 'Politically Motivated Property Damage'. *The Harvard Review of Philosophy* 28 (2021): 89–106. https://doi.org/10.5840/harvardreview20218337.

Somma, Nicolás M. 'Discontent, Collective Protest, and Social Movements in Chile'. In *Malaise in Representation in Latin American Countries: Chile, Argentina, and Uruguay*, edited by Alfredo Joignant, Mauricio Morales, and Claudio Fuentes. London: Palgrave Macmillan, 2016.

Somma, Nicolás M., Matías Bargsted, Rodolfo Disi Pavlic, and Rodrigo M. Medel. 'No Water in the Oasis: The Chilean Spring of 2019–2020'. *Social Movement Studies* (February 2020): 1–8. https://doi.org/10.1080/14742837.2020.1727737.

Sutherland, Edwin. 'White-Collar Criminality'. *American Sociological Review* 5, no. 1 (1940): 1–12. http://dx.doi.org/10.2307/2083937.

Sutherland, Edwin. 'Is "White Collar Crime" Crime?' *American Sociological Review* 10, no. 2 (1945): 132–139. http://dx.doi.org/10.2307/2085628.

van Weezel, Alex. 'Compensación Racional de Atenuantes y Agravantes En La Medición de La Pena'. *Revista Chilena de Derecho* 24, no. 3 (1997): 459–502.

Wilenmann, Javier. 'Artículo 14'. In *Derecho Penal Económico Chileno Tomo I*, edited by Bascuñán Rodríguez and Javier Wilenmann. DER Ediciones, 2023a.

Wilenmann, Javier. 'Comentario Previo a Los Artículos 12 y Siguientes'. In *Derecho Penal Económico Chileno Tomo I*, edited by Antonio Bascuñán Rodríguez and Javier Wilenmann. DER Ediciones, 2023b.

Wilenmann, Javier, and Antonio Bascuñán. 'Historia Del Derecho Penal Económico Chileno y de La Ley de Delitos Económicos'. In *Derecho Penal Económico Chileno Tomo I: La Ley de Delitos Económicos*, edited by Javier Wilenmann and Antonio Bascuñán. DER Ediciones, 2023a.

Wilenmann, Javier, and Antonio Bascuñán. 'Pretensiones de La Conformación de Un Derecho Penal Económico'. In *Derecho Penal Económico Chileno. Tomo I*, edited by Antonio Bascuñán and Javier Wilenmann. DER Ediciones, 2023b.

Wilenmann, Javier, and Mayra Feddersen. 'Contesting Authority in the Crisis of Neoliberalism'. In *Research Handbook on Law and Social Movements*, edited by Stephen Boutcher, Corey Shdmaiah, and Michael Yarbrough. Cheltenham: Edward Elgar Publishing, 2022.

Wilenmann, Javier, and Maite Gambardella. 'A Developmental Model of Sentencing Evolution: The Emergence of the Politics of Probation in Chile'. *The Howard Journal of Crime and Justice* 62, no. 1 (2023): 81–101. https://doi.org/10.1111/hojo.12510.

Wilenmann, Javier, Nicolás Del Fierro, Francisco Medina, and Esteban Olivares. 'La Determinación de La Pena En La Práctica Judicial Chilena'. *Politica Criminal* 14, no. 27 (2019): 456–490.

Winter, Jaime. 'Derecho Penal e Impunidad Empresarial En Chile'. *Revista de Estudios de La Justicia* 19 (2013): 91–125.

Index

For the benefit of digital users, indexed terms that span two pages (e.g., 52–53) may, on occasion, appear on only one of those pages.

References to notes are indicated by a note suffix after the para ID locator, as in this example: 77n.8

The manufacturer's authorised representative in the EU for product safety is Oxford University Press España S.A. of El Parque Empresarial San Fernando de Henares, Avenida de Castilla, 2 - 28830 Madrid (www.oup.es/en or product.safety@oup.com). OUP España S.A. also acts as importer into Spain of products made by the manufacturer.

Printed and bound by CPI Group (UK) Ltd, Croydon, CR0 4YY

29/09/2026

02224922-0004